Dearest Mum

I hope you.
this book.

Written by
here in France.

Love to you for ever
Caroline xxxx xxx
Xmas 2011

NO COPY OF THE SCRIPT

THE TRIUMPHS AND TRAGEDIES OF A CASTING DIRECTOR

SUE WHATMOUGH

ALS

First published by Authorhouse 29/12/10
ISBN: 978-1-4520-4959-5

This edition published by Alternative Literary Services 20/1/11
ISBN: 978-0-9569240-0-1

This memoir is based on the life experiences of the author. In some cases names have been changed to protect the privacy of the people concerned. Dates and the order of events are recorded to the best of the author's recollection.

Cover photograph by Alan Cunliffe 1966
Author photograph by Leaf Fielding 2008

Alternative Literary Services Ltd.
20 Rocliffe St.
Islington
London N1 8DT
www.alternativeliteraryservices.co.uk

To Leaf,
who has brought to my life the wholeness and fulfilment that has
enabled me to tell my story

"Every day of life is made up of happiness and sadness, pain and pleasure, dark and light, growth and decay in accordance with the ancient Chinese concept of Yin and Yang. It is not what happens to you but how you respond to what happens to you that will determine how joyous and fulfilling your life will be."
Liz Simpson 'Finding Fulfilment'

CONTENTS

PART ONE

LOST

1

ACCIDENTS WILL HAPPEN

'You know this is a crime, don't you?' A woman's voice close to my ear called me back to the present.

I opened my eyes and tried to focus through mist and sweat. My knees protruded from the steaming water like white islands. So did half my breasts. My arms rested limp and pale on the sides of the bath. Everything below the water line was vivid, lobster red and stinging, pricked by the needles of intense heat. A shiny pink face stared anxiously down at me. It was Claire, a woman I hardly knew. She held the kettle in her oven-gloved hand ready to pour.

'Can't take any more,' I muttered.

There was the gin bottle on the floor, almost empty, and the little bottle beside it. God knows how many quinine tablets I'd swallowed. Claire put the kettle in the sink then reached for my hand. 'Get out then, just get out,' she urged.

But I couldn't move, didn't dare, for fear of burning. I became completely leaden in the stillness of the scalding water, imagining it setting cast-like around me.

'Come on, Sue. You can do it. You must. Or at least try to pull the plug out.'

That meant putting my hand in and feeling around, churning the water. No, I'd have to wait for it to cool.

'Try, Sue, please try … please … you must … '

A dense hissing sound filled my ears, my vision blurred. I was about to faint, to shut out the world.

'Please, Sue … ' Claire's now frantic voice faded and was gone.

The drone of the Cromwell Road traffic woke me, at home, in our bed and alone. I could feel every lump and bump in the cheap mattress. Like the princess and the pea my skin hurt from top to toe. Then I remembered and wrenched the sheets off the bed. No blood, all was dry. The final attempt had failed. My baby had hung on, he or she was going to be and that was that. I looked at the alarm. It was five past eleven. What day was it? I'd no idea. I shut my eyes again trying to calm my thudding head. Right, it had to be Saturday and John must have gone to set up for the matinee and, God, I needed an aspirin.

I sat hunched over the edge of the bed staring helplessly at the yellow and purple bruises caused by a particularly violent jump down the stairs; one vain attempt of many to abort. And then I cried; cried at my misery, for my shame and not least for my naïvety. All John's words had been empty. The talk of marriage and a home together, far away from this draughty little bedsit, all lies, cruel lies. And last night, when I'd most needed his love and support, the shit had gone off to the pub leaving me alone with someone called Claire. Heaven knows if that really was her name, but it's kind-sounding and that's how I remember her. Who but the most long-suffering person would take responsibility for a pregnant teenager determined to abort herself? No doubt she'd brought me home too. But I didn't remember and didn't want to.

Strangely, crying helped lighten the heaviness in my head. I tried to be more positive. There was one consolation, wasn't there? John hadn't suggested a backstreet abortion. We'd decided we'd try and get rid of it ourselves or, more accurately, I would try. I'd failed. Ominous words echoed round the room, words I'd never forgotten. 'So don't come to ME if you get pregnant.'

It was 1956. I was eleven and three-quarters and things were happening to my body. Mother had explained, vaguely. 'Babies come out of ladies' bodies and periods are about preparing a place for them to grow,' she said, turning away to hide her embarrassment.

'How do they get in there, Mummy?'

'Well, Daddies put them there,' she said, returning to her fruit bottling and that irritating humming she went in for when there was no more to be said.

The doctor's children, who knew a lot about bodies, told me rather more. At first I couldn't stop laughing, but then, when they swore it was the truth, I was disgusted and ran home to tell Mother. She blushed and fussed with her hanky. 'Er, yes. But when you're in love and married it's, well, very nice.'

'I think it sounds horrible. Do boys really …?'

'If you simply must know more Susan, ask your father. He's very scientific and down to earth, he'll tell you.' She could be really prissy at times, probably something to do with her strict, post-Victorian upbringing. What she meant was Daddy would give me the details without being embarrassed. It was all terribly mysterious and I suspect some part of me didn't want to know.

In the Easter holidays Daddy asked me if I'd like to go down to the Montagu car museum at Beaulieu. There was an exceptional collection of vintage and veteran cars and he'd never been.

'Yes please.'

A day out with Daddy was bound to be interesting. Although he was a man who could see the funny side of things and loved a good laugh, his practicality verged on the eccentric. Nearly fifty and still wearing the same shoes. Well, not the exact same pair, but the same model. When the current pair were beginning to show signs of wear, they'd be reduced to gardening or garage work and new ones would be ordered from the factory, by serial number. Daddy liked neatness as well as consistency. The contents of his cupboards were so meticulously arranged he could tell you the pencil sharpener was on the third shelf up in between the inkpot and the brass set square. With Daddy nothing ever went missing. A mechanical engineer and inventor with the highest forehead imaginable, he spent much of his time taking cars to pieces, putting in new engines and improving on the originals. I'd often helped him in the garage handing tools or shining lights into awkward places. While he worked he liked to name and explain the function of all the components, so I could appreciate the workings of the internal combustion engine. I wasn't sure it was a necessary qualification for a young lady. On the other hand perhaps I wasn't going to be a young lady, not the sort you think of anyway. No, I was a tomboy and quite happy with myself.

The drive from Manor Lodge, our home near Camberley in Surrey, to Beaulieu took at least two hours and I'd have Daddy all to myself. Mother had a W.I. meeting, which she simply couldn't miss. Well, she'd made a plum jam sponge and Lady Lorinda Connors was to give a talk on her war experiences and Mother couldn't resist the chance to hobnob with the aristocracy. So I decided this was an ideal opportunity to ask Daddy about 'the facts of life' because he was driving and having to look at the road so I didn't have to see his eyes and he wouldn't see my blushes. I took a deep breath. 'Daddy.'

'Yes, poppet.'

'Er... what do people do when they …?'

'When they what?'

There was no turning back now. It came out in a gabble. 'Gotobedtogether.'

I knew he wouldn't answer immediately, Daddy always chewed over his words before speaking. And so I waited, as we did when he was about to hold forth on something or other. You could be sure his opinions were always well considered. 'Well, that's an interesting question. What are you now? Eleven, twelve? Yes, about ready to learn the facts of life.'

And so, for the rest of the drive he told me all about 'it'. About what happens to men and why and what they must do to make it nice for ladies. And what they mustn't do. What ladies can do that's nice for men and what happens when it ends. Then what happens if the lady gets pregnant and has a baby. It was all very interesting but revolting too. I couldn't imagine wanting to have a boy put his thingy inside me. After all that's where they pee from. As for having babies, I knew I wanted them one day but wished it were possible without 'it'.

Daddy talked about lubrication, ejaculation and masturbation and about something ladies have called a clitoris. He said it needs to be very excited for her to have an orgasm too. He told me some men don't know about that but that men who care about ladies do. And then he told me about VD, about syphilis and gonorrhoea and about contraception. Durexes were the best and most reliable method, he said.

15

By the time we got to Beaulieu, all my embarrassment had gone. He'd told me everything he could think of and it'd seemed like a biology lesson. His last words were 'Now you know all about intercourse. You're not an ignorant little girl any more.' He turned and looked at me over the top of his glasses, his expression suddenly stern and his steely blue eyes strangely cold. 'So don't come to ME if you get pregnant. Right?'

'Er... no Daddy. No!' I was completely amazed. Did he think I was dying to do it or something? No thanks. All those awful diseases were enough to put anyone off.

That was it. The subject was dropped and for the rest of the way to Beaulieu we sang songs—*The capital ship for an ocean trip, Abdul a bulbul emir* and *Wrap me up in your tarpaulin jacket*—all Daddy's favourites. As far as he was concerned, he'd done his duty; his daughter was now fully sex-educated.

In a way, I was grateful, but I was puzzled too. Never once had he mentioned the word love.

2

WHEN ALL ELSE FAILS

Six years later I left school, a Roman Catholic convent which I'd hated. If, as Mother used to say, schooldays are the best days of your life, then my future looked positively uninspiring. On the last day of term, my best friend, Annie, and I dumped our uniforms and worn-out satchels in the kitchen bins. Well, it was the best place for them. The stench of rotting meat cut-offs and vegetable peelings was so disgusting, we knew nobody would try and salvage them. Of course, with nuns you couldn't be sure.

It's no use pretending my parents' money had been well spent. I was the class daydreamer living in a fantasy world of romance and adventure. University was definitely beyond my reach. Of course, in those days you had to be extra brainy, one of the top two percent.

After school, if you weren't going to uni, you were expected to have some sort of career plan. I couldn't think of anything I wanted to do. I was too distracted by what was happening after school hours to worry about after school years. Parties, clothes, boys and pop music were much more interesting. My parents kept nagging at me about my future. Finally I got the point and, after a series of solemn discussions, we agreed that when all else fails, a secretarial course is a good idea.

'After all, dear, it'll tide you over until you get married,' said Mother.

'Nonsense woman, they're useful skills,' said Daddy impatiently.

I agreed with him; I wasn't into waiting for some nice young man Mother would approve of. Not for me a boring chinless type.

'Well, Mrs Hosters is the best secretarial college.'

'Don't be ridiculous, Joyce, we can't possibly afford to send her there,' said Daddy.

'Well, what about the London College? I'm sure Uncle Bert will help out with the fees.'

For years my great uncle had supported the family when they were short of a bob or two.

'Yes, Gruncle never says no,' I chipped in eagerly.

Daddy bristled and reverted to his native Lancashire. 'Shut up, our Susan, that's no way to talk.'

Mother threw him a dirty look. Her crisp Queen's English was an important attribute, a sign of class.

Gruncle's handouts always made Daddy mad. But he knew his Ministry of Defence salary couldn't satisfy Mother's aspirations, so finally, reluctantly, he agreed.

Happily, Gruncle considered my further education to be a worthy cause and paid for me to go to the London College of Secretaries. Mother thought it was a highly prestigious establishment, which meant I had to look highly presentable. She couldn't have her daughter overshadowed by the rich kids, so I was awarded a monthly dress allowance. 'Now, you're not to go spending this on records, and we don't want you frequenting those dreadful coffee bar places either,' she said, pursing her lips as she handed over a crisp blue five pound note.

'No, no of course I won't, I promise. Thank you.'

I'd never had this much in my purse before.

On the first morning of term, I came downstairs for breakfast clutching a briefcase and wearing a Black Watch tartan suit and green, square-toed mini-heeled shoes—stylish new outfit that any status-conscious middle-class mum could feel proud of.

'There, you do look smart.' Mother tweaked my collar and smoothed my new hair do—a neat little bob with ends flicked up, wing-like. 'Now a touch of mascara and some lipstick. I think you're old enough, don't you?' she whispered.

'She doesn't need to wear that muck, Joyce. She's perfectly pleasant-looking as she is.' Daddy didn't miss a chance to speak out against such unnecessary vanities. Make-up and high-heels were his pet aversions, especially the latter. 'Ruin your feet and the floor. You'll regret it when you're older.'

I spent a year at the London College of Sex, as the students called it. On manual typewriters with masked keys, we mastered the art of touch-typing to the beat of Booker T and the M.Gs' *Green Onions*. Apart from shorthand, office routine and book-keeping, we had to learn good deportment, presentation and efficiency. No big executive wanted a young lady who looked like she'd slept in her clothes, slouched in her chair and got all her papers in a muddle. That would never do.

My first job at the Design Centre near Piccadilly was dreary and undemanding. After four months as a dogsbody, I'd had enough and walked out in a fit of pique.

I hurried up the Haymarket, down into the tube and jumped on a train to Waterloo. But it's too early to be going home, I thought, as I emerged onto the mainline station. So I bought some chocolate and followed the exit signs for the Old Vic Theatre. There was a wee park opposite. It would be nicer there than sitting in the station.

I arrived just as a group of school children were filing into the matinee. They were going to see *A Midsummer Night's Dream*.

'Lucky things,' I muttered to myself.

Mother had always been an avid theatre-goer and had instilled the same love in me. We'd been to the theatre often and I already had a shoe-box full of programmes and an autograph book full of starry signatures. Our week at Stratford-on-Avon when I was fourteen had provided me with a whole host of goodies—Laurence Olivier, Charles Laughton, Albert Finney and other great actors.

I dug out my purse and checked the change. Hey, maybe I've got enough for a ticket in the gods? Why not spend the afternoon doing something I'd really enjoy?

I bought a ticket and climbed up and up to the very top of the auditorium.

The play was magical, even though the actors were far away below me, the seats were hard and it was hot. I drank in the atmosphere, the distant smell of greasepaint and scenery, sweets and ice-cream. By the time I left the theatre, I knew where I wanted to work.

The following morning I set off for London as usual, only this time I was heading for the Waterloo employment agency.

'I want a job in the theatre,' I announced after I'd done the obligatory shorthand and typing test. 'Preferably the Old Vic.'

The interviewer chuckled at my optimism. 'Not much call for secretaries there,' she said as she checked her list of vacancies. 'No, I tell a lie, the front-of-house manager is looking for someone. Only part-time, mind you. D'you want me to call him?'

'Yes, yes please,' I nodded eagerly.

She arranged an interview for the next day. Wow, what amazing luck! But I hadn't got the job yet, had I? There were bound to be lots of girls wanting to work in a theatre, and they'd probably be far prettier than me. I spent a restless night talking myself in and out of the job.

Mr Mortimer, front-of-house manager, twiddled his gold signet ring round and round his little finger. His hands were never still. Slender, perfectly manicured hands that gestured elaborately this way then that, adjusting his cuffs or straightening his bow-tie. The poor man's a bag of nerves, I thought.

'You're over-qualified, dear. I write few letters and there's little else to do apart from the daily check of the box-office receipts.'

'I don't mind that sir,' I said respectfully.

'Hmm, well, we'll see,' he said tossing his profile. 'I'll give you a month's trial. You can start next week.'

That evening my mate, Annie, rang to say our favourite band, The High Curly Stompers, were playing at the local jazz club. 'D'you want to go?'

'Rather. And wait 'til you hear my news!'

'What? What news?'

'Tell you later. Meet me at the bus-stop in half-an-hour.'

'Okey-doke.'

Wearing my favourite sloppy-Joe sweater, tightest skirt and dancing shoes I flew downstairs. My parents were in the sitting room listening to the wireless. I popped my head round the door. 'Bye. I won't be late.' And I was out of the house and away down the drive before they could object.

Just as the bus appeared, Annie raced round the corner looking amazingly French. Mind you, with a year in Paris, studying at the Sorbonne, and now a job in the French Department in Foyles Bookshop, who wouldn't be frightfully sophisticated? Her curly dark hair was urchin cut and she was wearing a shiny, pale blue, PVC mac with the collar turned up and the sweetest pair of ankle-strap patent-leather shoes. I was terribly impressed and wanted to look just like her. We jumped on the bus and climbed up to the top deck. Then I told her all about my new job and the strange Mr. Mortimer. Annie, being a woman of the world now, soon put me straight about him. 'He's probably one of them, you idiot,' she chuckled.

'What d'you mean?'

'A queer, homosexual.'

'Golly!' I'd never seen one close up.

'They don't bite you know.'

'I know they don't,' I said indignantly, not wanting to appear clueless.

'What about your parents? Were they okay about you getting a job in the theatre?'

'They were so furious I'd walked out of the Design Centre, they didn't say.'

'Typical,' said Annie. 'I think it's brilliant.'

'I'm jolly well not going to work somewhere I hate. I wish they'd treat me like an adult. I'm not at school any more.'

'Know what you mean. I'd forgotten what a bore parents can be.'

'Telling me.'

'After Paris, living at home and commuting is frightfully tedious. I've been thinking of getting a place in London,' she said airily.

'But what about us!'

'I meant us, dope. We could share.'

'Yes, yes! That'd be fantastic.'

'There are lots of flats to rent, I've seen them advertised in the Evening News. And in shop windows. I'll find us somewhere.'

Within days she'd put down a month's rent and I'd packed my bags. Mother was devastated, even though I promised to be back at weekends. 'But you're much too young. I'll be worrying about you, you know I will,' she whimpered. She was known for her worrying and getting into a state. I was used to it.

'Mummy, I'm eighteen. Everyone leaves home at eighteen.'

'I'm losing my little girl,' she sniffed and ran off upstairs.

'Thanks a lot,' said Daddy.

'Oh, gosh. I didn't think she'd be so upset, I …'

He raised his hand to shut me up. 'Go on, if that's what you want, and don't forget to take that confounded record collection with you.'

Annie and I moved into our poky Earls Court garret on a cold and blustery November day. The place was freezing. We turned on the gas fire, made a pot of tea and privately wondered if we'd done the right thing. We didn't say so, but each knew what the other was thinking. Our musty new home at the top of an old Victorian house had lumpy beds and wallpaper peeling off damp patches from the leaky roof. The traffic below was noisy and it sounded as if the couple in the next flatlet were into Scottish folk music.

'I know it's not great, but it was all I could find,' said Annie miserably.

I lit a Gauloise and passed it to her hoping she wasn't having second thoughts.

'Cheer up, we'll soon make it look homely and anyway, does it matter that much? The main thing is, we've left home and we're free.

3

AT THE OLD VIC

Mr. Mortimer's office at the Old Vic had a big desk, a comfy leather swivel chair and dozens of production pics around the walls. It looked out across the little park opposite and smelt of cigars and Air Wick. My office was the size of a broom cupboard, looked out at the brick wall of the next building and smelt of Chanel No.5—Annie's present from Paris. The work was routine and poorly paid. But I didn't mind that. I supplemented my weekly wage of four pounds ten shillings by usheretting and serving in the bar, which meant I got to see all the plays—over and over again. Each time they seemed fresh and exciting. Even so I became increasingly frustrated, wanting to be part of the magic, longing to be working backstage. Doing what, I had no idea.

One morning Mr. Mortimer asked if I could operate a plug-in telephone switchboard.

'Yes,' I said immediately, despite the fact I'd never touched one. The switchboard was located at the stage door!

'Ernie's getting on a bit and finding the hours too taxing. He needs a relief.'

Ernie, the stage door keeper, was the only person I'd met backstage. We'd had little chats when I collected the morning mail. He was a teddy-bear of a man with thick white hair and when he smiled, his round red face puckered up and his twinkly blue eyes completely disappeared. Every day he wore a different hand-knitted pullie and starched white shirt. His wife, Ethel, was a champion knitter. She'd been struck deaf during the war when a bomb dropped on the house next door and had to spend lots of time with her legs up due to varicose veins. They'd been together for fifty-two years and had four children and seven grandchildren and they were very proud of them all, well, except for that Mary, who'd taken up with a black man and gone off to live in Africa.

I said, 'Never mind, as long as they're happy.'

Ernie said, 'Hmmph, time will tell, time will tell.'

He'd been at the Vic for ages and knew everybody and everything that went on there and loved to share all the juicy tit-bits. I think he must've liked me. He wasn't the kind of man to waste time on people he didn't. 'Don't you worry about learning the board, ducks. It ain't difficult. And you being an educated young lady, you'll have it off in no time.'

He was right, I learned in an afternoon. My happiness was complete. I'd be backstage at last, well almost. He would do three afternoons and three evenings a week, I would take on the rest. With my other jobs that meant my wages went up to ten pounds ten shillings. Smashing!

I thought it'd be a doddle, sitting in Ernie's little cubicle working the board and greeting the actors as I handed out dressing-room keys. Leo McKern and Fulton Mackay were my favourites, always happy to indulge my girlish admiration and stop for a chat.

I was so keen I hadn't considered there might be a negative side to my new part-time position—the draught as the stage door swung to and fro on its automatic double hinge, the autograph hunters and theatre groupies, and Elsie, one of the local winos, who alternated between front-of-house queues and the backstage entrance performing a drunken song-and-dance routine. She looked like a scarecrow, sang like pork crackling and stank of dirty dustbins. Poor old thing, I felt sorry for her really, especially as Ernie said people like her often came from good families and had fallen on difficult times they couldn't cope with and started to drink and their good families had disowned them.

One problem I hadn't reckoned on was having to persuade the elderly actor, Wilfred Lawson, to leave the pub next door in time for his entrance as the Button Moulder in *Peer Gynt*. He seemed to be pickled most of the time, so it was quite a business. 'Wha was zat?' he'd slur, staring through me as if I wasn't there. He was a bit deaf and had bloodshot eyes that didn't focus.

'It's time you got into your costume, Mr Lawson. You'll be called soon!' I'd yell in his hairy ear.

'Wha costume?'

'The Button Moulder's. You're playing the Button Moulder!'

'Oh, yesh, so I yam.'

He'd heave himself up out of his seat and waddle precariously towards the door grabbing chairs for support and with me ready to try and catch him if he stumbled. He was a sack of bones with a crumpled face and a big red nose that looked as though someone had stuck it on crookedly. Once on stage he miraculously remembered his lines. But after the final curtain I still had to get him to his cab. I prayed Elsie wouldn't turn up and persuade him to join her in a double act that would be bound to end in a heap in the gutter. Thank goodness she'd usually collapsed in a shop doorway by the time I popped my head out to check the coast was clear.

With my new responsibilities, I thought I needed a new image—cropped chestnut coloured hair and a mac like Annie's, but black, which I wore with the collar up and tightly belted. My red patent shoes completed the outfit. I thought I looked frightfully French too.

It wasn't long before I got to know all the backstage staff at the Vic and, after the show, would go to the pub next door to drink with them and some of the small-part actors. I was now 'in the theatre' and felt accepted.

It was in the pub after work that I noticed one of the stage hands studying me. The tall, quiet man with the beard. I'd seen him around but had never spoken to him. There were prettier girls in our group so I must have been giving out strong signals, or at least a musk. He bought me a Bacardi and coke and led me to a table away from the others. 'I'm John and I work the flies,' he told me. His job was to operate the scenery from way up above the stage. 'I like it up there, away from the action.' He had a soft, caressing voice and an indefinable accent. When I asked where he came from he told me he couldn't remember and I'd have to ask the old witch. His mother was a clairvoyant and for all he knew had gypsy blood.

'And your dad?'

'Haven't a clue. Who cares?'

John's air of casual existentialism fascinated me. Soon we started seeing each other away from the theatre and bedding down on any old floor that would have us.

'You wouldn't like it at mum's,' was his excuse.

'And you wouldn't want to stay at our flat.'

Annie and I had recently moved into a dingy Victorian house in Cromwell Road. We had the two ground floor rooms, a kitchenette and a bathroom. There was a shifting population of around six of mixed sex and we slept, hemmed in by second-hand furniture and chaos, giggling like kids in a school dormitory.

John found us a place further up the Cromwell Road. A tiny room with a short, springy single bed, a cupboard with doors that wouldn't shut, two rickety chairs, a small, stained Formica table and a gas fire with a single ring at the side. The air was permanently stale and the constant traffic below made the front window rattle, but to me it was heaven. It didn't matter that I knew almost nothing about my new man; it made him all the more interesting. I was no longer an inexperienced convent girl longing to be promoted to adulthood. Like Angelique, the heroine from my favourite novels, I was in love with a tall, dark stranger, and life was going to be wonderful.

The reality of being with John delved deep into the night on a relentless round of smoky pubs and membership-only all-night bars, sleazy jazz clubs, wild parties and overnight crashes. His was a world of squalid extremes. Everyone drank heavily, everyone smoked and some took hard drugs. Most had the yellowy pallor of life in an underworld. Wherever we went there was the stench of stale beer and cigarette smoke. Secretly, I thought it was all pretty seedy but I tried to act cool.

John had a certain fondness for me, that was clear— he was a young man with a sexual appetite and obviously found me attractive. The sex was okay, as sex

29

goes, but there was little affection and John didn't go in for sweet talk, in fact he told me I was too much of a romantic. What I was looking for would only be found in slushy novels. On those rare occasions when we were alone together and not in bed, we were most likely to be high, usually on purple hearts, Mandrax or pot, and would fantasise about marriage and the flat we'd find and what it would look like. Those were the best times.

I hadn't meant to get pregnant, I'd used sperm-barrier jelly. John had flatly refused to wear durex and wouldn't be persuaded. 'Put one of them on my dick? Not bloody likely.'

After my failure to abort, the pregnancy became a taboo subject. John absolutely refused to talk about the future. For him the future was our forthcoming holiday in St. Ives, Cornwall. 'I'm going and if you don't want to come, I'll find someone else.'

'Is the flat really booked and … have we got enough money?' I dared to ask.

'It's all sorted,' said John, 'and we can hitch down, that'll save a few bob, so stop bloody worrying.'

But of course I worried. He was no whizz with finances; whatever he earned just seemed to disappear. Mostly spent on alcohol, cigarettes and drugs. My wages had to cover everything else. It was a constant struggle and we often went without dinner, making do on crisps or a plate of chips.

It was early July when we set off and for once it wasn't raining. Lifts were plentiful but I was feeling nauseous. I nibbled on dry biscuits and gazed out of the window, blind to the changing roadside scenery. It was impossible to switch off from what was happening inside me. What the hell was I going to do? The question hammered at my brain.

On Bodmin Moor the mist and drizzle obscuring the landscape and the road ahead reflected the hopelessness of my situation. How different from that trip to Cornwall two years before

~

It was the summer of 1961. Annie and I had just left school. We decided to go camping in St. Ives, the little Cornish town famous for its artists, potters and surfers. We booked a place on Clodgy Point where a friendly farmer allowed half a dozen tents to pitch in his cliff-top field.

Apart from having a good time, there was a special point to this holiday. Annie and I had agreed it was time to lose our cherries and we would do it before the fortnight was up. Get it out of the way, find out what the fuss was all about without risking the respect of our boyfriends who wouldn't know anything about it.

'It said in last month's *She* magazine that it doesn't really matter who they are or what they look like, as long as they're clean and gentle,' I told Annie. 'And we have to make sure they use durexes,' I added solemnly.

Annie giggled, puckered her pixie face and nibbled furiously at her nails. She was full of mischief and loved adventures; in September she was off to Paris to study at the Sorbonne, the lucky thing. I wished I was going too – the Eiffel Tower, the Champs Elysees, the Louvre, St Germain and Montmartre, they all sounded so much more romantic than shabby old England. I was convinced she'd never want to come back.

I think we both had notions of getting off with a couple of surfers but, sadly, two little white girls with boring hair-do's weren't in the least bit interesting to the beefy, bronzed Adonis's who rode the waves on Porthmeor Beach. We soon realised we'd probably have to make do with Andy and Alex, the train-spotters in the next tent. Andy, a thickset, dour sort with white-blonde hair and skin to match, was into electrics, whereas painfully thin Alex was full of enthusiasm for anything that chugged and puffed out smoke.

We got to know them quite well during the holiday but nothing even remotely sexy happened until the last night. After rather a lot of cider and Cornish pasties on the harbour wall, we wandered back to Clodgy holding hands. Alex had gone for Annie, so Andy had no choice. Luckily he didn't seem to mind and I reassured myself by remembering that if 'it' happened, it was to be a purely scientific experience.

Back at camp Andy tentatively slid an arm round my shoulder and leaned over to kiss me. Annie and Alex had crept away to the boys' tent and we were alone in ours. I was nervous and embarrassed and glad my blushes didn't show up in the dimness. I turned out the lamp, not wanting our shadows to provide a light show and wondered whether Annie and Alex were going to do it too. I hoped so.

The preliminaries amounted to little more than a fumble inside my bra, a painful tweak of my nipple and a couple of fingers up inside. I hoped he'd washed his hands. When he slipped on the durex I looked away.

'Er, I'm a virgin. I hope that's okay,' I whispered.

But Andy wasn't listening; he was too busy slathering on Vaseline to help him slide home. I was grateful for that. It hadn't occurred to me that some extra lubrication would be needed if it wasn't to hurt too much. In he went and after a few rammings and lots of puffing, he'd come. It was over. 'Was that good?' He lay heavy and sweating on top of me.

'Er, yes. Thanks. Very nice. D'you think you could … er … get off.'

He was squashing me. He rolled over and reached for the cigarettes. I pulled down my blouse and put on my pants.

'Want one?'

'Thanks.' It was a relief to take a long hard draw.

'We're off home tomorrow,' he said. 'Be leaving very early like.'

'Oh.'

We sat smoking in silence. Then I realised. Having intercourse hadn't been painful and, phew, there was no tell-tale blood stain on the sleeping bag liner. Perhaps using tampons from fourteen had already dealt with that little protective film Daddy had called a hymen.

Andy gave me a quick peck on the cheek and crawled out of the tent. 'I'd better be off then. Thanks, doll. Bye.'

I stubbed out my cigarette, straightened the sleeping bag and wriggled inside. I felt normal but I knew I'd changed forever. It was hard to believe I wasn't a virgin any more. Had 'it' really happened? If so, why had I done it with someone I'd only just met and hadn't any feelings for at all? It hadn't even been fun, and certainly not romantic. Oh God, Oh God! I was a slut. That kind of girl. Doomed.

4

DISGRACED

John and I walked the last few miles from Hayle to St. Ives and, even though only two months gone, I was exhausted. I staggered into our holiday flatlet and sank onto the bed longing for oblivion.

'Well, this seems alright, but I'm ready for a drink. You coming?' asked John.

'Don't think so,' I muttered.

'Suit yourself. See you later.' And he left.

I lay listening to his receding steps as he ran back down the stairs. Then I forced myself to sit up, needing desperately to understand where I was, to create a link between my body and this strange, ill-furnished room. The bed, a small double, was at least an improvement on our single back in Cromwell Road. An ugly wood and formica wardrobe dominated the room. As I opened it to put my coat away, I caught sight of myself in the huge round mirror of the art deco dressing table. My face looked drained and empty. Well, what did I expect? I turned my back on the miserable reflection. There was no way I wanted to wake up to that each morning, so I hauled the mirror round to catch the view from the big dormer window that looked out over a wide expanse of sea and sky. It was like standing on the prow of a galleon heading towards a never-ending horizon, an unknown future.

The next morning John announced that our accommodation was more expensive than he'd realised.

Arguing with the landlord was out of the question so our budget went down to a few quid. We were reduced to wandering around the town, having an occasional drink and eating burnt pasties, which were available and cheap at most bakers.

Mercifully our supply of hash was enough to alleviate my misery and keep John in a reasonable mood. The weather was hot and sunny and the tourist season hadn't begun. Much of the time we had the beach below our flatlet to ourselves and could lie listening to the swoosh of the waves and the cry of the gulls, imagining we were thousands of miles away on some exotic desert island.

By the end of the week we were completely penniless.

I couldn't face the prospect of hitching all the way back to London so we got a lift to Truro then caught a train to Reading. As there was no check at the barrier, we were able to slip on board without tickets.

The ride was a hell of hunger, exacerbated by the munchies of being stoned. It seemed that the oddest specimens of human animal were on that train and they were all eating. I spent a lot of time in the corridor, hanging onto the rail and gazing into the middle distance. I became fascinated by the different speeds of everything we passed—the nearer the faster, the farther the slower—and how looking forward with the direction of the train was looking into the future of the person sitting with their back to the engine and looking backward to where the train was coming from was the past. Weird notions like these got me through the journey. John slept most of the way.

Up until then neither of us had thought about how we could get out of the station at the other end. On the platform at Reading I phoned my old boyfriend, Maurice, who agreed to help us out. 'Get a train to Camberley, I'll meet you there. You can say you got on at Reading. I'll pay.'

It was the weekend and the Camberley ticket collector had gone home, so there were no awkward questions. Maurice insisted we crash at his place that night. He cooked us a meal too—baked beans on toast with an egg on top, a feast. After that John rolled a joint and sloped off to the sitting room. I left him to it—I'd had enough dope to last a lifetime.

Maurice and I sat in the kitchen drinking coffee. It was such a relief to be with someone I could entirely trust. He'd been my first boyfriend and although we'd drifted apart after leaving school, we'd always remained close friends. I still adored him. He was soft-hearted, generous and easy-going and reminded me of Cliff Richard, the idol of my early teens. 'You look dreadful, what's the matter?' he wanted to know.

My distress poured forth in a deluge of tears. He took me in his arms. 'Oh, Maurice, if only it'd been you,' I wailed.

'No, no. Not me! I'd have had to marry you.'

'Am I that awful?' I sobbed.

'You're not awful at all. You know that, you stupid thing. It's me. I don't want to get married or have children. It's too much of a responsibility.'

'John hardly talks to me now,' I sniffed. 'As if it's all my fault.'

Maurice wasn't in the least surprised. 'Frankly, I think he's a shit. You'd be better off without him.'

Back at the theatre I found it increasingly difficult to keep my emotional confusion in check. When I went round for my stage door shift, Ernie realised immediately that something was very wrong. 'You're not your usual self, what's the matter, ducks?'

'Nothing, Ernie, I'm fine, thanks.'

'Hmmph, can't kid me, you can't. Is it something to do with that layabout you've been seeing?'

'It's nothing. I'm just not feeling that well at the moment.'

He gave me a knowing look and reached for his coat. I could tell he didn't believe me, but I didn't want him to know. He'd warned me about John and I'd not listened. 'Night, ducks. And mind you're back to normal tomorrow,' he said sternly as he left the theatre.

I started my shift wishing I could've gone straight home. I loved my job but now everything seemed pointless and John didn't give a damn, he'd made that plain. Our working hours made it easy for him to avoid being alone with me, so there was no confrontation. Much was left unsaid, which was just as well; I couldn't have dealt with it I was so exhausted by the evening— morning sickness was all-day sickness in my case. When I'd finished at the theatre, I'd go back to our bedsit, eat something, if I could stomach it, and crash out. John would tidy up after the evening house, go to the pub and then on to some club or other. If he came back at all, it was probably nearing dawn. In the morning I knew better than to wake him before I left for work.

The next Saturday I went to a family christening—I was to be one of the godmothers. Not a role I could relate to but I'd accepted some weeks before. After the service little Rosie was passed to me. This could be my baby, I thought, as the pink bundle in a long white christening robe gurgled and wriggled in my arms. I swallowed a choke and managed a cheesy grin for the photo albums. Inside I was desolate. I simply had to talk to someone. What about my cousin Beth who was tending her latest in an upstairs bedroom?

She was wonderful. She didn't castigate or moralise. Instead she offered to look after me during my pregnancy. She and her husband lived in Dublin with their two-year-old son and baby daughter. 'You could help with my two,' she suggested.

'Oh, Beth, thank you, thank you,' I cried, flinging my arms round her.

'But I'm only prepared to have you if you tell your parents and they agree.'

Even though the idea terrified me, I knew she was right.

On the way back to London I gazed out of the train window in a trance of despair. Tell Mother and Daddy I was expecting John's child? They'd met him and it was obvious they totally disapproved. We'd been down to visit one weekend and he'd hardly spoken to them. Not only that, he'd refused lunch, which they found inexcusable. We'd caught an early train back to town.

'If I'd thought there was a bloody meal involved, I wouldn't have come,' he'd snapped. 'You know perfectly well I can't stand eating in public.' It was one of his hang-ups, something to do with his slightly protruding teeth.

So, considering their poor opinion of John, I felt sure the only way I could get my parents' help was to say I didn't know who the father was. I thought up a plausible story and decided to tackle this most daunting of revelations the following weekend. The persistent rhythm of the train over the sleeper joints brought Daddy's lecture, that had covered everything from technique to contraception, echoing into my brain like a death knell on my condition and my place in the family. ' … so now you know all I can think of to tell you, don't come to ME if you get pregnant.'

He'd called condoms rubber johnnies—how appropriately inappropriate, I remembered ruefully.

What would they do? Throw me out, I supposed. I didn't seriously believe that, but Daddy could be very brutal if really riled up and Mother … well, I could imagine what she'd have to say. The word 'neighbours' seemed to sum it up. She was a slave to respectability and, in 1963, unmarried mothers were socially unacceptable.

I packed my weekend case on the Friday night and took the coach home to Camberley and Manor Lodge, where I'd spent most of my childhood. On the way I tried to read, I tried to sleep, I even thought of striking up a conversation with the person sitting next to me, but what would I say? Nothing seemed worth saying. Daddy met me at the coach stop and gave me a big hug. That I didn't dissolve into floods of tears was a miracle. We drove home in a blur of trivial conversation.

Cousin Beth's mother, Auntie Tillie, and Johan, her second husband, were staying at Manor Lodge having recently returned from several years in Teheran. I loved them both and decided to speak to them before telling my parents the news. Auntie Tillie was outspoken and zany, quite different from Mother—she'd been the family rebel. Apart from being up to all sorts of mischief as a child, she'd later shocked everyone rigid by leaving Uncle Cyril, Beth's father, for Johan, the boy next door, a student of twenty-one. She was thirty-six at the time. Like Auntie, Johan was pretty down-to-earth, so I felt their reaction would be more practical than outraged. On Saturday afternoon, when Mother went down to the local shop and Daddy was, as ever, tinkering with some engine part in his workshop, I went to look for them. They were having coffee in the kitchen.

I'd been right. They took my news without a blink and asked no awkward questions. Perhaps they weren't that surprised. I'm sure they thought my wayward behaviour would get me into trouble sooner or later.

'Do you want us to tell your father?' said Auntie.

'Oh, yes. Please.'

They went off to the workshop to find him. I sat in my room until they summoned me. When I asked how he'd reacted, Auntie simply said, 'You know your father.'

I thought I did, but at that moment had every reason to doubt and didn't dare imagine.

'You'd better go and see,' she added.

I went down to the workshop quaking with nerves.

Daddy was ultra calm, passed no judgement and emanated a coolness that I found terrifying. 'Your mother must be told as if none of the rest of us know. You must do it at tea this afternoon. That's all.' I was dismissed.

If Mother noticed expressions were heavy when we gathered in the sitting room, she gave no hint, she was too busy pouring the tea and twittering away about the exploits of one of the neighbours. I was painfully aware of the loaded glances the others threw at me. When we were all settled with full cups and plates of jam sponge

I took a very deep breath then gabbled out my story. 'I'm pregnant. I got drunk at a party and had to lie down. A man came in. I didn't see who he was. I don't remember much more.'

Mother went ashen with shock. 'Oh God, what can we say?'

Daddy was immediately irritated. 'Not what can we say, woman. What can we do?'

Do? What did he mean? What could we do about it? I was going to have a baby and nothing was going to change that.

'Well, she simply can't, I mean, we can't have her...' Mother was crying now.

'Beth has a good gynaecologist. I'll get her number. I suggest you go and see if she can help,' said Auntie.

Mother was too distraught to respond but Daddy agreed it was a good idea and he would take me. There was no more to say except that Granny wasn't to be told. Granny, Daddy's mother, was now living at Manor Lodge and had her bedsitting-room on the ground floor where, most of the time, she sat glued to the television smoking cigarettes and oohing and aahing at the screen. She was a warm and loving Granny and I was hurt for us both that I was forbidden to tell her what was going on.

That night, convinced I'd shattered everything we'd ever known as a family, I cried myself to sleep. Mother did the same. I could hear her.

Helena Wright, the gynaecologist, was a woman of great tact and sensitivity. She was also an elderly eccentric, brimming with wisdom. She'd worked with Marie Stopes in the early days and been very active in the introduction of contraception for unmarried women. Up on her examination couch, she laid a red paisley scarf over my naked tummy—for modesty's sake I supposed—and pulled on lightweight rubber gloves before diving in. She closed her eyes and mumbled to herself whilst checking me out. If she had any notion I might not be telling the absolute truth, she chose to say nothing. 'Now, as there is no acknowledged father, I think we may have grounds for a termination,' she said as she emerged from my nether regions.

'Thank you.' My voice was weak with relief.

She smiled and picked up the phone. An appointment was immediately arranged with a colleague of hers at University College Hospital. Daddy was called in and gruffly informed of the situation. 'With luck you'll be able put this whole unfortunate episode behind you and get on with your life,' he said as we left the consulting room.

It was the only reference made to my dilemma. I had, however, to collect my stuff from the bedsit—it'd been decided that I should go sick from work and return home for the time being. Unsurprisingly, John wasn't in when we arrived and I was able to remove my belongings without interruption. I trudged up and down the four flights of stairs several times, thinking it would be a blessing if I aborted there and then, and saved us a lot of trouble. Daddy chose to wait in the car. Who could blame him? I imagine he just didn't want to see what he suspected to be a sordid little love nest. Although I'd avoided telling him and Mother we were living together, they probably had their suspicions.

I left John an explanatory note saying I'd be in touch when I had news and would he please ring me at home.

Our appointment with Professor Nixon at UCH was brief and conclusive. I was too far gone and he wasn't prepared to risk complications. I had to have my baby and if I wanted to put him or her up for adoption, Dr Wright would no doubt be able to help. I was coldly and neatly dealt with. Daddy and I left the hospital and drove home in stunned silence.

5

BANISHED

Under the covers at the bottom of my bed I lay curled into the tightest ball my body would allow. It was August and unbearably hot and entirely possible to suffocate beneath the weight of the bedclothes. As a little girl it was a place I could escape to when life became unbearable—because Mother wouldn't let me wear my sun-dress before the end of May or put on her pink nail varnish at Christmas or I'd been thwacked for climbing dangerous trees. When I felt better I'd crawl out and the air would be fresh and pure and things wouldn't seem so bad and nobody would say anything because I'd been punished already. But this time there'd be no escaping. The voices battling in my skull were relentless—maternal instinct versus the demands of middle-class society.

The main reason I'd lied was fear of the consequences of telling the truth. Had I been honest and admitted we were living together and the baby was John's, what would my parents have done? Insist he married me? They could hardly have dragged him up the aisle if he didn't want to go. So then what? They'd have had to accept this was to be a love-child, at least as far as I was concerned, and been faced with throwing me out to fend for myself in an unsympathetic society. In another life they might have kept us both at home. While I went out to work, Mother would be baby-minder, coping with the social stigma and the extra expense. But in this life, the idea was unthinkable. She'd be having to forego her silk undies for a bit, I thought sardonically, as well as fretting about my future marriage prospects. No man would be interested in taking her daughter on—after all, in those days, an unmarried mother was soiled goods and her child a millstone. So the alternative was they'd disown me and life would become a hopeless struggle for survival. Landlords weren't prepared to let rooms to single mothers, no crèches existed and there was no Social Security support. Even pregnant brides were still sneered at.

Alongside the cowardly self, a more responsible part of me admitted my behaviour had been wayward and disreputable with disastrous results. Now there was a price and I should be the one to pay it. I would carry my baby to term then give him or her up for adoption, thereby saving my parents even further anguish. After all, it was hardly their fault I was in this miserable predicament. After Daddy's pep talk on the trip to Beaulieu, the subject of pre-marital sex had popped up occasionally and their views were clear-cut.

'It's up to the woman to insist he wears a condom. She should never assume he'll marry her if she falls for a child. Shotgun weddings are a downright scandal. No man should be forced into marriage and, as far as I'm concerned, it's as simple as that.' Daddy was typically succinct.

'You know my feelings on the matter,' Mother would say primly. 'Men prefer to marry virgins. But if they must have … er, be intimate, then a gentleman would make sure he was protected and take responsibility if anything were to go wrong.'

'Huh! For goodness sake, Joyce, this is the twentieth century, not the dark ages.'

And so the ball would go back and forth across the net and I'd get quite weary. It never occurred to me that upbringing or past experience might have led them to think the way they did. I took most things at face value in those days. Daddy was a scientific man, so it was entirely logical that, in his opinion, there should be a sequence to relationships—attraction, dates, protected sex, engagement and trial marriage. Up to which point either party could back out with no harm done. If everything was going swimmingly—marriage, a couple of years' consolidation, family, if finances allowed, and then only two children because the world is becoming over-populated anyway. Mother was hung up on respectability—attraction, dates, falling in love, engagement, a beautiful white wedding, making love, as many babies as you like.

'Drat it, Joyce,' Daddy would say, 'sexual attraction and falling in love, as you put it, pretty much the same thing. All that romantic twaddle is foreplay. And as for breeding like rabbits, huh—darned irresponsible.'

'John! You know you don't mean that,' Mother would retort, looking hurt.

'For all practical purposes, I most certainly do.'

At that point I'd get worried that they weren't as happy as they appeared to be, even though Mother took care to tell me later, 'Your father's a sentimental chap really. He just doesn't like to admit it.'

So was there a right way and a wrong way of going about the love thing? Apparently not. Who could blame me for being muddled?

When I emerged from under the bedclothes, the air outside was heavy and my punishment still waiting but at least I'd made a decision. I would agree that Dr

Wright should be approached to arrange a private adoption. After that I had to get my life back. Start again.

I'd been so sad to leave the Vic, my new friends, Ernie and even Mr. Prissy Mortimer. As for John … every time the phone rang, I felt my heart thumping, it could be him begging me to go back. But this was a fantasy and I knew it. Admitting it however, was impossible.

I washed my face and went downstairs, relieved to have the house to myself that day—the weather was fine and the others had gone to admire the flowers at Wisley gardens. I made myself a cup of tea and carried it through to the sitting room. There, on the long window seat I could put my feet up and look out across the rockery which was a mass of colour in the summer months. My back was aching so I grabbed a cushion from one of the armchairs. Behind it were three orange W.H. Smith's spiral bound notebooks. There was nothing written on the covers; they were probably Mother's, she was always jotting down gardening or cooking tips. But no, when I picked one up and flicked through, I recognised the beautiful handwriting immediately. It was one of Daddy's diaries—the first entry read: *January 17th 1939. Bought engagement ring for Joyce.* Before putting the books back behind the cushion I just couldn't stop myself, I had to look at another entry—*August 4th 1963.* Three words and no more—*Bombshell from Susan.* Well, what did I expect? A bomb had been dropped on their lives and the sooner their daughter and her embarrassment were safely out of the way, the better.

47

Cousin Beth's compassionate offer still stood. Daddy had made all the necessary arrangements—Mother being permanently on the brink of tears and simply not up to practicalities. I was to leave for Dublin the next day.

In Ireland, Catholic girls who had fallen from grace were shown no mercy. They were bundled off to homes for unmarried mothers, where, after giving birth, they were required to nurse their babies for six weeks before giving them up for adoption. Perhaps, in the eyes of the Roman Catholic church, those weeks represented some sort of retribution. I doubt it was on the purely practical grounds that babies benefit from at least some breast-feeding. The homes were virtual detention centres, where the girls had to work from dawn to dusk, the diet was barely adequate, the conditions appalling and the air hung heavy with prayers for forgiveness. Invariably they were run by nuns and, if my convent days were anything to go by, there would be little comfort or understanding to lighten the misery of those unfortunate girls. On the other hand, here was I, going to stay with loving people in a comfortable home where the very idea that the wrath of a vengeful god would descend on me would be considered a sick joke. And although the prospect of losing my baby at birth was unbearable, having to give him or her up after six weeks would've been even more painful. I should think myself lucky. I tried to.

By the morning of my departure I still hadn't heard from John and phoning the Vic had proved fruitless. I suspected he was already seeing someone else and busied myself with packing, not that there was much to take. My small suitcase contained little more than a pinafore, a smock, a pair of stretchy ski pants, my red ankle-strap patent-leather shoes and a home-made elastic halter contraption designed to hold up my stockings when my waist disappeared. Beth had promised to lend me anything else I might need. The tiny innocent growing in my womb would keep me warm in the winter months. That was it. I zipped my suitcase with a hopeless flourish and went downstairs.

On the doorstep at Manor Lodge Mother wasn't the only unhappy one.

'Ee, love. I'm going to miss you.' Granny sniffled noisily and held out her arms. She'd been told I was going to *au pair* for Beth. 'Now you look after them wee mites and don't forget to write to your old Granny once in a while.'

I promised and hugged her tightly. Why the hell shouldn't she know the truth? There could be only one reason—she would've been vehemently against adoption. Granny was unashamedly working-class and believed families should stick together no matter what befell and bugger what anyone thought. I longed to blurt it all out there and then.

'Get a move on, Susan, you've a plane to catch.' Daddy sat in the car tapping his gloved fingers on the steering wheel. I climbed in and, as we rolled off down the drive, leant out of the window for one last goodbye.

There they were, two mothers—Granny, short and stout in her pinny with that shelf of a bosom resting on her tummy, how many times I'd snuggled up to her when I was little. Then there was Mother, straight, slim, immaculate in her green and white striped Horricks dress. Her face was inanimate, cast in the wax of sadness and disappointment—the slight crease in the brow, the misty eyes and the mouth set in a hard line.

One hand was raised as if she was taking a vow, but really she just couldn't bring herself to wave properly. Her hands weren't like Granny's, they were pale and slender, the nails manicured; she wore rubber gloves to do the chores. Granny rolled up her sleeves and got stuck in, hers were square and spatulate, working hands. At that parting moment one hand mopped her face with a big white hankie, the other waved for all its worth. Oh Granny, how I loved you. Blinking back my grief I rolled up the window as we drove through the gate and away.

6

MARMITE TOASTIES AND
A HALF-TIMBERED CAR

On the plane to Dublin I gazed down at the gauzy white clouds over the Irish Sea trying to imagine what kind of a household I would be living in for the next five months.

My cousin Beth, English rose, had escaped in 1959 from a step-mother she couldn't bear and married a pilot with the Irish airline, Aer Lingus. This was Dave Atkinson, dare-devil and francophile, who got a particular kick out of shocking people. As he would behave outrageously at the least sniff of a relative, living in Dublin meant that ritual family occasions could be avoided and Beth's embarrassment spared.

In 1960, Beth had baby Thomas, so grandma Tillie would pop over to Dublin whenever possible. In Auntie, Dave met his match. She too could be extremely contrary and enjoyed smashing him the odd verbal back-hander to keep him on his toes. She thought him a hoot and, I suspect, was happy not to be considered the only miscreant in the clan.

The noisy lowering of the under-carriage jerked me out of my reverie. We were coming in to land. Below me I could see the outline of the coast and Howth promontory, known as Ireland's Eye, where I was to spend most of my pregnancy helping Beth look after Thomas and baby Sadie. How ironic; I was going to Dublin to rehearse a role I wouldn't be able to play.

Beth and Dave's house had a stunning view over Dublin Bay, when you could see it through the persistent rain. From the moment I puffed my way up the steep steps to their front door, they made me feel welcome. It couldn't have been easy having a lump like me on the premises.

My cousin Beth was a strong, determined character with a soft-centred and sympathetic nature. Dave was a demanding, deliberately eccentric individual who thought of himself as ninety-nine percent French—goodness knows if he had any justification—so it was definitely in my favour that I could speak his favourite language reasonably well. Of course, being a pilot, he was away a good deal, so it was easier to tolerate my presence. When he came home he seemed to relish having another female to shock with his bilingual swearing and unmerciful teasing. I pretended to mind but didn't really and Beth, in mock disapproval, would always exclaim, 'Oh, Dave. Really!'

The room I had been given was small but comfortable and the crowded bookcase was to prove a sanity saver. I started at one end and worked my way to t'other. From Sagan to Sartre, Colette to Camus. It was humiliating to recognise that, until then, I'd filled my head with romantic slush and it was time I grew up, literally.

Despite my pain, I managed on the whole to be jolly, but every couple of weeks I'd lose my footing on the tightrope and topple into floods of tears. Then Beth would comfort and guide me out of my blackness and I'd struggle back up again, but it was impossible not to be constantly reminded of my hopeless situation.

Most of the time my days were full—changing nappies, preparing feeds, making Marmite toasties, potting and playing baby games. I painted a big ABC chart to hang on the broom-cupboard door, learned to cook quiche and filter coffee, went for long, lonely walks and read, read, read. I also had to go to antenatal classes and pretend I was married—I'd bought a cheap ring in Woolies as soon as my bump was too big to hide. When Dave was home, I helped pander to his whims and fancies and he had a few, particularly in the food department. He was certainly not the easiest of husbands or the most attentive father. There was no way Dave would think of changing a nappy. '*Zut*, Zaza, the yoke's done it again. Yuck, peanut butter. Do something!'

And Beth would say 'Oh, Dave. Really!' As usual.

There were *merde alors* galore, of course. French was spoken often in the Atkinson household and we listened to lots of Brassens, Brel, Aznavour and the like. Dave's francophilia soon rubbed off on me.

Despite all the evidence, I was still not convinced it was over between John and I. Daily I ran to the post to see if he'd written. For several weeks there was no word, but one day I recognised his writing on an envelope. I tore it open. He must still care, he wouldn't write if he didn't. It had to be good. Inside the envelope was another, which was covered in pencil-written words, all at angles: GONE, GONE, GONE AWAY, IT'S OVER, FINISHED, LEAVING, LEFT THE VIC and similar such phrases. I crumpled into a shaking heap, sobbing until I could scarcely breathe, could hardly see through my swollen eyes and my chest hurt from the racking. Beth hovered and made consoling noises but I had to go through the pain. Unbelievably, I was still not convinced.

In late October, she, Dave and the children went on holiday and I ran away. I had to get to London to find John and for him to say the words to my face. I caught the evening ferry back to England. Standing on the deck as we tossed in a very choppy Irish Sea, the sea legs I'd acquired on the family boat and from sailing days in my early teens, didn't fail me. I hung onto the rail and gazed at the moon enjoying the freshness of the wind, whilst others were throwing up all around. The extra weight of pregnancy kept me warm and, even though thoughts of my situation were uppermost in my mind, I tried to escape into the momentary pleasure of controlling my life, my getaway.

Annie and her sister, Rachel, were now sharing a small flat in Warwick Road, Earls Court, with a couple of girlfriends and various short-stoppers. The place was usually full but they found me a bed. The following day I set off on my search. I rang the Old Vic expecting to draw a complete blank, but John was still there, the job-quitting had been a lie. He agreed to talk, so we met in the coffee bar on Charing Cross Station; I couldn't bear the thought of any of my theatre friends seeing me pregnant.

'You look well.' John's tone was warm, even complimentary. Was he pleased to see me?

'I just had to get away. To be here again. Dublin seems to far.' Self-pity rose in my throat. I gulped it back under control. 'Where are you living now?'

'With Mum. You can stay if you want.' So casual, so easy.

I hardly hesitated. Maybe he still cared. 'Yes. Please.'

Mrs Williams was darkly eccentric and I was reminded that John had referred to her as 'the old witch' because she was into ritualistic magic and spiritualist stuff. She gave me the creeps, it was impossible to feel comfortable in her presence and I was relieved when we left her dingy house in Blackstock Road to spend the evening in the local pub.

For once with John, I managed not to drink but was nonetheless inebriated enough in spirit to sleep with him and subject myself to extremely discomforting intercourse.

The next morning he was up, dressed and gone before I could ask any questions. 'Have to go, see you.'

I too couldn't wait to get out of the dreary place. I didn't want to have to talk to his creepy mum. Feeling disillusioned, empty and used, I trudged back to Warwick Road to find Daddy had tracked me down and I was to ring him the moment I returned. I put off the dreaded phone call as long as possible. The girls were aghast, both at John's behaviour and my refusal to accept it was over.

'But I'm carrying his baby. I just don't understand,' I protested.

'You're an idiot, Sue. Men often ditch girls when they get pregnant.' Annie was clearly frustrated by me. 'Go on, you'd better phone your father.'

When Daddy arrived at the flat the next day, his detachment was harder to bear than the telling off I'd expected. With no wasted words on the way, he drove me to Euston station to catch the train back to Anglesey. He handed me two tickets—one for the train, the other the return ferry. 'Now this time stay put and get on with it,' he said offering a cold cheek, which I dutifully kissed.

That November I was shocked and upset by John F. Kennedy's assassination. But why? I was apolitical. Why did I care? It seemed that my leashed emotions were manifesting themselves in unlikely ways. The week before I'd wept inappropriately at an Ingmar Bergman film and had been particularly moved that Irish bus passengers crossed themselves every time they passed a church.

My sad little life was on hold. I could see no future. I was now six months gone and time seemed interminable. Only two thirds through my pregnancy, I had at last accepted that John and I were through. He felt nothing. I'd been a plaything, a diversion. In a way it was liberating but did little to lighten the anguish that came with every tiny baby movement, every gentle internal stroke. But I was getting on with it, as Daddy had instructed.

After a quiet Christmas just prior to which the baby had 'dropped' in my womb and was getting ready to push its way out into the world, I left Howth and returned to England to stay with Auntie Tillie and Johan who had by now bought a house in Wargrave. It was only half an hour from Manor Lodge and near enough to the Princess Christian private nursing home in Windsor, where I was to give birth. The doctor in charge of my delivery knew of my circumstances. 'Mr and Mrs Whatmough, I think it would be kinder, easier for your daughter, not to see her baby. I suggest we give her an anaesthetic as soon as the head appears. Do you agree?'

They did. Put that way it was hard not to.

My baby was due in early February so there was a month to get through—somehow. My body was really cumbersome by now. I tired easily and often had backache but was reasonably healthy. I'd made sure that my diet was good and had given up smoking and drinking too. I felt I owed it to both to my baby and his future parents.

Auntie's was a warm, comfortable household where there was much chat and laughter and the welcome distractions of reading, Scrabble and learning to do cryptic crosswords. But at the end of January there was work to be done and my evenings became incredibly hard to endure. A layette for the baby had to be provided and it had to be tagged. As there could be no proud initials to embroider, I spent several evenings sewing little crimson daisies on matinee jackets, nighties, nappies, towels and a beautiful shawl. With the exception of my dear Granny, our closest family members had been told of my condition and one kind auntie had knitted the jackets, another had crocheted the shawl.

I'd been trying not to think too much about the forthcoming birth, but now it was impossible. I was seriously frightened. All sorts of things could go wrong. In bed at night, my carefully controlled emotions surfaced. Questions, questions and no answers. Was I doing the right thing? How could I do it? Everything in me cried out to keep my baby. But there was no option. What else could I do? Who would the couple be? What would they be like? I'd never know. That it was guaranteed he or she would be truly wanted and loved was what mattered most. At least one family would be happy with this new baby, I had to remember I was giving them what they most desired. The cost to me was not their worry.

As my time drew nearer, the impending loss loomed and I found myself now relishing the new life in my belly. I would miss the flutter of my little interior butterfly, safe from the ruthless outside world, and so I wrote a poem and, in the haven of my bedroom, read it aloud praying that, by some miracle, my baby might hear and understand how I felt.

You lie beneath red marble cliffs,
adrift in a crimson sea.
So snug, so dark, so deep.
Quite content to grow
within the deepest part of me,
to live and breathe and sleep.
I'll never hold you in my arms
nor rock you on my knee.
My babe I yearn to keep.
There is an after-world of me
that's quite another place.
It's calling out to you.
And very soon your fate
will pull you screaming into space
all beautiful and new.
to join the other members
of the hardly human race.
There's nothing I can do.

On Saturday morning, 1st February 1964, Auntie Tillie and Johan went out shopping. I was still in bed. My time was nearly up, I wasn't sleeping that well and felt uncomfortably heavy. I dragged myself to the bathroom to go to the loo. There was a small show of blood. I knew this was it. I washed and dressed carefully and went down to ring my parents. They said they'd be over as soon as they could.

After lunch contractions started, but they were at long enough intervals for us to know I still had some while to go. Mother and Daddy arrived to take me to the nursing home. I climbed awkwardly into the back seat of the car. Mercifully my waters didn't break during the drive to Windsor. An embarrassing stain on the leather upholstery would have been a permanent reminder of a painful day.

As soon as I was installed in an upstairs room at the nursing home my parents left. I sensed their need to distance themselves. That way it was easier for them to dismiss the situation as an unpleasant dream from which they would be waking soon. I was never more alone than at that moment when I needed tenderness, comfort and a hand to hold. I was learning that it's best not to depend on anyone.

A nurse came to shave me and give me an enema. Then she plumped up my pillows, told me the doctor had been alerted and I was to expect a visit from the anaesthetist.

Between frantic rushes to the loo I lay staring at the polystyrene tiles on the ceiling trying to count the dots. Anything to pass the time between contractions. The anaesthetist arrived. He was a very tall man and thin, with sandy hair and a mass of freckles, not at all what I'd expected. I answered his softly spoken questions as best I could. He reassured me and thanked me politely before creeping out.

The doctor came next, checked me out and pronounced my baby was nowhere near ready to be born. He was wrong; within hours the contractions were coming harder and faster. I was given Pethadine to help ease the pain. It did, a little. Through each tortuous spasm I practised the breathing and relaxation method I'd learnt at the antenatal classes. It was after midnight when I was given the pre-med. In the middle of a particularly uncomfortable contraction I was transferred onto a trolley and wheeled into the delivery room where they rolled me onto my side. Right next to the table where I lay was a wire cradle. It looked cold and hard. But nothing much matters when you feel blocked and your loins are on fire from the intensity, the inevitability, of what is about to happen. There is no let-up, no escape when your bowels are threatening to explode. The combined agony in my heart, mind and body became unbearable. I longed for unconsciousness.

Nurses hovered. The anaesthetist loomed. I strained and pushed and cried with the pain. It felt like my baby, desperate to be born, was ripping my insides. Tears and sweat mingled as they poured onto the table. Then at last, 'Okay, Tom, here's the head.' I recognised the doctor's voice.

'You won't feel a thing,' said the anaesthetist as I shut my eyes.

The next morning I woke as if immediately after those words. I was back in my room. A young nurse I hadn't seen before came in. 'You've had a little boy. Seven and a half pounds. He's perfect.'

I smiled wanly. She probably didn't yet know my situation.

My breasts felt odd, my tummy was still swollen, my genitals were raw and delicate. I couldn't sit comfortably.

'Sister will be along in a minute, so let's get you cleaned up. We could start by brushing your hair, it's a mess,' she chuckled.

By the time the sister appeared I was looking halfway respectable. She said my baby was fine but obviously didn't want to tell me more about him. 'You'll feel uncomfortable for a few days. We opened your cervix so it wouldn't tear. But you're stitched up again now. And we gave you an injection to help dry up your milk. You'll need another one in a couple of days. How do you feel?'

'I'm alright … thank you.'

'We need a name for the birth certificate. Have you thought about that?'

I hadn't. I said the first name that came into my head. 'Sebastian, just Sebastian.'

The sister raised an eyebrow and swept out.

My parents came to see me later that day and informed me that everything was arranged. The adoptive parents would come for my baby the following Saturday. I could return home on the Sunday.

After that I had no more visits or visitors. The lonely week dragged painfully by. I read, rested and recovered, having Dettol baths as often as allowed to ease my discomfort. I rang my closest friends and got a message to John. Sebastian was the only baby in the home, I heard him crying down the corridor. It took the greatest act of will not to go running to comfort him, but my feet were leaden. If I'd gone there would be no turning back. I cried with him.

Saturday arrived. I stood by the window waiting to see the people who would take my Sebastian away. I was caught by the sister and told to go back to bed. But they couldn't watch me all day. Sometime in the afternoon a Morris Traveller pulled up in the drive below. A couple got out, took a carrycot from the back and disappeared through the door below me. It had to be them. I noticed he was tall with a crewcut and she was small but I couldn't see their faces. I darted back and forth from the bed to the window to be sure of being there when they left.

After what seemed an age, the man emerged with the carry-cot. A little pink head peeped out from the blankets. The woman followed with a large bag; the layette I'd so carefully embroidered. They opened the door of their half-timbered car and put the carry-cot on the back seat. Then they got in and drove away. Taking my baby out of my life, forever.

7

GRIEVING

The following morning I was waiting by the entrance when Patience, Daddy's car, rolled through the gates. Mother jumped out and gave me a quick hug, 'All right, dear?'

'Yes.'

What else could I say? There were no bandages, no crutches. My wounds were invisible. She could convince herself that now Sebastian had gone, so had my pain. I put my case in the boot and climbed into the back of the car.

'Hello, Daddy,' I said.

He didn't turn round, 'You're sure you haven't left anything behind?'

'Yes, I'm sure.'

We sat in silence while Mother went off to pay the bill.

From Windsor to Manor Lodge we passed through countryside awakening to spring, but all I could see was a desert; no future, just a huge expanse of nothingness. For the last nine months I'd had a purpose, a reason to exist; to give birth to another human being. But I wasn't allowed to be his mother. I was just a useless, empty shell.

When we turned into the drive at Manor Lodge the wild garden was a mass of snowdrops and the tiny tips of emerging crocuses. The sky was crisply blue—new life would soon be everywhere. As soon as we drew up,

I jumped out of the car. Granny would be there. She would welcome me, she would fling her arms round me and I'd feel warmth again.

Heedless of my still delicate condition, I sped into the house, down the hall to her room and charged in without knocking. The television was on and there she was, close to the screen, bent forward, intent and tense, her old wool crochet shawl pulled tight round her bony shoulders.

'Granny! Granny, it's me.'

'Ssh, ssh! Dixon's been hit.' She flapped her hand in my direction but didn't turn round.

This little rejection burst my fragile bubble. I flew up to my room and flung myself on the bed. Even Granny didn't care. What did you have to do to be loved, really loved?

Then a voice called up to me, croaky and urgent. 'Where's our Susan, where is she? Come on down, love, and give your old Granny a big hug.'

I wiped my eyes and ran downstairs. There she was, her wrinkly face glowing with love. 'Ee, I've missed you. Now come and tell me all about them two wee children of Beth's.'

Clasping her knobbly, outstretched hand I followed her into her little bedsit. The television was still on, the credits were rolling; she'd been watching one of her favourites, *Dixon of Dock Green*. She switched off the set and sank into her wing armchair. The gas fire was on, the room was hot and smoky. I drew up the old leather pouffe and sat down at her feet. She settled her hand on my shoulder. It felt warm and comforting. I took a deep breath. 'Thomas is adorable, he has white blonde hair, a round face and the pinkest cheeks,' I started. 'And Sadie looks like a baby Auntie Tillie.'

Granny giggled croakily. 'Ee, I can just imagine,' she said. 'Go on, love, go on.'

And so I told her about my time in Howth, about sweeties and potties and baby clothes, and about Dave and his capriciousness and how I loved Beth. It was like telling a story. Whenever I felt emotion rising to the surface, I stifled it. How I longed to spill out the whole truth, to tell my dear Granny I'd had a baby. But I didn't, there was always the chance she might've had a heart attack.

Gradually a protective shell began to form, fragile at first but becoming harder as time went by. In those days there was no such thing as post-traumatic stress, you were expected to return to normality as if nothing had happened, to concentrate on the moment and make plans for the future. In front of me was a rocky path up the side of a dark mountain. When I reached the top I'd be able to see clearly. In the meantime there was the humdrum process of existence, the 'getting on with it.'

Three weeks later, on the fourth of March 1964, we came home from the cinema to find Granny in bed and struggling to stay alive. She'd had angina for some years and with the weakening that comes with old age, her heart was no longer able to bear the strain. As her life slowly drained away, we sat holding her hands and praying silently for a reprieve, knowing there could be none. When finally I crawled into bed it was four in the morning but I felt suspended in time and most of all, in disbelief. Downstairs my Granny lay pale and still under her brushed cotton sheet. The doctor was filling in the death certificate. I'd seen her die, I had to believe it. But I didn't have to accept it.

At Granny's cremation, Daddy cried. It was the first time I'd seen tears roll down his cheeks and, despite my own great sorrow, I rejoiced in his show of emotion. He was capable of tears, they were there and that was all that mattered.

Dear Granny, how I missed her. Whenever I'd felt really low, she'd been there to rescue me with a hug, a laugh or a story. Now, like Christopher Robin, I'd sit by the window watching the raindrops racing down the panes. In my misery there was comfort in pretending I was a little girl again, innocent, loved and safe. But, most of the time, disillusionment and bitterness gnawed at my insides. How naïve I'd been to take for granted that the love of my parents was guaranteed—no matter what, I could feel secure. And I was angry too. How could they be so dominated by middle-class morals that they'd allow their daughter's baby, their grandchild, to be given away to strangers? My emotions were still in turmoil, seesawing, jolting from up to down and back again. A future with love, laughter and a career in the theatre was unimaginable, but the alternative, a pathetic mire of self-pity, would be far too depressing. It was pointless wallowing around in my misery, I had a life and I would make something of it. Determination would give me courage, wouldn't it? Somehow I'd be okay, wouldn't I?

As for my body, that was a mess too—saggy, stretch-marked tummy, droopy boobs and no waist to speak of. I'd lost my figure as well as my baby. Lonely in my bed, in the early hours and sleepless, I'd snuggle under the cosy patchwork quilt of happier memories.

Granny was still with me. The vivid moments came and went. Death ends a life not a relationship.

She was a champion farter. She invented the trumpet voluntary. She'd accompany them with rows of ee's and oo's then clap her hand to her mouth as her giggles turned to coughing fits. Granny smoked—clandestinely. She'd slip me a florin to buy her cigarettes and whisper, 'Don't tell your mother, mind you. And keep the change for yourself, love.' Always the same words.

Granny knitted socks on four needles for Daddy and made Lancashire hotpot and a wonderful cake called parkin—until her arthritis got too bad. Then she had to get out from under Mother's feet and, with terrible grace, finally relinquished her role in the kitchen. After that she rarely left her room. There she'd sit reading the Daily Express, listening to the wireless and smoking. If Mother knocked she'd stub the cigarette out and shove the ashtray under her cushion. Granny was a fire risk and her room stank. I worried too about her little budgie, Pookie, getting asthma.

Granny said, 'Budgies don't get asthma, love, but I'll open the window if you like. But not for long, mind you. I can't have my little Pookie getting a cold, can I?'

Such was her logic.

In 1959 we bought her a television set. It had a wooden case, three knobs—on/off, brightness and volume control—and a magnifying glass screwed over the 9-inch screen. Granny was thrilled and settled into her wing armchair with the antimacassar to become a telly-addict. She liked *Double your Money, Take your Pick* and *Dixon of Dock Green*, of course. I think she had a bit of a crush on the leading actor. 'Ee, that Mr. Dixon, he's a proper gentleman. Just like your grandpa,' she crooned.

'Granny, he's a policeman!'

'Don't be so daft, child. Your grandpa's not a policeman!'

'Not Grandpa. Jack Warner!' I giggled.

'Who's Jack Warner?'

'The actor who plays Sgt. Dixon.'

'Dixon's not an actor, love, he's a policeman.'

'Dixon's not real, Granny.'

'Get on with you! You think what you like and I'll think what I like,' she retorted.

Dear Granny, she wasn't really with it. But she did have an eye for Grandpa.

He was Mother's father and a pillar of society, or should I say a rod. He stood so straight you'd think he had one up his back. Actually I remember Mother telling me that she, Auntie Tillie and Uncle Donald had a walking stick threaded through their elbows and across their backs if they didn't sit up properly at table. Grandpa was a tartar who terrified me. He was always immaculately dressed, rarely smiled and disapproved of just about everything. Picturing him in a policeman's helmet was so comical I just had to tell Mother, ' … and I think Granny's in love with him,' I said.

'Don't be so silly, dear,' said Mother, her hand flying up to smother the spluttering hiss that was her laugh.

Normal out-loud laughter had been severely reprimanded by Grandpa. 'Stop guffawing, child. It's most unladylike,' he'd said. Grandpa was a very strict man who'd never emerged from the Victorian era. To him little was a laughing matter. In Granny's eyes, however, he was the epitome of desirability.

Dear, dear Granny. I could no longer go to her room. Even though Daddy had cleared most of her stuff away, the stale smell of cigarettes and her favourite boiled sweets still lingered. Her crackly laugh and the ee's and oo's were still in the air. To think she'd left us so soon after her great grandson had been born. The child she never knew about and I would never see again. How callous life could be.

Not long after Granny left us, so did her little budgie, Pookie. I was sure it was from loneliness. We buried him in a bluebell patch in the wild garden.

8

A CAP AND A TUBE OF JELLY

I had six months to change my mind about Sebastian's adoption. The final papers were to be signed in August. Mother was visibly nervous, no doubt worried sick that at the last minute I might refuse to give him up—I saw it as a case of finding the strength not to. But although I would've given anything to have my baby back, I knew there'd be no last minute miracle, no way I'd be able to look after him myself. Even though it was against my every instinct and I might regret it for the rest of my life, I had to sign.

I busied myself getting my body back in shape. Exercising in the vain hope my tummy would flatten and my boobs return to the nice roundness of a year ago; they'd given in to gravity and needed encouraging back up. The stretch marks on my stomach turned slowly from reddish-purple to silver and my cervix recovered from the stitches with the help of cauterisation. None of these restored my emotional equilibrium—I felt scarred, both inside and out. Mother at least had the sensitivity to spot when I was particularly down, but couldn't bring herself to talk about it. She preferred to pass the buck. 'We can arrange for you to see a psychiatrist, if you like,' she said at dinner one evening.

I'd come downstairs tear-stained and puffy in the face. 'No!' I was adamant. Mother looked flustered and Daddy carried on eating as if nothing had been said. I calmed down. 'Thank you. I'll be alright.'

If I'd had the courage I'd have suggested she was the one who should see a psychiatrist. A woman who was more concerned about her reputation than the welfare of her own child needed more help than I did.

I resolved to keep out of her way as much as possible. Whenever I could persuade a few bob out of either her or Daddy, I would scoot up to London to see my friends. They were still living in Warwick Road, still secretarial and still making whoopee in their spare time, except weekends when they trundled back home with a big bag of laundry. It was a long-needed relief to talk about Sebastian, John, my anger and my hurt and everyone was very supportive. Annie's sister Rachel, older and more sophisticated than Annie, asked if I'd thought about sex in the future.

'No. I don't think I could ever trust a man again. Anyway, who'd want me now, I'm a mass of stretch marks? It'd be too embarrassing.' I said feebly.

I was greeted with a chorus of poohs and pahs.

'Most men wouldn't know what they are. Anyway, you can still look fabulous. It's time you got some new clothes and your hair looks awful,' said Annie.

'She's right. Smarten up and get some durex. Just in case,' said Rachel.

'You never know,' said Annie.

'I s'pose you're right,' I said, trying to be more positive.

They were wise, my pals, but I wasn't looking for a boyfriend, I'd had enough of men for the moment. However, when I went for my regular check-up with Dr Helena Wright—the only contact I had in the gynaecological department—the subject reared its head again. From below the familiar red paisley scarf draped, as before, across my tummy, she um'd and ah'd most expressively as she delved into my lower depths. 'Given the circumstances, dear, you're in reasonable shape,' she announced. 'Now have you thought about contraception?'

'Er, no. But…'

'The Brook, dear. The Brook.'

I was none the wiser but didn't want to admit it. She picked up the phone and made an appointment for me that afternoon—Dr Wright, being a pioneer for women's rights and freedoms, had influence. When I arrived at The Brook and joined the other girls in the waiting room, I had time to wonder what on earth I was doing there. Sex was the last thing I wanted. I got up to leave.

'Susan, is there a Susan here?'

'I'm Susan,' I said automatically.

'This way, dear.'

I had no option but to follow the nurse into the consulting room.

The Brook Street Clinic was the only clinic in the country catering for the contraceptive needs of single women. Here there was no moral posturing, no questions were asked and no judgements made. I was simply required to give my name, age and an address. I used Warwick Road. I was then introduced to the Dutch cap. A dome of fine yellowy-pink rubber mounted on a springy metal ring. I was checked for size and taught the insertion technique, which involved squatting on my haunches, squeezing the lubricated dome into a figure of eight shape and pushing it in, up and over my cervix where, upon release, it would spring back into shape. After a few giggly failures, I mastered it. Now at least I was prepared, although actually using

72

the thing seemed a very remote possibility. In a daze of disbelief, I left the clinic armed with the cap in a case, a pot of rubber-preserving powder and a couple of tubes of spermicidal jelly. Back at the flat, when I told the girls, they were amazed and impressed and lost no time in booking appointments themselves. At home I secreted my cap in my undies drawer and sat down on the bed to wade through the sits vac columns of the local paper.

By the end of a fortnight I'd applied for several jobs, been for a number of interviews and accepted an offer. Secretary to the works manager of Inferation, a local engineering company who made ice machines, beer coolers and hot food cabinets. I needed money and it seemed the least depressing option.

Within a week I'd discovered the work tediously routine and most of the people from another planet, where soaps and scandals were the favourite topics of conversation. The idea of a wider world full of opportunity and adventure was not for them. I knew I could never fit in, not that I wanted to. No, I just had to make the best of it for the time being. It's only temporary, I told myself; before too long I'll have saved enough money to get back to London and look for another theatre job.

At home Mother and Daddy did their best to cheer me up. 'Now's an ideal time for a serious attempt at learning to drive,' said Daddy.

He was right and I was glad of a constructive distraction. Before leaving home at seventeen I'd had a few goes in Patience on the disused runways at Blackbushe Airport. The car was Daddy's pride and joy. He'd bought her in 1949 when he sold Sally, the old Ford 8. Patience was a 1935 Vauxhall Big Six 7-seater limousine. Although hardly a new model, she was nonetheless a very smart affair; just the car for Mother to practice her royal head-inclined waves—although I hardly think this was Daddy's reasoning. He spent several months restoring her to her former shining glory and when, ten years later, the old girl's innards finally gave up, he replaced them with a bus engine! Consequently Patience was pretty heavy to handle and had almost put me off driving altogether. I was glad when Daddy came to his senses and bought something more modern. With much sadness and a grand farewell, Patience took her final leave and rolled away down Manor Lodge drive with her new owner, a budding young mechanic called Norman (Spotty) Barnstable, at the helm. Daddy was now the proud owner of a Wolseley saloon and I didn't need much persuading to have another go behind the wheel.

Naturally he taught me all he knew, from basics to technique, and this inevitably included instruction on what was happening under the bonnet. 'Now, there's no need to over-rev—just listen to the engine. It'll let you know when it wants to change gear,' he said. Or, 'Don't wrench the gear lever! Feel your way smoothly through neutral. Double de-clutch if you like. Your passengers shouldn't feel the gear change so ease up off the clutch gradually, don't just whip your foot away and give everyone a nasty jolt.'

Wow, was he fussy! I was relieved when a formal instructor took over the last couple of lessons to get me ready for my test.

I passed. It was great being the only one of my girlfriends who had her licence. What was even better was that Daddy, having taught me to his own exacting standards, was prepared to let me use the Wolseley. Those were the times when I felt almost worthwhile.

9

I HAD A SISTER ONCE

For me the weeks trudged by, but my parents were caught up in a whirl of house-hunting. With Granny gone, they'd decided to sell Manor Lodge and find somewhere smaller. I didn't want to leave. I loved the old house. It'd been our home for fifteen years.

Now we would be moving and I was even more dispirited when my parents chose the Triangle, a chalet bungalow in nearby Yateley. It wasn't a patch on Manor Lodge.

The place needed decorating, and Daddy preferred to do it alone, Mother was allergic to paint fumes. She's good at allergies, I thought cynically, gets her out of all the grotty work.

'Daddy thinks we should take a holiday and so do I,' she told me.

'Where?' I said suspiciously, fearful I'd have to spend time alone with her.

'How about America?' said Daddy.

'Daddy thinks it's time we went to visit Dorothy.'

'Wow! Oh yes, please.'

America! And my sister—fantastic! It'd been so long since she'd left us, I'd given up hope of ever seeing her again.

When I was born, my sister, Dorothy, mostly called Dossy, was thirteen and evacuated to a boarding school somewhere. I wasn't really aware of her until three years later when she finally came home to live with us in our flat in Roehampton. At first I thought she was Mother's daughter too but it was explained to me that Daddy had been married before and that Dossy was actually my half-sister. I was completely baffled; I thought that she was a whole person and they'd made some sort of mistake.

She had eyes that crinkled up when she giggled and long, dark chestnut hair which I loved to brush. She looked after me whenever Mother and Daddy wanted to go out or Mother didn't feel up to it, which was often; I was a hyperactive child and frequently exhausted her. Then she'd become irritable and take it out on Dossy. Accident or otherwise it wasn't difficult to get her in a tizzy. One day, when reaching in the cupboard for the marmalade, the top came off and the pot slid out of my hand. It bounced off the kitchen counter and globbed all down the front of my new dress—candy striped with loads of smocking on the bodice. Mother, alerted by the noise, charged into the kitchen. 'Dorothy, where are you? Look what this child has done,' she shrieked.

We heard the loo flushing. Then Dossy rushed in and stood to attention to find out what she'd been accused of this time. 'I'm sorry, I was in the lavatory.'

'You know you can't turn your back on her, so kindly time your lavatory visits for when I'm in charge.' With that Mother yanked the dress over my head and sped off to the bathroom tutting frantically.

Dossy picked up the jar and started mopping the floor. 'What a waste, Sukie. Oh well, never mind.'

But I did mind and I think she did too. A whole jar of our favourite, Nell Gwynne marmalade, had gone west. In 1947, we were still frugal; a hangover from wartime days, when everything is precious.

As well as being rather clumsy I had a habit of disappearing—the minute backs were turned I'd scamper off to explore the outside world. When we went shopping, I had to wear a leading rein—a harness made of pale blue leather with bells on—and if Dossy let go for a moment, I'd be away down the street as fast as my legs could carry me. Once, in the chemists, I managed to give her the slip completely. Poor Dossy, she was weighed down with shopping, struggling to find the right change in her purse while I was straining at the leash. It was all too much for her. One hefty pull and I was off. By the time she'd paid and run out of the shop, I'd disappeared.

Five hours and a search party later, I was discovered toddling across the mud at the edge of the Thames near Putney Bridge. Dossy was in disgrace for several days.

She drifted from one job to another, mostly hairdressing salons and beauty parlours where, to Daddy's disgust, they experimented on her. She'd arrive home with her hair in some elaborate style, heavily made-up and with her long nails brightly varnished. She'd creep in hoping not to get caught before she'd had a chance to clean up. We had no idea that, before long, there'd be nobody telling her to get the muck off her face and brush her hair properly.

It was 1948. I was four and Dossy had just turned seventeen when contracts were exchanged on Manor Lodge, our new home.

'So, there you are girls, isn't it exciting?' said Daddy.

We supposed it was.

'Naturally, as we'll be moving away from London, Dorothy won't be coming. We're going to find you a nice flat somewhere. You'd like that, wouldn't you, dear?' said Mother brightly.

Dossy was totally bewildered. 'I don't know,' she stuttered.

'Of course you would. Independence, the chance to do just what you like. Maybe you could share with another young girl. Then you'd have company in the evenings.'

'Who? I don't know anyone I'd want to live with,' close to tears, Dossy was becoming seriously alarmed.

Daddy, on a high and not in the mood for an emotional scene, left us to it. But Mother was not prepared to argue. 'Lots of our friends have young daughters. I'll ask around. Right, I'm off to make the tea. La, la, la, la …' She bustled out of the room, which meant the conversation was over.

Dossy ran off to our bedroom. I scuttled after her but didn't get far; as I crossed the hall, Mother shot out of the kitchen. 'Come and give Mummy a hand, there's a good girl,' she said, grabbing my arm.

Within a week a suitable flat and flatmate had been arranged. Dossy was packed and ready to move out. I was very unhappy; I loved my big sister and had become used to having her around. She played with me, made me laugh and, at night, when we were tucked up in our little side-by-side divans, she'd tell me her secrets. It didn't matter that I was far too young to understand them.

She looked so forlorn standing in the hall, hat, coat and gloves on and her big suitcase at her feet. Just like she was going back to boarding school.

'Oh Dossy, you will come and see us, won't you?' I whimpered.

'Of course, she will,' said Mother who stood at the door waiting for Daddy to fetch the car.

'Yes, of course I will.' Dossy tried to sound cheerful, but her lips were quivering as she bent down to give me a kiss.

I whispered in her ear, 'I've got a present for you,' and slipped her a brown paper bag tied with one of my hair ribbons.

She loosened the bow and sneaked a peep. Inside was a small jar I'd filled with Nell Gwynne marmalade pinched from the kitchen cupboard. Dossy giggled and thrust it in her pocket. She whispered, 'Thank you, darling,' then gave me a big cuddle and stood up and, for Mother's benefit, said sternly 'Now, I want you to promise to be good and not go running off.'

'I promise.'

Daddy's footsteps echoed on the stairs outside the flat.

'I have to go,' Dossy cried and fled.

Soon after she left Roehampton, she fell in love. His name was Jerzy and he was twenty-three. Jerzy was a student and penniless, so when Dossy told us they were engaged, Daddy was not amused. 'She's far too young to know what she's doing,' he stormed.

'John, John. If that's what she wants, then let her have her way, for heaven's sake.'

'No, Joyce, absolutely not. The man's not suitable. He'll be too much for her to deal with. After all he's been through, he'll hardly make an ideal husband.'

The walls of our flat were thin, so I could hear them. What's Daddy talking about? I wondered. Jerzy's a nice man even if he does have a very funny way of talking. He was Polish and the first foreigner I'd ever come across. Perhaps foreign men didn't know how to be good husbands, I reasoned. It was some time before I found out what Daddy meant.

With or without his approval, Dossy was determined to marry her Jerzy. Not surprisingly, when she rang to say she was now Mrs Dorothy Gruszczynski, Daddy was livid.

He steamed for so long, I thought he'd never forgive her. Mother, in the meantime, was very light-hearted, as well as being preoccupied with the news that later that year a far more important wedding would be taking place—Princess Elizabeth to Prince Philip. It was the first big royal celebration since the war and everyone was happy. Mother said it would be great for the country's morale. 'There's considerable bomb damage to mop up, and lots of poor people are living in prefabs and we've still got food rationing to put up with. So, I'm quite sure the palace will choose a simple menu. For diplomatic reasons.' Mother enjoyed talking about goings-on at Buck Pal. What she didn't read in the papers, she imagined. She went on to tell me that after the big event we'd be going on an important shopping expedition. 'The Queen is bound to be wearing a splendid hat. I want one just like it.'

'Why?'

'Well, er … for commemorative reasons, dear.'

What that meant, I had no idea.

After the wedding and having studied Picture Post magazine photos of the event, we set off to find 'the hat'.

Inevitably, anything remotely resembling the Queen's ceremonial headgear proved impossible to find. After much traipsing round all the smart shops I was desperate to go home. Something had to be done to distract Mother. I pulled on her sleeve. 'Mummy, Mummy, my nose hurts.'

'You haven't got one of your asthma attacks coming on, have you?'

'No, but I think I put a button up it,' I wailed.

'A button! Are you mad, child?' she screamed so loudly I burst into tears.

It caused a huge fuss, which only abated when hospital was threatened and I admitted I might have made a mistake.

The episode did not, however, deter Mother in her search. Finally she bought a truly remarkable hat; it was like a sort of double beret which perched high and slightly askew and had bright green ostrich feathers cascading over the sides. The colour was probably totally wrong but Mother only had black and white photos to go by. Needless to say, she never had occasion to wear the hat. It remained wrapped in tissue paper in a variety of bedroom cupboards until, many years later, she gave it to me to wear to a fancy dress party.

By the time I was seven, Jerzy had completed his studies and Dossy had given birth to their first child, Mark. I thought being an Auntie was very funny, but we didn't see much of them. Daddy didn't appear to be in the least interested and Mother actively discouraged visits. 'Daddy's very disappointed with Dorothy,' she told me. 'Really, we've both had a lot to put up with. You can't imagine what a dreadfully moody child she was. And I tried so hard, I did everything I could to be a mother to her. Your half-sister is an ungrateful girl.'

'But I love her, Mummy.'

'Yes, well, you only see the good side of her.'

Once, after much persuasion, I was allowed to go and stay the weekend with her and Jerzy in their tiny Putney flatlet. It was high up under the eaves of a tall Victorian house and, being summertime, the place was pretty stifling. Jerzy sat down to tea in his vest. He had a square face, a chunky build and a heavily accented voice to match, often difficult for a little girl to understand. On his arm I noticed a tattoo. Not the ordinary sort with a heart or a crest or something, this tattoo was just a row of numbers. When later he went out for a beer, I asked Dossy about them.

'Jerzy was a prisoner of war. They were for identification,' she explained.

'Like dogs wear collars with their names on?'

She laughed wryly. 'Not exactly. My poor Jerzy was in a concentration camp, two in fact, Auschwitz and Birkenau they were called. Dreadful, dreadful places.' Tears sprang to her eyes, so I thought I'd better not ask any more.

In February of 1952, George VI died, the country went into mourning and Mother was with the royal family in spirit.

Princess Elizabeth was to be crowned on June 2nd the following year, and elaborate preparations for the event were under way. I was kept abreast of all the news by an eager Mother who had already arranged for us to visit friends with a television. Then, at the family get-together for my ninth birthday, Dossy made an announcement that distressed me horribly. She and Jerzy had booked their passage to New York. 'America's the land of opportunity and we're going to seek our fortunes, Sukie. And when we've made lots of money, we'll pay for you to come and visit us.'

'Oh yes, yes please, Dossy. Please make lots of money soon,' I sobbed.

The coronation came and went. We'd seen the whole ceremony on television, in black and white and a bit blurred as the reception wasn't good. It was exciting of course, but I was unhappy. I was going to lose my sister, maybe even forever.

The day before departure Dossy and Jerzy packed everything they owned into two large suitcases—the flatlet had been rented equipped and furnished, so they had few belongings—and as most of their savings had gone on the fares, they were going to start with virtually nothing. I thought that was terribly brave.

The night before they left, I dreamt I was standing in the shallows of a deserted beach and gazing out to sea. The blue-green water stretched from my feet to the straight line of the horizon. All around was silent and absolutely still, except for the slowly diminishing shape of a ship. As it got nearer and nearer to the line, I had to strain to make it out. Then it became a tiny black dot and suddenly disappeared altogether. My sister had sailed off the edge of the world. I was awoken by the sound of sobbing. It was my own, but when I opened my eyes there were no tears, but only for a moment, until I remembered today was departure day.

Daddy drove them to Southampton. Mother sat in the front and I sat between Dossy with Mark on her knee and Jerzy. I held their hands and tried to be strong. We arrived and made our way to the embarkation point. Although she was a no-big-deal ocean liner, to me the boat was gigantic; you couldn't see both ends at the same time and she towered over the quayside. When the time came for Dossy, Jerzy and little Mark to walk away up the plank, my flood-gates opened. I didn't know when I'd see her again and I expected I might be grown-up by the time I did, if I did. Dossy cried too. I could see her blowing her nose in her big white hankie as she waved back down to us. Then a huge horn sounded, they cast anchor and were tugged out towards the Atlantic Ocean. On their way to the other side of the world.

Dossy's departure was still a vivid and painful memory. Eleven years had passed and I could still hear, as if it were yesterday, the words she whispered before they left. 'I love you, darling. And one day I'll explain everything.'

10

REUNION

We were going to be with my sister for my twentieth birthday. She would be a stranger, this mother of three with a modern life-style oceans away from mine. My brother-in-law, Jerzy, after further extensive studying, had become a nuclear physicist and been taken on by General Electric. He was now racing up the career ladder and we gathered they were living very comfortably indeed. My only contact with Dossy had been by the occasional letter. Nonetheless, our rather formal correspondence, sparse though it had been, had made me want to know her. I couldn't believe the appalling press she'd been given by Mother. 'Now dear, don't forget Dorothy has always been very jealous of you so she may well behave most strangely. She can be moody, snappy and rude,' she warned me.

'I think I'm old enough to make up my own mind about her now,' I replied firmly.

I had a funny feeling I'd think she was great and we'd get on really well.

'Yes, maybe, but she hasn't changed. Don't forget the letters she's plagued us with over the years.'

How could I? They had an underlying anguish I couldn't comprehend. And I certainly couldn't understand the almost uncanny glee Mother displayed when she showed me yet another of those sad outpourings of accusation and bewilderment.

'You see how ungrateful and unkind your half-sister can be,' she'd say.

I didn't see. I was determined not to. She'd robbed me of my child, she wasn't going to rob me of my sister too. 'I may not know her, but she's my sister—half or not, and I'm going to love her.' And with that I shot off to my room.

Our arrival at Philadelphia airport was overwhelmingly emotional. Dossy and I flung our arms round each other and cried. Even Mother managed the odd tear. I couldn't imagine what her ominous warnings were about. Dossy's welcome was genuinely loving. Of course, she'd changed—a little slimmer, bobbed hair and, most of all, an air of self-assurance. Out of reach of Mother's jibing, she'd blossomed. My sis was full of fun, a bundle of giggles, a busy-bee sort of person with twinkly eyes and limitless energy. She loved adventures, was utterly forthright and scared of nobody. She was also generous, soft as blancmange and extremely affectionate. I adored her from the first. After everyone else had gone to bed, we'd sit up chatting well into the small hours. If Mother woke for a pee, she'd see the light still on and thrust her head round the sitting-room door, bristling with curlers and resentment. 'Now, you girls, it's high time you went to bed.'

'Yes,' we'd chorus and carry on talking.

Tutting frantically, she'd haul her head back out of sight and stomp off to her room.

Dossy and I were getting to know each other, trying to capture the missing years, see things from the other's point of view. Of course, we talked long and hard about my little lost Sebastian. We cried. We wished it'd been different. I think the most loving and unselfish of gestures had come from my sis. My real, total and extraordinary sis. She would have taken him, looked after him as her own. She felt that that was the right thing for families to do, to stand by each other. I was shattered when she said she'd been told her offer was highly unsuitable; the matter was being dealt with and she should mind her own business. How unutterably cruel, not to say ungrateful. Why was she excluded, made to feel like an outsider and not a member of the family? No wonder her letters were so full of distress.

Our new-born relationship suffered few setbacks; we shared the same opinions on many things. But there was one area we just couldn't agree about. My future. And here I was adamant, after all, it was to be mine, wasn't it?

'Sue, Daddy spent a lot of money on a good secretarial training for you. The best. You could get a job with high wages in any number of big companies,' Dossy insisted.

'I'm not interested in big companies. They'd be like Inferation only larger—yuck! Boring, boring, boring.'

'Everything's boring if you're not interested in it. You use that word a lot. You're pretty intolerant, aren't you?' said Dossy fiercely.

'I don't know what you mean. I'm only saying that I won't sell my soul for money. And there's only one business I want to work in. I'm sorry.'

'Sell your soul,' she laughed, 'don't be ridiculous. As for wanting to get back to the theatre, that's the last place you should be thinking about. You've already blotted your copybook there, haven't you?'

I opened my mouth to object.

'An immoral lot, if you ask me,' she added casually, lighting up another of her menthol cigarettes.

That was it. I realised there was absolutely no point in pursuing the discussion, we'd never agree. What it had achieved, however, was to increase my resolve. Nobody, not even my sister, was going to persuade me to do a job I didn't enjoy for some company or other producing something I couldn't care less about just because the salary was good. Not bloody likely. I was going to get back to the theatre no matter how long it took. That was where I would one day make my mark. I glanced at the clock, it was coming up for two a.m. 'Dossy, I'm sorry, I know you only want the best for me. Thank you for that. Can we go to bed now?'

'Yes, darling,' she said giving me a conciliatory hug.

I crept up to the spare-room. Mother was snoring gently. Despite her love for the theatre, she'd probably have agreed with Dossy, I thought grimly. I was glad I hadn't been battling with both of them.

Our three weeks went by far too quickly. The house was constantly buzzing with activity. The children— Mark now joined by Susan and Geoff, seven and four respectively, were demanding bundles of mischief and energy and even Mother was drawn into playing games and trying to keep control. Dossy arranged several outings and there was always shopping to be done. I was amazed by everything I saw. It was all so big, so streamlined, so advanced, so easy. I even got to drive the Chevy round the parking lot at the local shopping mall. We certainly didn't have them in England. Dossy and I whiled away several afternoons cruising the stores. We meandered from aisle to aisle looking at all the goodies. I bought a pile of Beach Boys records for nuppence and Dossy had great fun indulging her dress sense and guiding mine. I was keen to go home with a different look. I was now desperate to find a fella, any fella who'd make me feel I was still attractive. A few new outfits might just give me the edge.

It was the night before we were due to leave when I finally broached the mysterious subject. Mother had gone to bed and instructed Dossy not to keep me up late. But I didn't care how long I stayed up, I wanted to know. 'Dossy, will you tell me what happened before I was born? You did promise.'

'Only if you swear not to tell Mother and Daddy that you know.'

'I swear.' I was puzzled though.

'Well, I guess Daddy's told you he was married before. To my mother. Her name was Delia.'

'Is she dead?' I asked.

'I don't know.' She held up her hand to stop me questioning, lit a cigarette and settled comfortably into her corner of the sofa to tell me the story.

—11—

ABUSED

In 1923, Granny, Grandad, Daddy and Uncle George moved to Huddersfield from Wigan, soon after Daddy had matriculated with very high marks. He'd gained a scholarship to technical college there and Granny was cock-a-hoop to have such a clever son. The family were poor but very proud, particularly Granny, who doted on her older boy. Uncle George, who was five years younger, soon left to join the Air Force.

Daddy studied mechanical engineering and studied hard. Not long after qualifying he got engaged to Daphne and Granny was thrilled. Daphne was a quiet, dutiful girl who would make her son an excellent wife. She was also a devout chapel-goer and determined to stay a virgin until they married. Daddy, however, couldn't wait, and Delia, a local girl with a reputation, was prepared to take the edge off his sexual appetite.

When Delia announced she was pregnant, her brothers threatened Daddy with violence unless he married her. Daphne was broken-hearted and vowed never to trust another man.

With wedding present money, Daddy and Delia were able to put down three month's rent on a small terraced house. Daddy began to look for work. Good jobs were hard to find in Huddersfield so he searched further afield through the columns of national newspapers. The best offer came from a small engineering company in Middlesex. For Daddy this was too good an opportunity to miss, he accepted. He would come home at weekends. Ever supportive, Granny insisted that she and Grandad move down south with him and they rent a house together. As usual Grandad had little say in the matter.

'My boy must eat properly. Our Ernest'll just have to find a job down there,' said Granny.

As he was a bus driver, it wasn't difficult.

They rented a place in Kenton and Grandad was taken on by the local bus company.

By the time Dossy was born, Daddy's job had become more demanding and travel more expensive. He wouldn't be able to get up to Huddersfield often and would see little of his baby daughter. He tried to persuade Delia to move south, but she absolutely rejected the idea. All her family were in Huddersfield and that was where she wanted to be. And so it was for two years.

In the summer of '33, a new secretary came to work at the engineering company. Well, that was it. Daddy was smitten by the attractive brunette with the cultured voice and impeccable manners and soon he and Joyce started going together. She was flattered by his attentions and his exacting approach to dating. He never forgot to bring flowers or chocolates, always turned up on time and his little love notes were written in the most exquisite handwriting she'd ever seen. As for his working class origins and down-to-earth manners, she could overlook them; John was a man with a brilliant brain.

Soon they were seriously courting but to marry Joyce he had to divorce Delia and he had no grounds. Five years separation seemed the only option. In those days there was no such consideration as irretrievable breakdown of the relationship. Joyce agreed to wait but was not happy when Daddy went up to Huddersfield to see Dossy. 'Must you, John? I thought we could go to the theatre on Saturday.'

'You know I don't give a damn about Delia, but I want to see Dorothy. It's not often I can afford it, but when I can, I'm going. Sorry, but that's the way it is.'

Joyce knew better than to argue.

Delia would be cold and unwelcoming when he turned up on her doorstep. 'Take her out if you must. I don't want you hanging around here under my feet.'

So Daddy would piggyback his little girl to the park and buy her an ice-cream cornet. She would lap it up as quickly as she could but often as not she'd go home with ice-cream all down the front of her coat. Delia was not amused. 'Sloppy kid. And you're as daft as a brush, John Whatmough. Fancy buying the little tike a cornet. Oh, but then, it's not you as has to wash her clothes. Go on, get off with you.' Then she'd snatch the envelope with Daddy's maintenance money and shoo him out of the house. Dossy would run down the road clinging onto his hand begging him not to go. The visits were heart-wrenching for them both and Daddy wished he could just scoop her up into his arms and take her home to Kenton.

One day Delia sent him packing for good. 'And don't come up here getting the kid all in state. In fact, you'd as well just bugger off back down South and leave us alone.' She grabbed Dossy's hand and dragged her back into the house, bawling her eyes out.

When, back in Kenton, Daddy told everyone what had happened, Joyce found it hard to mask her relief. Grandad noticed and scowled at her insensitivity. Granny wiped her eyes on her pinny. 'Poor, poor, wee mite. It's proper terrible. And she's my granddaughter,' she sniffled.

'If the child's going to be upset by the visits, it's best John doesn't go, in my opinion,' said Joyce firmly.

And so he stayed away, until one morning, in the spring of 1937, a letter arrived from Huddersfield. It was from Delia's father. He thought Daddy should know that Delia had a new boyfriend and was expecting a baby. Little Dossy, now six years old, was unwanted and being cruelly mistreated. Frequently she was sent out with a pail to beg potato peelings from the neighbours. When the pail was full she had to trudge to the edge of town to the pig farm where she could sell the peelings for a penny. Enough to buy her a bun. She was permanently hungry and seriously under-nourished. When Delia and Fred went out, they'd tie her to the pipes under the kitchen sink, that way they could be sure she couldn't get into the larder.

Daddy was desperate. He had to save her somehow. Then he realised he'd be able to sue for divorce on the grounds of adultery and possibly even get custody of his little daughter. First though, he needed proof that Fred, the boyfriend, was the father of the new baby.

Aunt Milly, Granny's sister, lived in Newtown, Wales, and Delia had never met her. She was the ideal person and keen to help. Daddy took two days off work and he and Aunt Milly caught the train up to Huddersfield. It was teatime and dusk was closing in on a drizzly day when they arrived. Daddy had bought a trilby hat. With it pulled down hard to hide his face and the collar of his mac turned up, Humphrey Bogart style, he waited across the road while Aunt Milly knocked at Delia's door. She was in; the lights were on. She opened the door heavily pregnant. 'Yes?'

Aunt Milly said, 'Is John Whatmough in?'

'He doesn't live here any more,' said Delia.

A man appeared behind her. A man in a vest. 'Who is it, love?'

'Someone for John.'

'Tell them…'

But Aunt Milly had gone. She had the evidence. Not only was Delia pregnant, but Fred was very obviously at home in the house.

Daddy now had proof of adultery and with the letter from Delia's father as evidence of Dossy's maltreatment, his solicitor was confident he'd be granted custody. Determined to rescue his little girl before any further harm could come to her, Daddy didn't wait for the court's decision. He borrowed a car, went back up to Huddersfield and waited behind a wall opposite Dossy's school. At the end of the day nobody came to meet her. Daddy emerged from his hiding place as casually as possible, so as not to alarm her. 'Hello,' he said.

'Hello.'

'D'you know who I am?'

'Yes, you're my Daddy.'

'Do you want to come and live with me?'

'Yes. Yes, please.' Her eyes filled with tears.

Daddy took her by the hand and led her to the car. It was parked outside the ice-cream shop. 'Would you like a cornet?' he said.

'Yes, please. Yes, please,' she cried.

She jumped up and down with excitement. It was the first ice-cream Dossy had had for such a long time and she wanted to make it last. She was with her Daddy, her hero, and he'd bought her an ice-cream, just like he used to. She'd never forgotten his wonderful visits and how he'd always been so loving and kind to her. She'd dreamt about him often and longed for him to rescue her from that other man. How she hated Fred and she knew he hated her too. Now she'd be safe and she would have her very own Daddy to herself.

Not so. Back in Kenton, Joyce was waiting. Apprehensive, resentful and ill-disposed to welcome the scruffy child with suspicious eyes peering out from beneath the fringe of her pudding basin haircut. Wrinkling her nose, Joyce tossed her haughty head in Granny's direction. 'My God, she's filthy! Mother, fill the bathtub!'

The next day Daddy wrote to Delia threatening her with the police if she tried to take Dossy back. She didn't reply.

Daddy won his case and Dossy never saw her mother again.

At last she was well fed and looked after, particularly by Grandad who she adored almost as much as Daddy. But, for the skinny little girl, life in Kenton was only happy when Joyce was not around. Granny could be very strict but nowhere near as mean as Daddy's fiancée, my mother-to-be. Dossy had a permanently runny nose, and a strong northern accent which was certainly not music to Joyce's ears. 'I just don't know how long I can bear that ghastly Yorkshire twang. I shall arrange for elocution lessons. And for goodness sake, child, blow your nose,' she shuddered. As far as she was concerned, Dossy was a damned nuisance and, when nobody else was about she made sure she knew exactly how she felt.

~

As she told her story tears rolled down Dossy's cheeks. I was crying too. 'Why didn't they tell me? And how could Mother have been so horrid?' I wailed.

'She wanted him all to herself. And so did I. And then the war came and she had the perfect excuse. She said I had to be evacuated. It was too dangerous in Kenton so I was sent to a boarding school.'

~

Dossy was desolate. Dolforgan Hall, an isolated pile of a place near Kerry in Wales, was bleak and Dickensian. The staff were brutal. The old building was dismal and draughty. Ice formed on the inside of the multi-paned windows in winter. If one broke, cardboard replaced it. The children shivered in their beds under threadbare blankets full of darns. The sheets were grubby grey because detergent was strictly rationed. Laundry days were infrequent anyway. Except in Dossy's case. She wet the bed, often. When it'd happened back in Huddersfield, she'd been forced to sleep in the cupboard under the stairs.

'Until you learn cleaner habits, you little runt,' Fred would say.

At Dolforgan Dossy was permanently miserable. Discipline at the hall was ruthless. Any child who wet the bed was punished, humiliated, made to carry their soiled sheets into morning assembly. Dossy's bed was always damp—from tears, urine and not having enough time to dry after she'd scrubbed the sheets each morning. Predictably her schoolwork was hopeless and she was often singled out for ridicule. Her classmates were merciless.

Lonely for a friend, any friend, and anxious to curry favour with the other girls, she was persuaded to steal a box of Black Magic a teacher had carelessly left in the classroom. The girls promised to share the chocolates with her. Inevitably she was found out and sent to Coventry. She was forced to wear a sign *'I am a thief'*, even on school walks, and was fed on bread, sugar and water for a week.

Life was wretched but her spirits were cheered when she heard Auntie Tillie would be bringing five-year-old Beth to Dolforgan Hall. Maybe, despite the seven-year age difference, they could be friends.

Beth stayed for one term. When Auntie found out what the place was really like, she whipped her little daughter away immediately. Dossy was on her own again. And to make her life even more wretched, Joyce, now married to Daddy, refused to have her back in the holidays and rarely visited her. 'Far too dangerous, John. And we can't afford to go traipsing up there. She's fine, don't you worry.'

So he didn't. Daddy was involved in a top-secret project. He had to spend a lot of the war years in America and Canada. Dossy was sure he didn't know how bad things were for her. She had to believe that of her beloved father, her rescuer. He couldn't have known, could he? Joyce certainly wouldn't have told him. If he had known he would have made sure she came home for Christmas at least. And even though they begged to have her, she wasn't allowed to stay in nearby Newtown with Aunt Milly and cousin Mary either.

~

We couldn't figure out why.

'Maybe Mother was afraid I'd tell them how mean she was to me and how miserable I was at Dolforgan and they'd find out what a hellhole of a school I'd been sent to.'

I agreed. 'Yes, and I can just imagine what she would have said to them—Milly dear, we can't possibly expect you to take the girl on. It's far too much trouble and expense. I absolutely won't hear of it.' I imitated Mother's imperious tones and a bit of a laugh helped lighten our spirits a little. We both knew how formidable she could be.

'Of course, Auntie Milly was far too sweet to argue,' Dossy continued.

She remembered hearing some years later from Mary that Daddy had once passed through Newtown on his way to a meeting. An official car had pulled up outside their little terraced house and Daddy, with a briefcase locked to his wrist, had come in for a cup of tea. He'd told them he didn't have time to see Dossy and when they'd asked again if she could come and stay with them he'd said, 'That's Joyce's department. You must talk to her.'

There was a side to Daddy neither of us could understand.

~

On the 14 June 1944, Dossy received a telegram. It read 'Baby Susan arrived today. Love Daddy.' She was choked; she hadn't even known Mother was pregnant.

Actually I might not have existed at all. Mother's first child had been stillborn, so during her pregnancy with me, she had to spend a lot of time with her feet up. After I was born she was advised not to try for another baby.

As far as Dossy was concerned, I was another obstacle between her and her beloved Daddy and life was going to get even more wretched. She locked herself in one of the lavatories and wept the hopeless tears of despair.

The war ended the following year. Dossy was just fourteen. Mother insisted she complete her education at Dolforgan, after all she'd been there since she was eight.

She finally left in 1946 and came back to where Daddy, Mother and I were now living, a flat in Roehampton Close, London.

~

It was nearly five o'clock. We were both emotionally exhausted. Two lost souls who'd found comfort in each other. Our hankies were soaked and our eyes were swollen. But we were complete sisters at last.

'I'm sorry, so sorry. I never realised. Nobody told me.'

'Darling, please, don't cry for me. It was all a long time ago. I'm alright now,' Dossy squeezed my hand.

'But telling me brought it all back, didn't it?'

'Yes, but I can see things more clearly now. At first there was only my side of the story and then what little Daddy and Mother wanted me to know. But as I grew older I grew curious. There were gaps, inconsistencies, so I turned to Granny and cousin Mary to fill them in. And now I feel a whole lot better. I've been able to tell my little sister. Come on, time we got to bed.'

I was desolate to have to leave her and go back to England, there still seemed so much more to say. The long flight home gave me plenty of time to reflect. Dossy's story explained why Daddy had reacted so coldly to my pregnancy. And I think I understood Mother a little better too; inheriting someone else's child and a damaged one at that. Then losing her first baby and only just being able to hang onto her second. How bitter she must have felt sometimes. But does understanding lead to forgiveness? Would I ever, could I ever, forgive them? Was there really anything to forgive? I just didn't know.

Signing Day arrived. The day Sebastian's adoption would become final. This was my last chance to back out. But I didn't, I couldn't. I signed. That was it, I'd given up all rights to my baby. He would never know his real mother and I would never know him. I had to close a door in my heart and throw away the key. It was an agonising decision but, in those circumstances and at that time, I was convinced it was the right one.

Outwardly oblivious of my pain, Mother appeared a lot jollier and had resumed her irritating humming habit. 'La, la, la, (nothing more to be said) la, la.'

Daddy said, 'Now you can put the whole unfortunate experience behind you,' and went back to his garage.

Of course he was right. I had to look forward not back. Some kind of life lay ahead and I had to get the best out of it. My child was someone else's and that door was finally, irrevocably, closed.

With Mother, Daddy, Dossy
& Granny 1947

With Mother and Dossy
1948

Daddy with Patience

Manor Lodge

PART TWO

LIGHT YEARS

12

BEATNIKS AND SQUARES

During the long, slow climb back to normality, Sebastian was never far from my thoughts. It'd been really tough. Some days I'd go around hating myself for having messed up my life, then I'd hate myself for being a pathetic blob. But gradually, over the months that followed the signing, I learned there is life after pain. Being a sad case didn't make you popular, you had to be fun and carefree. Dressing in the latest fashions and having a good time were all that mattered. The best way to survive was to be just like all my girlfriends, on the surface anyway. 'I know what I want and I won't find it in Camberley. I'm giving in my notice,' I told Annie.

'You don't mean you're actually going to do something about it at last.'

'I've been in the bloody place for long enough. I suppose if you worked in the research and development department, you could get excited about ice-making machines, hot food cabinets and in-line beer coolers, but for the rest of us, work is just a job and a pay-packet at the end of the week. No, I've had enough.'

For once I wasn't being unrealistic. Dear Gruncle had recently died and left me some money. Enough to put down a deposit on a bedsit in London and survive until I found a theatre that needed me, wherever and in whatever capacity, it didn't matter. I'd had time to mourn the loss of my little Sebastian and to find a perspective I could live with, but it was hard to stop myself imagining someone else helping him to walk and talk and teaching him to call her 'Ma-ma'.

Life hadn't all been miserable. Although I was still at home and Annie was living in London, I caught up with her and her crowd at the weekends. She was now going out with Jock, a left wing intellectual studying at the London School of Economics. They and their group of beatnik friends had saved me from sinking into maudlin retrospection. Frankly I was a bit in awe of them, particularly Jock. A dishevelled sort of person with a lumbering walk, a shock of untamed curls, startling eyes and a lisp. He was part of the advance guard of the youth movement of the early '60's, campaigning for CND and human rights and against social injustices. At parties he was usually to be found in the kitchen dissecting the latest news and expounding his political theories. 'Western society is heading for disaster. If we're not all blown to smithereens, we'll be mown down in a lemming-like rush over the cliffs of capitalist greed.'

Annie wasn't the only one with a boyfriend, I was going out with Richard, Jock's best mate and fellow radical, a handsome, brooding character with a bohemian lifestyle and a gift for writing poetry. He was at teacher training college in Southampton and being a student, couldn't afford a car, so during the week I'd borrow Daddy's Wolseley or hitch down to Southampton after work. We spent most evenings in, having a quiet smoke and listening to our favourite jazz sounds—Coltrane, Davis, Monk and Mingus. If we felt particularly flush we'd pop out to the pub for a Newcastle Brown. It was all very lovely—when Richard was in a good mood. When he was down he was impossible. Some months back we'd decided to go to Morocco in the summer, and I'd been looking forward to it, but now I was having severe doubts. The down swings were becoming more and more frequent. Richard was smoking too much, or in a mood, or full of apology for being in a mood and it wouldn't happen again—but it always did. I was plucking up the courage to break it off when he told me he was planning something really special.

A lot of the students at his college were anti-establishment and spent their weekends at rallies and demos. Richard thought it was time they organised their own event and got permission to use the main hall. And so, one Saturday night in May, a *Happening* came to Southampton.

It was an evening of improvisation where everyone joined in. There was music and poetry but there was also lots of action. A big wall of painted cardboard boxes divided the hall and we charged at it shouting and singing and breaking down the barrier that divided the rich and the poor. The atmosphere was electric. Protest poems were read and the music got wilder and wilder. We danced and sang and expressed ourselves in whatever way felt right. There were no rules. The instigators of this extraordinary event were painter and poet Adrian Henri and poet Brian Patten, both from Liverpool—the happening city. The music, an eclectic mix of rock, jazz and soul was provided by a group called the Clayton Squares, Liverpudlians too.

Afterwards everyone came back to Richard's place for a wind-down smoke. They were friendly, easy-going, interesting to talk to and, despite the seriousness of their disillusionment with modern society, full of fun. I was hooked. I could easily have become a

Happening follower. I neglected Richard that evening and he noticed.

'For my twenty-first I'm gonna have a helluva party and the Clayton Squares to play at it.'

'I hardly think so, dear. You'd need somewhere with a stage and plenty of room.' Mother was already looking worried. I knew she'd try to steer me away from the idea, but I had my inheritance money and I was going to decide what to do with it, nobody else.

Besides my plans for moving back to London and the party, I had my eye on a Bedford Dormobile, which would be good for holidays. Also I owed my parents the two hundred pounds they'd lent me for the nursing home where I'd had Sebastian. They weren't well off, despite Mother's pretensions or because of her lacy undies, who knows. Although I was pissed off about paying them back, I thought it was better to do it with good grace and no arguments. That way, should some other ticklish situation pop up in the future, they couldn't remind me I was in their debt. Anyway, dear Gruncle had left me loads of money—twelve hundred pounds! I'd have more than enough left over for a wowee of a party.

'We could hire the big hall at Hawley Hotel, do the food at home and they could provide the drink, which we'd pay for up to a certain amount, then people would have to buy it. The Squares charge seventy-five pounds a night and we've arranged that they can stay at Graham's, and altogether it'll cost about a hundred and fifty pounds,' I told Mother.

'Who's this we you keep talking about?'

'Annie and I, of course.'

'Well, you seem to have it worked out already.'

She was right, we had. In fact we'd been planning it for some time. The prospect of a big celebration had helped keep me going through months of scrambled emotions.

It was the 14th June, 1965, and I was twenty-one at last. Thoroughly nerved up at the thought of all that had still to be done, I felt too sick to face breakfast. Annie was due to arrive at the hotel early to help me put up decorations and arrange the hall for the party. Soon the Squares would be on their way down from Liverpool and Richard was coming up from Southampton later. Telephones were buzzing as friends bubbled with enthusiasm—to be invited to a party where the latest Liverpool group was to play, was something to get really excited about.

For the occasion I had a brand new outfit; a shiny ivory shirt with pearl buttons and Peter Pan style collar under a black pinafore with the skirt just tipping the knee. My shoes were black patent leather, strapped and sling-backed and I'd had my short bobbed hair tinted copper. I hoped I looked great but wasn't sure: my hands were shaking so much my eyeliner had to be re-applied several times. But finally I was ready.

By seven most of the eager friends were at the hall and drinks had started flowing. Beatles music played in the background to get us all in Liverpool mood. I noticed Richard hadn't turned up yet, but was too distracted by the other arrivals to care. They were excited and impatient.

'Can't wait to see them!'

'They're super!'

'How did you get them to come?'

'It was easy. I negotiated with their agent.' I tossed my head and moved on, glancing at my watch. Quarter past seven.

'What time are they due?'

'Any minute, but... er... they've a long way to come, so they could be a bit late.'

Richard arrived and I pulled him aside. I needed calming. He wasn't interested in my worries and made for the beer. I felt worse. By seven thirty I was having trouble fending off the questions. Had I really booked them? Had I got the right day? The right week? The right anything? It was unbearable. I was going to be a laughing stock at my twenty-first birthday party. I felt so sick, I fled to the loo, stuck my finger down my throat and brought up precious little. I caught sight of my reddened face in the mirror. The tears welled up. Annie came to find me and mop up my distress. We emerged in strength with the announcement that the Squares were obviously lost and we were going off to find them. We'd cruise up and down the A30 for as long as it took. Beer and cider were flowing and eats could wait.

Three quarters of an hour later, we gave up. It was a pointless exercise, but at least it got us away from ridicule. We parked the car behind the main building and braced ourselves to go back in and serve the food. Then we heard them. They were playing Sam Cook's *Good News*. Joy enveloped us. They'd made it. My reputation was restored.

The evening was a huge success. We danced ourselves footsore and at midnight went back to a friend's place to continue celebrating. By morning I'd fallen for saxophonist Mike and promised to go to Liverpool the following weekend.

13

JE VOUS AIME BEAUCOUP

I spent the week in a froth of expectation. In the mid-sixties Liverpool was meant to be the in-place and I couldn't wait to find out for myself. I made excuses not to see Richard and felt guilty. Our relationship had been floundering for a while and I was too fired up with excitement to risk a row. Annie knew what was going on and she was sworn to secrecy.

'I'll break it off when I get back from seeing Mike,' I told her.

'But what about your Moroccan trip? You were really looking forward to it.'

'I know,' I said miserably.

'All that talk of floating about in a burka and sandals practising your French and gazing at Mediterranean sunsets and smoking great dope.'

'Don't rub it in.'

'*Comme tu es folle, ma petite.*' Annie enjoyed practising her French. She'd learnt in Paris.

'I'm not nuts.' I'd learnt most of mine in Evians-les-Bains when I was twelve.

~

By the summer holidays of 1956, the nervous eczema that plagued me around exam time had gone and I just had to wait for my results. Gruncle asked me how I thought I'd done.

'The French paper was okay, but I don't think I've passed much else,' I said miserably.

He puffed on his smelly pipe, his brown eyes twinkling. 'Oh well, not to worry, dear. I'm sure you're doing your best.'

I adored him and not because he was rich and generous with it, but because he was unfailingly optimistic, even-tempered and loved to laugh. It was hard to believe Gruncle and my strait-laced Grandpa were brothers.

He brushed the stray strands of tobacco off his grubby tie, took a deep breath and heaved himself out of his chair. He was uncomfortably overweight and permanently scruffy, even though his tweeds were of the very best quality. He put an arm round my shoulder to steady himself. 'Now, how about an exchange with a French girl? I'll pay,' he said.

'Wow!' I was thrilled and shocked too. Cousin Beth had exchanged with a Parisian girl and come back speaking enviable French. Would I be as successful?

'Thank you, Gruncle. I'd really like that,' I said.

When the agency confirmed that my partner was to be a girl called Marie-Francoise Philippe whose family had a summer place at Evian-les-Bains on the French side of Lake Geneva, Mother was most impressed. 'Very smart. A resort for the rich, you know,' she declared.

Daddy said, 'I hope you realise what a lucky girl you are.'

'Yes, I do. It sounds … lovely.' Secretly I was unsure, nervous really; after all I would be spending three weeks with complete strangers.

When I walked out of Arrivals at Geneva airport and saw Marie-Francoise and her mother, my heart sank; they had the best tans ever and I felt like a white hankie next to them. Marie-Francoise kissed me on both cheeks, pulled me to one side and told me to call her Frankie, not Shoo-shoon, which was her family pet-name. She hated it because it made her sound like a baby and now she was twelve, she wanted a grown-up name. She had a brother, Marie-Pierre, who was fourteen. His nickname was Boulou and he hated it too, but I wouldn't be meeting him so it didn't matter. He was away on holiday somewhere. I wouldn't be meeting Papa either, he was very important and had offices in Paris and Lyon.

She rattled off this information almost without drawing breath while Madame stood smoking a smelly cigarette and waiting for the chance to greet me. When Frankie let go she swooped in. '*La petite Suzanne. Bonjour, ma cherie,*' she gushed, planting two more kisses on me.

She was wearing bright orange lipstick. Oh golly, I thought, it's bound to have left marks on my cheeks and I'll look really stupid. Whether I did or not became a matter of little importance when I saw their car—a red, open-topped sports car with black leather trim.

Frankie jumped into the back seat, pulled me down beside her and snuggled up. Madame started the engine and we roared out of the car park. She drove like a demon. We whizzed through picturesque villages and beautiful hilly countryside with occasional glimpses of the sparkling lake the French call *Lac Leman.* Several times we passed men peeing by the side of the road. I was shocked but Madame whistled and Frankie laughed. Mother was right about the French being terribly *risqué*. She hadn't told me they'd also be fun, affectionate and easy-going. Yes, I was going to have a super holiday and as Frankie and her mother spoke not a word of English, my French was going to get loads better and everyone at home would be pleased.

Within two weeks it'd improved no end. On the other hand my self-confidence had suffered a shaking. Frankie was very pretty, had long blonde hair and wore short shorts almost up to her bottom. All her clothes, and there were loads, were colourful and flattering. Mine were drab and boring. Her hair looked wonderful hanging loose or plaited and draped over one shoulder. Mine was mouse-brown, straight and horrible and only came down to the bottom of my ears and had to be set. I wished I didn't look so English and had hair like Frankie's. She was far prettier than any of the girls I knew at home.

Madame didn't look like the sort of mothers I was used to either. She was madly glamorous. She wore lots of make-up, tight tops with the beginnings of her bosoms showing, flared skirts and very high heels. Frankie told me *Maman* had been the beauty queen at Evian-Les-Bains the summer before. The idea of my mother posing in high heels and a bathing costume in front of a panel of judges was inconceivable.

If I thought I'd be shown the local sights, I was mistaken. Our days were spent by the lake, which looked far more inviting than it felt: the water was goose-pimplingly cold and the big pebbles on the bottom stubbed our toes. Mostly Frankie and I played jacks and read comics while Madame sunbathed or plucked her leg-hair out with tweezers. Occasionally she'd sigh, '*On va faire les courses.*'

So we'd leap in the car and roar down to the town to do the food shopping. Sometimes Madame allowed us a quick visit to the *plage* with its pedallos, slides and diving platforms. On dull days we stayed at home and explored the grounds and outbuildings or played *cache-cache*, hide-and-seek, in the dark cellars below the building with the girls in the next apartment.

The other thing we did, but only when Madame was out, was play *Vous et votre garçon-ami*—a game of our own invention where we pretended to be a couple in love. It seemed very rude and naughty to me, but Frankie said, *'C'est normal.'*

I consoled myself that we were only experimenting and as we were in France, it was alright and I did want to learn how to kiss.

Whilst at Frankie's I decided the French were not only relaxed about bodies but not much else seemed to phase them either. If you wanted to do something, you just did it, no fussing and discussing. It was just *'Oui, pourquoi pas? On y va.'* Indeed, why not? And off we'd go.

Frankie came back to England with me and we had fun and giggles camping in the garden and watching pop shows on Granny's little television. But the sightseeing outings Mother had arranged weren't a big success. Wherever we went, into the countryside or to Windsor Castle or Buckingham Palace or the Tower of London, Frankie would shuffle along looking at her feet, humming or singing *Nous marchons comme les militaires, toi devant la belle mère derrière.* I didn't realise at the time that she was laughing at us marching around the place like soldiers with mother bringing up the rear. Frankie wasn't a bit interested in historical monuments and certainly wasn't bothered about learning English. To Mother's annoyance, we nattered away in French. 'Now, dear, Frankie is supposed to be learning English. What will Madame say if she goes home not having learned a thing?'

'I shouldn't think she'll care, she's probably having an affair whilst Frankie's away,' I said casually.

'Susan! What a dreadful thing to say. I can only assume you don't understand what you're saying.' Mother's mouth dropped so far open, I thought her teeth might fall out. I had to stifle my giggles.

I wasn't meant to know Mother had false teeth, nobody was, but I'd spotted her spare pair in a box in her undies drawer. Often, when she was out shopping, I would dive in and try everything on. Parading in front of the mirror in her frilly bras and panties, I could pretend I was a grown-up. And now I'd been to France, I thought I was. 'All married people have affairs in France. *C'est normal.*'

Mother stamped out of the room making blowing noises. I didn't know why. She was the one who'd told me they were very *risqué*.

When the time came for Frankie to say goodbye, Granny got very emotional. 'Ee, that wee girl from that France, she's reet lovely, she is. I'll miss her,' she said to Mother.

Frankie smiled sweetly and gave her a cuddle. '*Au 'voir Gran-nez. Je vous aime beaucoup,*'

'Ee I don't understand a word you say, love.'

'She said, bye, bye, Granny. I love you lots ...'

'Ee, ee ... ' and with that Granny burst into tears and had to go to her room.

At the airport Frankie and I clung onto each other until the last possible moment. When the flight was called, she whispered in my ear, '*Au 'voir, ma chère Susie, à l'année prochaine.*'

We'd agreed to ask if we could exchange again the next year and I thought there was a good chance; I'd come top in the French exam.

14

MOVING ON

The weekend in Liverpool was a revelation and quite the best fun I'd had in ages. I stayed, no-strings, at Mike's flat in 10 Canning Street, in the heart of Liverpool 8 where most of the beats lived. Although he was a bit shorter than me, I found Mike very sexy. He was refreshingly laid-back, such a change from Richard's moody temperament, and had a deep, gurgling laugh and a strong accent—Liverpool tinged with Welsh. He played wonderful sax and I loved his throaty singing voice—very Leonard Cohen. In his pink shirt, tight pants and pointy toed-shoes, he'd sway to the music as if it came from inside his body.

That Saturday night the Squares were playing at the Cavern and I joined the girlfriends in the band-room. We arrived well before the mob. Sue, who'd been with Bobby, the drummer, for years, explained how unpopular girlfriends were—jealous fans were pretty horrible and best avoided. After the gig we went on to the Blue Angel nightclub, where fans were banned. On the Sunday Mike showed me the sights—the Liver buildings, the old cathedral with its spooky swastika-graffiti'd graveyard, the new rocket-shaped cathedral, Lime Street station, the incredible murals in the lifts at the Adelphi hotel and the Phil (Philharmonic) pub with its panelling, stained glass and long marble bars which were usually draped with a selection of colourful, alternative types. Then there was The Crack, quite another sort of pub. The Crack lived up to its name, unlike the Phil, it was tiny and intimate and Mike knew everyone there. 'John Lennon used to sit under that table and spout poetry. And this is Mike, Paul's brother, he's with The Scaffold.'

He also introduced me to painter Sam Walsh, and poets Roger McGough and Pete Brown. It was all so thrilling. Liverpool had given birth to The Beatles and a whole host of alternative talent.

I wanted to be in amongst it and passed the long train journey home planning my future. Mike had suggested I could rent the empty first floor flat at No. 10. He'd arrange it with the landlord. The invitation was irresistible. I was picking up my second-hand Dormobile van the next day, so I'd be able to move my stuff in that.

Telling Richard wasn't going to be easy and as I knew I'd need some moral support afterwards, I persuaded my old boyfriend, Maurice, to come to my rescue again. 'You and your men,' he sighed.

'You were one once, don't forget,' I said blowing him a kiss.

It was dusk by the time we arrived in Southampton and I was full of foreboding. I climbed the front steps wondering whether Richard would let me in or slam the door in my face. Strangely it was open.

The stairs were dark as I climbed up to the flat. All the rooms were dark too. A thin shaft of light from a street-lamp slanted past the sitting room door and across the landing. I tiptoed in. Richard was sitting in the big armchair, which he'd turned to face the bay window. He didn't budge but I knew he must have heard me on the stairs. 'It's me,' I said feebly.

He got up and I could see his distress. I felt the biggest bitch ever. 'Are we finished?'

I nodded, explanations seemed futile. 'I'm sorry.'

He didn't probe and he didn't push, he merely asked me to take him to London. He didn't want to stay in the flat. I agreed but had to explain I had Maurice in the van.

'Charming.'

We drove to London in silence and dropped Richard at Jock and Annie's. By this time it was too late to go in, so we turned round and headed home to Surrey. Maurice tried to distract me with jokes and silly stories but I was tired and feeling horrible. I was driving erratically anyway, not being used to the van. When I had to brake suddenly to avoid a jaywalking drunk, we skidded and ended up in a ditch. My beautiful second-hand Dormobile juddered, choked and cut out completely. We were stuck. I burst into tears; as usual my emotion spilled onto Maurice's shoulder.

It was somewhere around four in the morning when we finally found a phone-box. Daddy came out to rescue us without a single complaint but his coldness was unbearable. He put a 'broken down' notice on the van but I was worried someone would steal it. 'Drat it, girl, get in the car. You can call the garage in the morning.'

By the time we'd dropped Maurice at his place, the drizzly dawn promised a thoroughly miserable day. When we got home Mother made tea and plonked my mug on the kitchen table without a word. She and Daddy went back to bed leaving me to drink it alone. I realised then they were probably sick and tired of their wayward daughter. I'd overstayed my welcome. As an only child you have to get it right—it's the one chance your parents get. I stared into the tea-leaves at the bottom of the mug, wishing I could interpret them. Liverpool seemed like a dream. Was I really going to live there? What about finding a theatre job? Would I ever make a success of my life? And where was my baby?

15

THE ENTRY OF CHRIST
INTO LIVERPOOL

My parents took my news very well. Yes, they'd had enough of me. 'There's your Uncle George in Woolton, if you need anything,' said Mother.

I'd forgotten that. Uncle George was Daddy's younger brother, a gentle, good-looking man, who seemed to be constantly grappling with some problem or other and consequently permanently miserable. His childhood had been thoroughly overshadowed by Granny's pride in, and obvious preference for, Daddy. He was the originator of the silent but deadly. We dreaded car rides with him knowing that if we weren't frozen stiff from the open windows by Mother, we'd be gassed by Uncle G. But for all of this, he was a kind man who, I discovered later, had a predilection for naughty nude magazines though not the courage to buy them. As he apparently ranked me as broad-minded, I became his paper-girl. I supposed even windy uncles had their needs.

I couldn't wait to leave my job but had to work out my notice, so I spent every available moment making endless lists of what I'd need to take with me. Of course, they were far too long. But every snail needs its shell even if it's a helluva of a tight fit. Daddy, family packing expert, was impressed when I managed to squeeze several bits of furniture, two large suitcases full of clothes, my record-player and albums, books and other essential-to-life-and-well-being treasures into the back of my dented Dormobile and headed North.

Looking at the map of the UK, I saw Northwards as uphill all the way. My van apparently did too. We chugged by Oxford, laboured past Stafford, barely made Bromsgrove and arrived at Canning Street totally exhausted but triumphant. Everyone was in: Mike, Adrian Henri and his wife Joyce, Bobby the drummer and Sue so I had plenty of help unloading and carting my stuff up to the first floor flat I was to rent.

That night, after a rather lengthy 'welcome to Liverpool' lay, I discovered Mike had an amazing sexual appetite which I alone could never satisfy. Hey ho, I thought. He's a really nice guy but I'm on an adventure, so, if he wants supplementary satisfaction, well never mind.

10 Canning Street was a Victorian House with three floors and a basement. The decor was predominantly dark blue. The lower stairs walls were hung with Adrian's latest paintings—dead pigeons stuck on canvas and splashed with paint—I'd hold my nose and looked straight ahead whenever passing. Up to the top floor, large white canvases, decorated exclusively with minute paintings of plates of salad, reflected light down into the dark well outside my two-room flat. Although these eccentric works didn't appeal to me, I was thrilled to discover Adrian's biggest and most famous canvas hanging in my front room; it was there because it was the only wall in the house large enough to carry it. *The Entry of Christ into Liverpool* was literally crowded with everyone who was anyone on the Liverpool scene of the moment, including the Beatles, all set against a background of Lime Street station and the Adelphi with

the Liver Buildings on the horizon. It was a wonderfully vivid painting which I delighted in studying on a regular basis to see who else I'd met who might be featured.

The next few weeks were spent in nesting mode and because my van was making alarmingly expensive-sounding noises, I swapped it for something much smaller, a Renault 4L—christened Semolina on account of her colour. I also explored the streets; Liverpool 8, I discovered, had a reputation. Kerb-crawlers were a regular feature and street fighting between the locals and the black population from Upper Parliament Street meant going out at night alone was not a good idea.

Mike's life centred around the music scene; if a good group came to Liverpool, we saw them. I was transported by the Walker Brothers at the New Brighton Tower and the Spencer Davis concert was extraordinary. Mike knew Spencer and singer, Stevie Winwood, so we went back to their suite at the Adelphi for drinks after the show.

The rest of my inheritance from Gruncle and my savings disappeared alarmingly fast, so finding a job became a priority. I went to the nearest temping agency knowing work with pay at the end of each week was pretty well guaranteed—being a secretary as opposed to a shorthand-typist gave me the edge.

Monday came and I turned up at my allocated temping job in a solicitor's office. After a day of copy-typing with no punctuation where I thought punctuation ought to be, I was stiff with boredom and sore with typist's bottom. The two consolations were, knowing

I'd only nine more days to endure and that the evenings would be entertaining; Liverpool nightlife was buzzing and I wanted to experience it all.

After the solicitors I spent a week at an engineering company where the smell on the factory floor reminded me of sessions in the Manor Lodge garage, helping Daddy as he dismantled and reassembled bits of car. Interminable evenings holding a lamp and miscellaneous tools—like a theatre nurse, with greasy hands.

The following week it was a Catholic publication where I kept my opinions to myself. I'd learned about Catholicism at school.

Farnborough Hill was a Convent College where nice young Catholic girls could be well educated, both intellectually and morally, and if God willed it, take the veil, thereby ensuring not only God's pleasure but future teachers to keep lay staff to a minimum. The school was classed as minor public and was inordinately proud of its reputation. Even so, they'd agreed to take me. It didn't matter that I'd failed the eleven-plus and was a 'non-Catholic'. My parents' money had the same value at the bank, so it was acceptable, if perhaps a touch tainted. I'd seen nuns before but knew little about them except they couldn't marry, did good works, prayed a lot and usually wore black and white. I found out that they were actually 'Brides of Christ', weren't good to everyone, prayed very fast and their habits were rather smelly.

In Religious Knowledge lessons they told us that newborn babies are stained by original sin, and therefore unacceptable to God and his angels. As only a Catholic baptism could wash the stain away, it was best to see to it double quick in case the unfortunate child died inopportunely. With particular relish we were also informed that non-Catholics, being unbaptised into the chosen faith, would be in a permanent state of original sin and as St. Peter only lets Catholics into heaven, they would end up in Limbo or hell. If you didn't fancy spending your afterlife floating around in nothingness, conversion could be a good idea.

When Catholics committed some sin or other, there was always Confession. They'd to go into a booth with a see-through grille, tell the priest sitting behind it absolutely everything and then he'd give them Absolution. For little venial sins to big mortal ones, this was the road to purification. As long as they recited Hail Mary, Our Father or Glory Be as many times as prescribed. When I asked my classmates if they were truly sorry, they said 'of course'. Although, often as not, they'd commit just the same sins the following week. I'd have been damned (oops!) if I'd had to tell the priest the stuff I actually regretted, let alone my innermost secrets. Luckily, being a non-Catholic, for me confession would've been pointless; I'd still have to go to Limbo. 'Father, I've thought lewd thoughts and touched myself in rude places.'

'What were your lewd thoughts and where were your rude places, my child?'

Yuck! If God had wanted us to have only pure thoughts, we wouldn't have babies, and if we weren't meant to touch our rude places, it'd be pretty hard to wash.

I also couldn't work out why there were so many desperately poor people who put money into the offertory of an incredibly rich church. Surely God had no use for money.

No, Catholicism was not my scene. It just didn't square with my values and anyway I preferred to figure out the mysteries of God and creation for myself rather than blithely accepting what others pronounced on the matter.

But I did smile at the thought of what Reverend Mother would've had to say about the wanton young lady I'd now become. 'A non-Catholic, what do you expect? You mark my words, that one will surely end up in hell.'

'Up yours, Reverend Mother, I'm having an adventure!'

But by the end of my time with the Catholics and having spent a month playing Miss Take-a-Letter in dreary set-ups, I began to wonder if Liverpool had been such a good idea after all.

I was discussing my plight with Bobby's girlfriend, Sue, in the Phil one night when a jolly-looking black guy, who must have been eavesdropping, plonked himself down at our table. His eyes bulged and his huge white teeth gleamed. 'You looking for a job? I know a good one.'

'Whoops!' I thought but didn't want to appear rude. 'What is it?'

'The manager at the Everyman is always complaining he ain't got no assistant. I'm there in *Jack of Spades*. I could introduce you.'

'What on earth is he talking about?' I whispered to Sue.

'The theatre, the Everyman Theatre!' she exclaimed.

I needed no persuading. We left the pub immediately. I met the Manager, Michael; we got on okay and it was agreed I'd start the following week. How extraordinary to have had such luck again.

I rushed home to tell Mike who took advantage of my high spirits to say he'd met a rather gorgeous brunette and was thinking of moving in with her. I wished him lots of luck and love and we agreed we were parting friends.

Jack of Spades turned out to be a musical about Jamaicans coming to Liverpool looking for work and lodgings. The poignant dialogue and beautiful songs reflected their difficulties and the ignorance and prejudices they came up against. Sadly it disappeared without a trace, probably because of inadequate publicity but also, I think in retrospect, because it was not the genre of the moment. However, I enjoyed every performance, and I saw most of them.

During *Jack of Spades,* the actors for the next season came up to start rehearsals. Life soon became full of interesting 'thesps' although my closest mates were the stage management team. One of them, Nick, became my live-in boyfriend. With a regular chap came regular sex.

Let's face it, the Dutch cap is a chore. You have to put it in on spec and that uses up a whole lot of jelly, and if you're on a sex marathon, you have to keep topping it up and that's a mess. I was becoming thoroughly fed up with the thing when I heard about the latest development—The Pill.

I decided to ask my GP. I thought he might be agreeable as attitudes to unmarried sex were becoming more relaxed. In fact the liberated young were starting to do it wherever attraction was reciprocated. For women the pill represented freedom, for men a relief.

The doctor was a bit reluctant at first, but as I was in a live-in relationship and, having had one baby, didn't want to risk another, he agreed to put me on Ovulen. I was to take one at night for twenty-five days or so, come off for a week to have a period, then restart. It was easy and I felt no ill effects. The cap and accessories were ceremonially dumped in the bin. Part of me was sad to be moving from one contraceptive to another. I was mad about Nick and if he'd wanted to get serious and have kids, I'd have been overjoyed, but I knew the last thing he had in mind was to be tied down. And even if he had, it probably wouldn't have been to me.

Nick had acting aspirations and with dad Griffith Jones and Gemma as his sister, it was hardly surprising. He'd been marinating in theatre and films all his life. He was tall, blonde and good-looking with a brown velvet voice, younger than me, full of fun and optismism and I didn't doubt he'd make it one day. I had no such aspirations, never having fancied myself as an actress and guessing I'd be pretty uncastable anyway. Too tall, not a beauty, a comedienne or a character. What exactly I was heading towards I'd no idea, just being there was enough.

We were paid a pittance, so it was a struggle to get by. The hours were often long and we were frequently worn out, but nobody clock-watched because the days were exciting and varied. Apart from duties I was familiar with from Old Vic days, I was stand-in at lighting rehearsals, helped out wherever anyone needed help and got to drive the theatre van—none of the stage staff had a licence. All in all we were a happy and dedicated crew and life was great.

Sadly the rosy glow blinded us to the volcano of trouble that was about to erupt. Terry Hands and Peter James, our directors, had very different ideas about the plays they wanted to put on. Terry was into the *avant garde* while Peter was more inclined to the 'bums-on-seats' approach. Their constant clashes split the company into two rival factions. At the end of the season, the governors, who were more interested in money than art, sacked Terry and all his supporters. The actors were moving on anyway, but for those back-stagers who were behind him, which included Nick and therefore me too, it was a major blow.

So, disillusioned and thoroughly dejected, we left. After that I couldn't even face passing the theatre and would detour to avoid it. We were lost and broke. So while Nick wrote around to all the drama schools, I took a two-day course in selling encyclopaedias door-to-door. I was hopeless; after the first week I hadn't sold a single set but had drunk endless cups of tea and polished off lots of cake and biscuits in friendly houses in North Wales—my patch. It was pointless to continue although one useful contact had come through my failure as a salesperson.

I had another car, Bluebell, a beautiful blue Triumph Roadster coupé. Bought for forty pounds from one of the actors. Sadly my trusty Renault, Semolina, had been written off; Nick in charge but not his fault. She'd been towed away to death-by-rust in a car graveyard and the insurance company had paid me fifty pounds. Unfortunately, Bluebell was operating on only one kingpin and was rather dangerous so I was delighted to discover, at one of the houses I visited, the husband was a mechanic.

'Always wanted to get under the bonnet of one of 'em', he said rubbing his hands in rude glee. To my delight he agreed to fix her for nothing.

Just before I was condemned to a new stretch at temping, Nick got a letter from the Bristol Old Vic drama school calling him to a weekend assessment. And so fate spun us in another direction, South.

We quit the flat, stored the bits of furniture at Uncle G's and crammed our most essential belongings into Bluebell's dicky seat—a sort of separate boot and back seat combined. We drove back to London via Nick's interview in Bristol and stayed with his parents in Earls Court. A week later he heard he'd been accepted. We were thrilled.

But then he delivered an unexpected blow. He wanted to make a completely fresh start at Bristol and I wasn't part of his pictured future. I was devastated. How could he chuck me just like that? Had he no heart? But then I remembered how I'd felt telling Richard it was over between us and how he thought I didn't give a shit. Could there ever be a clean way to break off a relationship?

So now I was back where I'd started from, it was as though a rosy future with Nick, Liverpool and the Everyman had only existed in my dreams. Now I had no boyfriend, no flat and no job. Thank God there was still the safety net. My parents took me back.

'What a pity, dear,' said Mother.

'That's life,' said Daddy. 'You've got to shop around to find the right partner.'

'Really, John, you make it sound so sordid. Nick was a very nice young man, and from such a well-known theatrical background. I feel sure he has the makings of a fine classical actor.'

'Well, classical or not, he's obviously not ready to commit himself and I don't suppose that was ever his intention,' said Daddy, eying me over his glasses.

I burst into tears and fled to my room. What was wrong with me? Would I ever get things right or was I a no-hoper? Just when I was beginning to feel really happy, life, like a house of cards, had to tumble down around me again.

Mother appeared with a glass of whisky. I could have done with the bottle. She put her arm round me. 'I know it's horrid for you but Nick has his ambitions. What about yours, eh? Neither Daddy nor I want you to get stuck in a job you hate, but you must be realistic. The chances of finding a worthwhile career in the theatre are very slim.'

I blew my nose and downed the whisky in one. 'I know that, but I must still try. It's where I want to be. Where I belong.'

'Well, good luck, darling. And do try putting a price on yourself. Don't keep falling for all these young men.' Mother had a knack of giving with one hand and taking away with the other. She'd fired my enthusiasm again but at the same time had insinuated I was an easy lay. Perhaps, by her standards, I was. But then how could she possibly understand how I felt. How desperately I longed to meet the right man. I often wondered if I'd recognise him when he came along anyway, if he ever did. But, whatever happened, I absolutely couldn't think of myself as a total failure, not yet. I'd go back to London and find another theatre job.

16

THANK YOU JONATHAN MILLER

By now Annie and Jock had drifted apart and she was living with school friend, Rhoda, in Notting Hill. Annie was working part-time on the locks at Little Venice and Rhoda imported sandals from Morocco. Their flat was all Indian prints, cushions and the heady perfume of joss sticks, mixed with marijuana and the sounds of Dylan or Baez. Their hippie lifestyle and philosophy were most appealing. I slept on their floor and hung around with them and their friends whilst combing the Sits Vac columns for theatre work. There was nothing for several weeks. Then I saw it … and made a huge red ring round it; the Mermaid Theatre needed a stage door keeper and it had to be someone with experience. Hooray! That's me! I wrote off immediately. A couple of days later the phone rang. A friendly voice called Judy arranged the interview with Ken, the general manager.

'He thinks it should be a man. But I persuaded him he should at least see you,' she told me.

'Thank you.'

My spirits nose-dived—female and only twenty-two. What chance did I stand? I should've realised. I rehearsed answers to every question I imagined he would ask. I even practised lowering my voice. I must have sounded daft. Annie was practical as usual, 'Just go and be yourself. Putting on an act is stupid.'

I took her advice and got the job. Heaven knows why. Maybe there wasn't any competition. Once again

I'd be where I longed to be and that was all that mattered. The sickly backstage smells of size and greasepaint would greet me every morning. The swing of the stage door would freeze my legs as I sat at the switchboard with its wires and plugs and little round pop-down extension indicators. The keys would jingle on the dressing-room board and a hotchpotch of people would come by. People selling things, delivering things, looking for autographs, carting props and costumes. And there'd be the actors. Many of them would just greet me, but others would stop for a chat. The stage door was a sociable sort of place.

The downside of the job was the money—eight pounds a week. I arranged to supplement it by working front-of-house in the evenings. Connie, in the bar, needed help and there was always usheretting and ice-cream sales. I'd be okay. I found a dreary but clean bedsit in Chelsea and consoled myself with the thought that I wouldn't be spending too much time there. I'd be working late most nights.

The warm blanket of theatre friends soon wrapped itself around me. I got to know Judy; a straight-talking girl with neatly bobbed hair and athletic legs who was far too sensible to bother with such frivolities as fashion. With her you knew exactly where you stood and I liked that a lot. Then there was Andrew in lighting; an absolute sweetheart with a problem. He thought he was gay but he wasn't sure. He'd scoot round to the stage door on a regular basis. There we'd wrestle with his confused emotions. I became best friend, mother figure, punch-bag and, occasionally, we'd fall into each other's arms through sheer exhaustion.

The Bedsitting Room—a Spike Milligan special, Shaw's *Man of Destiny* and *Treasure Island* provided me with a stream of actors to fantasise about. After the evening show, I would tag along to the late-night theatre watering holes. The Buxton club, Jerry's in Shaftesbury Avenue and the Borsch 'n Tears Russian restaurant with music in Beauchamp Place. Here I met the crowd from the Royal Court Theatre, among them Dennis Waterman, *enfant terrible*, best known as William in the television series *Just William*. When we hooked up together for a while, I got very little sleep.

Luckily I could recover discreetly. My little cubbyhole behind the switchboard offered adequate cover for cat-napping. Andrew wasn't impressed however and we fell out for a while.

The Bedsitting Room was usually a sell-out, but Spike didn't always turn up for the show. His psychological problems were famous and his mood swings spectacular. I certainly saw both sides of the man; the stage door hinges were frequently tested for strength when he slammed through in the bleakest of moods or on a complete high. We never knew what to expect. When he was up he was absolutely great—fun, affectionate, kind and totally dotty. For some reason he called me the Welsh Guardsman—I couldn't think why. But at least he'd given me a nickname. Sometimes he'd stop by the stage door for a chat. One day he spotted me reading a book of Edward Lear limericks. He snatched it from me and scribbled in his versions of some of the last lines. They were a great improvement. And when Mother was going through a tie-making stage and had dumped a load on me to sell, Spike took

135

the box, grabbed my hand and pulled me round the dressing rooms. Nobody dared refuse him. We sold them all.

When it came to dottiness, Bernard Miles ran a very close second. I never figured out whether he was a genius, seriously unhinged or knew something the rest of us couldn't possibly grasp. Whichever, and perhaps all three were applicable, it was impossible not to be impressed by his energy and dedication.

He had founded a small theatre company in an outbuilding in his back garden. Some years later, through dogged perseverance, he'd raised the finance and acquired the permits to bring his little rep into the heart of London. Not central enough nor grand enough to be classed as West End, the Mermaid Theatre, Puddle Dock, Blackfriars was, as far as Equity was concerned anyway, a provincial rep. Ridiculous, but it probably suited the budget—actors in the West End could command far higher fees.

Although life was good and I now had a new boyfriend—a lovely guy called Peter who was in that year's *Treasure Island,* I knew that stage door keeping was taking me nowhere, not that I had any idea where I wanted to go until one morning when Judy came down to collect the post for the production office and announced she was thoroughly fed up. 'I hate being cooped up in that darned office all day,' she told me.

'You should be so lucky,' I said. 'My shorthand and typing speeds must have gone right down by now. Tell you what, why don't we change places?'

We both burst out laughing.

Two days later I was summoned up to see our general manager, cool, calm Ken, with bushy hair and beard to match and penetrating eyes that made me feel like a stupid schoolgirl. I wondered what on earth I'd done. Perhaps someone had complained. Oh God, was I about to lose my job?

'I didn't know about your secretarial training, why didn't you tell me at the interview?'

'I didn't think it was necessary for stage door keeping.'

'It isn't, but it's useful up here. Judy seems to fancy the idea of swapping jobs. What do you think?'

'That would be good. Thank you.' I said. I'll feel cut off up here, I thought, but a possible pay rise and a busier day will be worth it and anyway, it was a sort of promotion.

'Right, you can start Monday, nine o'clock sharp.'

In the production office I worked hard for my extra two pounds a week. My duties involved liaising with agents, typing letters and contracts, making sure the office ran smoothly and, inevitably, filing. The system was efficient but antiquated, so I spent every available moment up-dating it. I kept running across old letters signed by someone called Anthea Lynex.

'Who's she?' I asked Ken.

'Used to be our casting director.'

It was as if someone had redirected all the meandering lanes of my directionless existence into one major road. I knew in an instant what I wanted to do with my life and the more I thought about it, the more sense it made.

I knew better than to discuss it with Ken. First I had to research the idea. By now I'd struck up telephone acquaintance with several actors' agents. After all, I was their stage door. Through me they could find out what plays were coming up, put forward their suggestions and hopefully get some of their actors to tread the boards at the Mermaid. It paid them to be friendly. I would broach the subject with one of them. Peter Browne and I had a good rapport. He called soon enough. 'Hello Flower.'

'Hi Peter.'

'Anything happening?'

We were waiting for confirmation of the next play.

'No news yet, but I wonder if you could give me some advice. I want to know about casting directors. What they do exactly.'

'Of course. If you're free, why not let's have lunch tomorrow and I'll tell you.'

And so we did and I learned all about the casting process. My gut feeling had been right—if I'd been one already, I'd have cast myself in the role.

I would need to get to know the capabilities of a huge range of actors. This meant seeing as many plays, films and as much television drama as humanly possible. Then, armed with a memorised repertoire, I would put forward to visiting directors my suggestions for each of the parts. Once the actors had been chosen, I would negotiate fees with their agents.

As a casting director, I'd be approached by agents who would take me to see their clients in work or ask me to grant them general interviews. Their aim was to familiarise me with everyone on their books so I would include their names when suitable parts came up.

Those were the basics of the job. I was convinced I could do it. I knew I wanted to.

I decided to wait before asking Ken if he'd consider me as an apprentice successor to Ms Lynex. Instead I spent lunch and after hours going through the Spotlight directories which contained photos of the vast majority of British actors. It took me about three weeks to compile a list of all those I'd seen and to add my comments on their performances. I was amazed how many I already knew.

Jonathan Miller, fresh from his controversial *Alice in Wonderland* for the BBC, came to direct a Robert Lowell play, *Benito Cereno*. The cast was predominantly black. Whilst formulating a character breakdown to give out to agents, Jonathan admitted to me that his knowledge of black actors was very limited. If my moment was going to arrive this was it. I plunged in. 'I know some very good people.'

'Marvellous! Let's get to it.'

He was terrific to work with; receptive, appreciative, kind and fun. When I asked if he'd put a good word in for me with Ken, Jonathan sung my praises and said he'd like me credited in the programme.

'Too late, I'm afraid. It's already gone to print.'

I was very disappointed but not deterred. I'd gained credibility if not creditability. I asked Ken if I might act as casting director on future productions. 'If you must, but don't think of asking for a pay rise.' The Mermaid's meagre budget probably gave him endless sleepless nights already.

'Thank you. I won't let you down.' I sped down to Connie's bar to find Andrew and celebrate. My career was truly launched.

17

BREAK A LEG

The Mermaid Theatre was the start of my apprenticeship and I soon discovered that my Jonathan Miller experience had been unique; not all directors were a joy to work with. Some were bloody damned difficult—couldn't make decisions, wanted all top names on a tiny budget, had horrendous egos or appeared to be off their rockers—like Bernard Miles.

Being the owner, founder and boss of the Mermaid Theatre, he got to choose the plays, and sometimes, heaven help everyone, he would direct as well. Unfortunately, for me in particular, he showed little interest in his fellow actors. 'Why would I want to go to the theatre? Dreadful places, boxed in by God knows who, on a hard seat with no leg room. And as for the thespians, waste of time most of 'em.'

'D'you feel the same about the cinema, Bernard?' I ventured.

'Load of worthless rubbish, all of it.'

I reckoned the number of actors he knew would have fitted in his dressing room, and then he would probably have forgotten their names—he had an appalling memory and non-existent listening skills. Working with him was going be a pretty unfulfilling experience.

The summer season was coming up and he'd decided to treat the tourist trade to not only one but three classical Greek tragedies, in rotation—which meant a cast in rotation too. Help!

I set up weeks of interviews. Bernard wanted to meet half the actors in Spotlight. We waded through an endless stream of hopefuls. I traipsed up and down ferrying the victims from the stage door to the interview room and back. All were required to read a script extract with Bernard playing opposite them. He fancied himself as Queen Hecuba. As he was mostly known for his Long John Silver in *Treasure Island* or the yokel in the egg commercial, this was enough to put anyone off.

By the time we were into the third week, I was not only exhausted but beginning to wonder what on earth I'd got myself into. That day, someone had cancelled and I sat on the top of the stage door steps snatching a coffee. Just as the previous interviewee reached the corner by Blackfriars station, I saw him spin round and race back towards me. 'Terribly sorry. Forgot my umbrella,' he said breathlessly.

'Don't worry, there's nobody with him. You can pop up and get it.'

He was gone for a quarter of an hour. When he came back down his face was a picture. 'You're not going to believe this but he's just interviewed me all over again,' he spluttered.

'Oh, yes I certainly can believe it. I do apologise,' I said ruefully.

Then we burst out laughing. Although it was completely disheartening for both of us, we couldn't help but see the funny side.

The plays were finally cast from the actors Bernard saw in the last few days of interviews and, even then, he had terrible trouble remembering who they were.

During the run I got to know one of the young actresses playing a series of small parts in all three plays; a small but striking brunette whose name was Candy. She'd recently been working at the Old Vic. Of course, we got to compare notes. 'My fiancé's on the stage staff,' she said.

'Really, what a coincidence, so was mine, once. His name was John Williams. Is he still there?' I asked.

Her mouth fell open. 'I don't believe it. He most certainly is, and he's the one. In fact, I'm going to have his baby,' she told me proudly.

Oh God, oh God, oh God! How I managed to stop myself from telling her my sorry tale, I'll never know. 'Great, super ... wonderful. Congratulations,' I said in a rather high-pitched voice. 'Must go ... meeting someone.' And with that I fled.

Spike was back. It was Christmas, we were doing *Treasure Island*, again, and for once Bernard was not directing or playing Long John Silver. It was such a relief to have actor/ director, Ron Pember, in charge.

Someone had the bright idea of getting Barry Humphries for Long John with Spike Milligan as Ben Gunn—I was left to get my teeth into the pirates. It all sounds great, doesn't it? And so it should have been. Unfortunately Bernard just couldn't let go; after weeks of lurking at the back of the auditorium he emerged from the shadows two days before the dress rehearsal, to announce he hated the show and wanted to re-direct the whole thing himself. How Ron managed to deflect him, I do not know. And Bernard wasn't the only one to get right up noses. So did Jack Sprat, his parrot, who was used to perching on her master's shoulder and wasn't at all impressed by Mr. Humphries.

Spike's Ben Gunn was a triumph of improvisation. Had he learned the script? I doubt it. Could he remember his moves? Of course not. Was he a Goon out of bedlam or a monkey with a banger up its bottom? He was certainly elsewhere, particularly when he forgot to turn up altogether. Predictably the audience thought him hysterical and the rest of the cast thought him a trial.

As for Mr. Humphries, well, I don't think I ever saw him smile.

During my time at the Mermaid I got through a selection of fellas, as we did in those days, and Andrew came and went. Having made up his mind he was more gay than straight, his social life was leaning at a pretty steep angle.

I had outgrown my little bedsit by now and found a flat in Battersea but needed some sharers. One of the visiting actresses, Cyd Hayman, said she was looking for a place. We agreed to give it a try. Then I approached Carol Drinkwater, a friend on Stage Management. She said she'd like to come in with us as her working hours were pretty unsociable, rushing to catch the last train back home to her parents' place in Bromley was proving impractical. The timing was just right for her; she was about to start acting training at the Drama Centre in North London.

The flat was roomy and comfortable but it wasn't long before Carol and Cyd became disenchanted with the way I was running things and ganged up against me. Cyd shut herself in her room and refused to come out, Carol took me to task. 'Your trouble is you're too damned bossy and all you seem to think about is paying the rent and the bills. Just get off our backs, will you.'

Had I been that horrendous? 'I'm sorry, I didn't realise. I really don't mean … I worry about it you see.'

'Yes, well stop it, okay?'

'It's alright for you, it's not your responsibility.'

'Come on, don't give me that, Sue,' she said fiercely. She looked so irretrievably pissed off, I slumped down at the kitchen table and burst into tears. Carol can be pretty formidable, but she is also very kind and loving and it wasn't long before we were weeping all over each other. We made up and I stopped fretting.

At work I was really happy. Casting suited me and I discovered I had a good memory after all—for something that genuinely interested me. As my head wasn't jam-packed with stuff to get me through exams, I had plenty of room to develop a brain like a filing cabinet—of photos, details and the CVs of literally thousands of actors. Luckily I liked them.

In those pre-celebrity-culture days, they were ripe for ridicule and often dismissed as egocentric, loveys, exhibitionists, or psychological misfits. Undoubtedly any of these labels could be applied to some, but they could be applied to people in any walk of life. Not too many thought to call them courageous.

Actors go to interviews knowing that not only is their ability under scrutiny, but so is every detail of their physicality. Few professions require such an all-inclusive appraisal—enough to knock anyone's self-confidence out of touch. And it's easy to say they don't have to be actors if they can't cope with it. In my experience, serious actors are driven and I don't suppose too many could give you clear-cut reasons and why should they? Maybe they're hungry to project into a wide range of emotion, to portray a variety of very different characters, to understand more about the human condition, to leave their lives in the dressing room and step into the shoes of someone else for a while. Seems to me the opposite of egocentric.

The average working actor will meet hundreds of fellow thespians as well as directors, producers, stage staff and television or film crew members. Everyone is thrown together on the first day of rehearsal. There is no time for circling round, examining, getting to know each other gradually. It has to be instant and it's very intimate. Small talk is as unusual as china cups at coffee break. Remembering all those names, as well as your bloody lines, is well nigh impossible. Hence 'darling', or should I say 'lovey'?

I doubt many exhibitionists or show-offs suffer from stage fright but I haven't yet spoken to an actor who doesn't. In fact visiting their dressing room before the show is taboo. Some can be physically sick before going on stage or camera—although, once in character and performing, the nerves usually disappear.

Psychological misfits? Who isn't these days? It's unusual to meet people who aren't hiding their weaknesses behind the curtain of a dysfunctional childhood, or who aren't afraid of just about anything—deep and meaningful conversation, admitting they're sick, an addict, impotent, out-of-work or broke. Actors, at least, have found a pretty good way of taking a break—becoming someone else for a bit. How sensible!

I discovered very quickly that good actors are usually dedicated and hard working, often brilliant raconteurs and a lot more open and fun than the average mortal. I also discovered that, just like the rest of us, they could be disgruntled, bitchy, ungrateful, insincere, neurotic or even totally unbearable if they became successful.

Over time I came to number several among my closest friends.

After a couple of years at the Mermaid I wanted to try casting for films and television, but to do that meant getting a 'ticket'. The union, The Association of Cinema and Television Technicians (ACTT), was a closed shop. The only way I could get in was by working for another casting director as an assistant. I wasn't proud, I didn't mind. I had much to learn anyway. I was introduced to Jimmy Liggatt, freelance and about to start casting for a psycho-mystery television film series for Hammer Films at MGM studios in Elstree.

He took me on and Hammer got me the required union membership. I was now legit although, after the series, I would be out of work again. But I had every reason to be optimistic—there were only about a dozen freelance casting directors in the business and the demand was increasing. I would survive.

As Elstree was only reached from Battersea via Timbuktoo on public transport and I was carless, having had to sell Bluebell during my job-hunting period, Daddy came to the rescue and found me a second-hand Ford Popular. I was all excited until I saw her. If MGM studios called for a good vehicular image, I'd not qualify. Gherkin, as I christened her, was more like tenth-hand. Daddy had sorted the engine and cleaned out the black dust; the previous owner had used her for humping sacks of coal about.

'She's a good little bus—for seven pounds,' purred Daddy 'and you'll soon get back into double-declutching.'

Gherkin was a sort of down-market Patience. I smiled bravely and drove her back to London. She was fine, but embarrassingly slow on hills. I resolved to trade her in as soon as decent and possible. In the meantime at least I could make it to Elstree and there I was going to get into the film and television world.

LEARNING THE HARD WAY

MGM was fun and, under Jimmy's kindly gaze, I learned a lot. *Journey to the Unknown* was a back-to-back series—two in filming at the same time—so we were kept pretty busy. It was over all too quickly.

I was now back out in the real world, jobless and afraid. At night I would lie awake worrying—maybe going freelance hadn't been such a good idea. I might never work again.

After a couple of weeks I was rescued by a director I'd met at MGM. He offered me a film to cast at the other Elstree Studio—ABPC, Associated British Picture Company. *Moon Zero Two* was no masterpiece but it was work.

Two more B films came along and I was glad to practice where it didn't matter too much and to learn about the seedier side of the business. At one interview, after I'd reeled off my credits, making them sound as grand as I could, I was amazed when the director, Peter Collinson, leaned across the lunch table, stared unwaveringly into my eyes and whispered, 'And do you fuck too, Sue?'

'Yes, of course,' I replied quickly, hoping he didn't mean him.

Luckily I was able to lay on a bevy of much more attractive propositions and luckily too he behaved himself at their interviews. Doubtless he made a note of the odd contact number, but I shall never know.

Another director, Robert Hartford Davis, slimed all over the young actress playing the lead. Her elderly female agent became apoplectic and insisted I protect her client from the drooling sleezeball. I had to spin out my contract until the end of the shoot and lurk in dark places like a sleuth.

Casting these educational gems was soon over and once again I had nothing to move on to. It was a testing time grubbing around for something that would pay the rent and I became pretty dispirited. There was always the old temping possibility, but that would feel like a retrogressive move. I decided to take on anything but. I wanted to feel like a 'resting' actor; just filling in until the next casting job. I waitressed, canvassed, shop-assisted and took photo-proofs round at wedding receptions. The latter was not a great success. Tipsy and insistent guests would thrust glasses of champagne at me. Fatal—it goes off like a scatter-gun in my head. I made a complete muddle of the orders and was told to get lost—without pay of course.

Work came along eventually, spasmodically. I moved from film to television and made good contacts for the future. But the in-between times were tough and, during a particularly barren patch, I reluctantly applied for a permanent job, casting commercials.

I was taken on and started as a nine-to-fiver at Young & Rubicam advertising agency. At least I'd be able to survive and would be dealing with actors and agents again.

It turned out to be particularly demoralising. I had little respect for many of the prima donna directors and as for the art directors and copywriters, I thought they were a brigade of moods, ultra trendy and terminally trying. Their egos eclipsed any I'd had to grapple with so far.

'Now hands that do dishes can feel soft as your face …'

'If I have to find one more young mum with angelic girl-child, I'll drown in washing-up liquid,' I said to Kip, a producer's assistant in the television department.

He laughed. 'Know what you mean, but you shouldn't take it so seriously.'

'Just one squirt will cut through all that horrid grease and the bottle will last for simply ages,' I chanted.

'Stop it!'

We might have giggled but the words haunted my dreams, troubled my conscience and made a nonsense of my ambition.

What was I doing stuck in an advertising agency? It had nothing to do with acting ability and everything to do with 'look'. This wasn't casting. This wasn't the career I'd envisaged for myself. I had to get back to the real thing.

A short freelance spell at Yorkshire Television prior to Young & Rubicam days had given me hope. I'd kept up regular contact with Muriel Cole, the head of casting. Her replies were always full of encouragement and ended with the same words every time, 'You're top of my list as soon as a vacancy comes up.'

So, with the possibility of a job in the casting department of a big television company, I was able to cling to optimism. In the meantime, I simply had to get out of Y & R.

Lynda Marchal, an old friend from Liverpool days, was currently living in Maida Vale with her sister, Gilli

Titchmarsh, and we'd become good friends too. Sometimes I stayed overnight at their place and more than once they'd put up with me moaning about my job.

'You'll just have to leave and take your chances,' said Lynda.

'Tell you what,' said Gilli, 'why don't you come and join me. Most of the time I've more work than I can handle.' Gilli was a freelance casting director working almost entirely in advertising but at least her clientele were from production companies specialising in quality. It had to be a better option. I gratefully accepted and, the next day, handed in my notice.

During my last month at Y & R, Maggie Cartier, another casting director friend, took pity on my imminent departure into, as she saw it, penury.

'I'm casting a Polly Peck tights commercial next week. You've got nice long legs, I'll put you up for it,' she said.

'You're not serious,' I laughed.

'I most certainly am. Give you a chance to find out what it's like to be on the other side of the casting process,' she said mischievously. 'The fee is forty pounds a day for three days plus repeats.'

'Well, I could do with the money.'

'Right, that's settled. I'll be in touch,' she said firmly and bustled off.

For the interview we were asked to wear hotpants and very high heels. The rest of the hopefuls in the crowded waiting area were models and dancers. Fearing I might be recognised from some casting session I'd overseen myself, I selected a chair in the darkest corner and buried myself in my book. Finally Maggie called me in. 'Don't worry, I'll do all the talking,' she whispered. 'Terry's very nice. You'll do fine.'

Terry was the director Terence Donovan, a teddy bear of a man with a great smile and a London accent. The choreographer was Leo, a weasly American with a big ego and a sadistic streak—he asked me to bunny-hop round the interview table. Unsurprisingly, and despite a boned bra, my size 38c's objected vehemently to such torture. Terry looked both embarrassed and amused. Maggie came to my rescue. 'Thanks Sue, that'll be enough.'

Feeling thoroughly ridiculous, I struggled up from my haunches barely keeping my balance on the high heels. As I made for the door …

'How tall are you?' Leo asked.

'Five feet ten … and a half,' I replied.

'So with those heels, about six two, six three?'

'Yes, I suppose so.'

'Okay, you can go.'

As I shut the door behind me, I heard the nasty little man say, 'Hmm, well we do need a giantess and the legs are okay, but the rest …'

Luckily, I didn't hear what the rest was. I removed the wretched heels and sped for the door.

I was amazed when Maggie called the next day to say I'd been chosen to sing and dance with half a dozen other sets of legs. Oh my God! 'Maggie, I haven't danced for years and as for my singing voice, well, excruciating would be putting it kindly,' I squealed.

'Nonsense, you'll be great. Don't take any notice of Leo, everyone knows he's a shit.'

'Can I think about it?'

'Nope, I need an answer now. Come on, you know how it is.'

'Alright. I'll do it. Sorry if I seem ungrateful. Thank you.'

'My pleasure. Bye.'

What on earth was I letting myself in for? The last thing I wanted was to be in front of the cameras! Oh well, at least the money would be welcome.

How I got through the whole affair I can't imagine, but I did, with the help of a couple of the other girls.

To the tune of *The Long, The Short and The Tall*, we had to sing the immortal words:

> *Love 'em all, love 'em all,*
> *The long and the short and the tall.*
> *Ladies with fat legs and ladies with thin,*
> *Whatever their sizes we fit 'em all in ...*

Wowee! My job as *The Long* was to lead the troupe of five across the screen and into a little dance routine. After several failed attempts and much embarrassment, I mastered the art of four-inch heel balance and we were in the can without going into overtime.

The morning after the first television showing I expected a barrage of phone calls from friends and family, but no—the only person who spotted me was Mother's cleaning lady!

19

A SIGNIFICANT MEETING

In the spring of 1968 I moved from Battersea to a semi-basement flat in Shepherd's Bush with Pat, a friend I'd made at MGM, as flatmate. She was tall, dark and Canadian and could seduce pretty much anyone she fancied. And she fancied often. She'd flutter her false lashes, gaze tellingly into their eyes and they knew she was dying for it. I tried to discover the secret of her *fatalité* but it was no good. I consoled myself with the thought that at least my eyelashes were my own. Pat's sexual appetite was ruthless enough to pinch one of my boyfriends from under my nose, but my dented pride soon healed—quite honestly his equipment was far too large for me.s

We realised pretty quickly that there just wasn't enough money coming in so we needed a flatmate to share the expenses. A friend introduced us to Eileen, a sock buyer who had bad circulation and knitted. She also didn't smoke dope. She was of the 'it does nothing for me' school. We suspected she'd never tried it.

'You sure there's nobody else?' said Pat. 'What about a guy?'

'Not likely! I refuse to play gooseberry in my own home. She'll be fine. We don't have to socialise if we don't want to,' I replied.

So Eileen moved into the room at the end of the corridor and we got along okay.

One Sunday in the May of 1970 the three of us drove over to Barnes Common. It was hot and sunny. We found a quiet clearing and stripped down to our bikinis. Eileen mentioned there was a football friendly going on nearby—between a couple of advertising agencies, one of which was Young & Rubicam. I wasn't interested but she knew some of the players; she worked Wednesdays on the door of a jazz club they frequented. She toddled off.

Pat and I turned onto our stomachs to expose doughy white bodies to the sun. After a while Eileen returned with two guys in tow—Evan, round, red-headed and very jolly looking and Terry, slim, smart and balding but with sideburns to make up for it. Nothing special but pleasant enough we thought.

At a party the following weekend we met Terry and Evan again and they introduced us to another friend, John. We drank and flirted and predictably Pat wasted no time. John was soon under her spell and they disappeared off somewhere. Terry and I joined the crush of dancers in the sitting room. He had a natural sense of rhythm and a mischievousness I found pretty appealing. When he asked me if I was, 'One of those people who turned on.'

I said, 'I'd love a little smoke.'

We giggled and went out to his car.

The joint, which he rolled with the speed of a practised smoker, was pretty strong. I'd had too much drink and this tipped me first onto Terry's lap then out of the passenger door as I brought up all the nibbles I'd consumed. Surprisingly it made no difference, he liked me enough to take my phone number.

A week later he rang and asked me out and before long we started going together. Unlike most of the men in my life to date, he was even-tempered, reliable and refreshingly forthright. Terry meant every word he said. As a child, I thought Daddy was a typical man and had taken for granted that what men said was what they meant and what they said they would do, they did. That way you knew exactly where you stood and could react appropriately. In other words, you had a copy of the script. I'd discovered quite the opposite and was becoming seriously disillusioned. I couldn't figure out why males seemed to feel obliged to come across with a hotchpotch of lies about how sexy/beautiful/special you were and, most insulting of all, how much they loved you, when all they really wanted to do was get your knickers off.

No, I got none of that from Terry. He would chat away happily about all sorts, then suddenly reach for my hand and say, 'Let's go to bed.' Like it would be greatest fun for its own sake.

Gradually I learned that this straight-talking guy whose company I enjoyed so much, came from a very poor family who lived in a Trust flat in West Kensington. His mum was a cleaner, his dad a decorator and he had two older brothers. His mum was an Irish Catholic who'd left Cork when she was still in her teens to go into service. She was a beautiful person who'd sacrificed herself for her husband and three sons. Terry was very aware of how much she went without to provide for them and he adored her. He had no feelings or respect whatsoever for his dad, a drunk who blew his wages in the pub on Fridays.

Terry left school at fifteen having been written off as useless—dyslexia wasn't acknowledged in those days—and the only reason he became an apprentice hairdresser at a small salon in the North End Road was because he couldn't find anything else to do. To the surprise of family and friends, he had a 'flair for hair' and by his mid-twenties he'd worked his way up to a top salon in Belgravia.

With the job came a taste for the quality only riches can afford. He still lived at home and spent most of his money on hand-made suits, cashmere and silk. He'd had a few girlfriends, but now wanted someone a bit more classy to go with the gear and obviously thought a well-spoken, fairly presentable, middle class, ex-convent girl with a career would do well enough. His friends indulged him, but I could tell they wondered who on earth he'd got hold of now—sort of Princess Anne character with a silly laugh.

'Don't you worry about them taking the piss out of your accent. I like it,' said Terry.

Soon it became obvious this was not going to be a short-lived affair. But were we ready to get a place together? Terry was staying at the flat every night but would go back to home base in the morning to change into his work suit and catch the number 9 bus to Belgravia. To him leaving home meant making a major commitment.

And as for me? Being in a secure relationship with a thoroughly decent guy was just what I needed and had always wanted. But was Terry the right man? Could this lead, at last, to marriage and babies? Was I really in love?

20

HOUSEHUNTING

At last the day came that I was able to box up my files and walk out of Young & Rubicam to become a freelancer again. It was particularly good to be away from the routine and formality of a nine-to-five existence. Although I was still desperate to get back to television or film drama, I was grateful to have been offered work at GilliandSue, where there was plenty of variety and a lively atmosphere. We were three very different personalities—Gilli, a gentle soul, controlled, earnest and hard-working, Sue One, dynamic and outspoken and me, chaotic but caring.

The GilliandSue office buzzed with activity and overflowed with photos, props, costumes and visiting actors trying to make a good impression. This could be difficult when Gilli's King Charles spaniel, Willy, decided to upstage them by making love to his tasselled cushion in the corner. There were other regular poppers-in to divert us, including Gilli's sister, Lynda, a brilliant mimic and raconteuse, who could whip us into a giggling sundae whatever the prevailing mood.

As I had no regular clientele, I mainly looked after Gilli's over-spill. It was the time when such directors as Alan Parker, Ridley and Tony Scott, Hugh Hudson and Adrian Lyne were dominating the classy production output. Apart from Tony and Adrian, they terrified me. I dreaded those awful words. 'Haven't seen anybody I like. We'll have to go again.'

On those occasions I felt stupid, inadequate and a let-down to Gilli.

The most arduous aspect of casting commercials was having to get to know the models of the moment; every Zed card—two to four photos plus contact details—looked fantastic. How on earth could I tell who was really gorgeous? I couldn't so it was trial and error; if they look right, call them in and hope they live up to their photos. I came to hate being handed a brief for a beauty product—perfect hair, skin, hands and most tedious of all, prepared to strip off for body lotions, soaps or deodorants. Those briefing instructions would go something like this: 'Right, Sue, you can see from the story-board that we want a full-length shot of her body, side view with the arm raised. So we don't want to see anyone who won't take off the lot.'

Of course I couldn't say what I thought—'oh fuck, I hate these sessions, they're so degrading'—I had to present a businesslike, neutral front. 'And they'll have to strip at the casting session, I imagine.'

'Definitely, we don't want any stretchmarks, unsightly moles or flab, do we?'

So, if they needed the work, the poor girls had to agree to take everything off for inspection by not only the director, but the art director, the copywriter, frequently the client and anyone else who had come along for a leer. They made me sick and even more convinced that if I didn't get back to casting actors and not types or models soon, I'd lose heart completely. Then I had a call which cheered me up considerably. It was Muriel Cole from Yorkshire Television. 'Sue dear, I can't guarantee it, but I may have something to offer you in a few months' time. Maureen Riscoe is thinking of leaving. I don't have a date, but I'll be in touch as soon as I know.'

'I'll look forward to hearing from you. Thanks so much,' I said, trying not to sound too eager. At last there was light at the end of the advertising tunnel.

Terry and I became a couple and agreed to try living together. Although there was no talk of an engagement, at least setting up home would move us on a stage.

'Hmph, a trial marriage, eh? Very sensible,' Daddy's reaction was predictable. 'Hope you're on the pill.'

'Yes, she is. Don't want any kids thanks,' said Terry.

'Er … no,' I murmured glancing at Mother.

'Coffee anyone?' she said in a high-pitched voice as she leapt up from the table.

'Hang on, hang on, Joyce, I want more pudding,' said Daddy indignantly.

'Then help yourself, dear,' said Mother and sped off to the kitchen.

We were with them for Sunday lunch and I'd spent most of the meal summoning up the courage to say we were thinking of buying a house.

It wasn't difficult to find a building society who agreed we were eligible for a mortgage and we managed to get enough cash together for a deposit. As Terry worked Saturdays, it fell to me to do most of the house-hunting. At first I was bubbling with enthusiasm but it didn't take long to realise we wouldn't be able to afford anything decent. Some of the places I looked at were downright disgusting. Once, having collected the key from the agent, I let myself into what was supposed to be an empty house to discover squatters in bed and aggressively indignant at my arrival. The place was a complete dump and the air thick with the smell of dirty socks, sweat, cigarettes and stale beer. I stuttered an apology and fled. Could there be anywhere worse? Yes—when I found myself in a doss-house full of hopeless drunks. The atmosphere reeked of rancid sick and the mattresses and pillows were so high I nearly choked. As I stumbled down the grimy staircase to the front door, I couldn't even touch the banister for fear of contamination.

'Sorry, but I refuse to look at anywhere else on my own,' I told Terry that night. 'I can't believe places like that exist. I thought I was going to throw up. No, I've had it with bloody house-hunting, you can look for a change.'

'Alright, alright. There's no point getting worked up. Organise some houses for next Monday and I'll go along and check them out.'

Strange things happen at strange times—later that night Terry's mate, Steve, rang. They'd worked together in Reading and remained good friends ever since. Steve now had a successful salon in Brighton and was thinking of expanding. Would Terry be interested in a partnership? He could start at the existing salon, create a clientele and then they could look for a new premises together. Terry broached the subject with me rather tentatively. 'What do you think? It'd mean finding a place to live in Brighton? And … you'd have to commute.'

'No problem,' I said gaily. 'I like Brighton.'

The notion of being a commuter appealed—I'd have time to read, write or do the crossword. On the London to Brighton line the grandest old lady of a train, the *Brighton Belle*, was still running. You had to pay a surcharge for the privilege of travelling on her, but it was worth it to be able to slip back in time to the thirties, to sink into her well-padded seats surrounded by exquisite wood panelling and deco lighting. Hot breakfasts *en route* were also above average for British Rail. I didn't know the Belle was soon to be taken out of service—I think she was considered rather crotchety by modern standards.

The other attraction to Steve's offer was the chance to live near the sea and the South Downs in a pretty, lively town. The houses would be cheaper too. No, I didn't need to think, it sounded ideal.

Here was the possibility of a brighter future for Terry. He'd begun to tire of Belgravia where there were no prospects of promotion. His boss had plenty of life left in him and his clientele was as up-market as they were ever likely to be—Lady this and Lady that and lots of Mrs Riches, draped in silks and furs and sparkling ornaments. No wonder he had such expensive tastes.

Unlike me, Terry didn't make decisions easily, but this time he hardly hesitated. He phoned Steve back. 'You're on. We'll be down at the weekend.'

I took the Monday off and, after lunch with Steve, we did the rounds of the estate agents to see what houses were on offer. We found one that day. I knew the moment I walked in that this was where I wanted to live and there was no need to look any further. Terry needed some persuading. 'Why did they show us the place? We said our limit was seven grand and this is seven and a half,' he protested.

'We can manage it, I know we can,' I said confidently.

Two months later we moved into 53 Westbourne Street, our first proper home. We were on the lowest rung of the property ladder and it felt great.

21

JUST ANOTHER SOAP OPERA

Six months later Muriel Cole from Yorkshire Television called and offered me a permanent position in her Casting Department. I was delirious. I might be on staff again but I'd be back in drama. I couldn't wait to get home to tell Terry.

'You haven't accepted!'

'Of course I have. It's proper casting again and steady money.'

'Well, you can forget about us then. I'm not moving to fucking Yorkshire!' He snapped and stormed out.

I rushed after him. 'It's not in Yorkshire. It's at their London office.'

Silly bugger, how could he have thought, even for a moment, that I'd want to leave our lovely new home. We were a few minutes walk from the sea, the air was pure and I felt fitter than I had for ages. Our three-storey, four-bedroomed Victorian terraced house was my ideal nest. No, I certainly didn't want to be anywhere else in the world.

Muriel Cole was portly and formidable and wore her grey hair in tight bun. She led me to a small office at the end of the casting corridor and thrust the door open. 'And this is Margaret, who will be your secretary,' she said grandly.

The face occupying the desk by the door glowered at me from behind a curtain of blonde hair.

'Get up, girl, get up. Now, whether you like it or not, Maureen has left and Sue here will not be putting up with any of your nonsense. So tidy that desk and snap to it.' With that our imperious head of department swept out.

'Hello, Margaret,' I said holding out my hand.

'The name's Maggie, only the old cow calls me Margaret.'

'Right, yes, okay, Maggie.'

'There's a script on your desk. I've done a cast breakdown and the director'll be in this afternoon.' She slunk back behind her desk to attack the morning mail. Every envelope torn open was accompanied by a disdainful groan. I wondered if she was in the right job. Or, more to the point, was I?

Deciding it was best to get stuck into the script and ignore her, I survived until lunch-time. When one of the other casting directors, who I'd met during my freelance stint, popped her head round the door, I was extremely relieved.

'Fancy lunch at the pub?' she said.

'Yes, great. Thanks.' I leapt out from behind my new desk and grabbed my coat. 'See you later,' I threw at Maggie and left, not waiting for a response and not expecting one anyway.

Over a cider and a sandwich I learnt that Maggie was seriously pissed off that Maureen had left. She'd adored her. And now she'd was lumbered with me and was convinced I couldn't possibly replace her. No wonder she was hostile. When I got back to the office, I broached the subject. 'Maggie, I may not be Maureen, but I'm not so bad and you mustn't believe any advance publicity you've heard from Muriel. I think it's important we try to get on together. Okay?'

Maggie's lip quivered for a moment but then she managed a little smile. 'Okay. Sorry.'

After that we became good friends. She was Em and I was Wattage.

Life under Muriel's regime was reasonably paid, but boy, did I earn that comforting cheque at the end of the month. The projects kept coming. It was nothing to be allocated several programmes at once. For instance, whilst I was working on a series as well as setting up a period drama adaptation, Muriel waltzed into the office waving more scripts. 'I know you're busy with *Hadleigh* but you can fit this in. It's not all prestige drama, you know.'

She plonked the script on my desk. The title was *Emmerdale Farm*. 'Goodness knows why they're bothering with this. Minority taste if you ask me. Still, ours not to reason why. Anyway, it's a bi-weekly soap opera,' she said as if someone had stuck something foul-smelling under her nose. 'It's to go out at lunchtime for the moment but if it catches on, they'll re-schedule it to early evening. Toodleloo,' she trilled and swept out with a mischievous smile.

Not a big cast, not particularly demanding roles, I thought as I skimmed through episode one. Ought not to be too taxing. Wrong. Muriel hadn't told me the producer wanted several options on the regular characters for future episodes. Even I, with my limited experience, knew that most successful actors shied away from long-running series. Once identified with a particular character, they would be considered uncastable in any other role except, perhaps, in a panto at the end of a pier somewhere when they would be billed something like this:

with
Jo Bloggs from CORONATION STREET
as Widow Twanky

'Oh shit, Em,' I moaned. 'I really don't fancy this. D'you think I could bow out?'

'I'd like to see her face if you try,' she giggled.

At that moment the door flew open again. It was Muriel. She dumped another paper on my crowded desk. 'The budget. Not brilliant, but I'm sure you'll manage.'

I glanced through it with increasing horror. Nearly everyone was expected to work at minimum rate. 'God! I mean, yes. Well, I'll do my best.'

'Knew I could rely on you, dear.' Tossing her head and billowing her nostrils, she turned to leave but then, halfway to the door, spun round with a disgusted snort. 'Those appalling cigarettes, the air in here is quite ghastly!' She marched over and thrust open the window, 'Smells just like a French brothel,' and off she went holding her nose.

'Just how d'you think she'd know that?' asked Em.

'Well,' I said, 'there's obviously more to Auntie Muriel than we realised.'

After a year of casting for Yorkshire Television, my repertoire of actors had passed well into the thousands and I'd met a wide range of directors and producers. Our office resembled a railway terminus with their comings and goings. If I got on with them and the job went well, they asked for me again. To be busy meant you were sought after and that was great. But no matter how busy you were, you were expected to take time out of the office to attend the read-through—a get-together of all the actors, director, producers, wardrobe, make-up, the writer and the casting director. Everyone would sit round a big table and the producer or director would introduce cast and crew to each other. When the time came for the actors to read the script, I would cross my fingers and hope they came across well. Although they would rarely give any kind of performance at this initial stage, I always enjoyed hearing the script coming to life.

However, on one occasion I found myself the centre of attention. After months working on the enormous cast, it was finally read-through day for the thirteen part serial of *South Riding*. Rehearsals were about to begin. James Ormerod, one of the two directors, was waiting outside the hall when I arrived. 'Hello, Jimmy.'

'Morning, Sue. Can I have a word?' He took me to one side. 'I'd like you to introduce everyone.'

I froze. 'Jimmy, don't do this to me.'

'Sue, you know the parts and you know everyone's name, you're the obvious person.'

'Must I?'

Jimmy grinned mischievously. I knew I couldn't refuse. He took my hand and lead me in. The hall was full, the tables were arranged in a large square. People stood around chatting, drinking coffee and greeting the arrivals they already knew.

Finally, when everyone was present and correct, we took our places round the tables. I sat next to Jimmy. He stood up. 'Welcome, everyone. I hope you've all got copies of the first three episodes. Don't look so alarmed, we're only going to read episode one today.

Afterwards, and before you go, please make sure you've checked in with wardrobe and make up. That's Jo over there and Hilary next to her.' Everyone looked. Jo and Hilary nodded and smiled. Jimmy continued, 'And sitting next to me is Sue, our casting director, who's going to introduce everyone. Over to you, Sue.'

Nerves jangling, I levered myself out of my chair. I felt the heat rushing to my face. There were about forty members of cast and crew present and I was going to have to remember them all. Their names and the parts they were playing, or jobs they were doing. I was praying I wouldn't freeze halfway through. 'Good morning,' I said tentatively. 'Right, here goes. This is Dorothy Tutin who's playing Sarah Burton and Nigel Davenport who's Robert Carne. Lesley Dunlop is playing Lydia Holly and …'

How I got through I don't know. I took it slowly, allowing myself to match the character to the actor. It would have been easy to stumble, or dry as they say in the profession, but I managed. I sat back down with a big 'Phew!' of relief.

Jimmy patted me on the back. 'Well done, Sue.'

My performance was over, the spotlight was off me, well, almost. Someone clapped then everyone joined in. It was the first time I'd ever received a round of applause.

Play reports, play reports, Muriel Cole's wretched play reports. All theatre and cinema-going for casting purposes was paid for by YTV but our dear boss ruled that her casting directors submit a full critique of whatever they'd seen before they could put in an expenses claim. The report would be circulated round the department with the top copy going to the head of drama. So, busy or not, if we wanted our expenses paid, we had to find the time to write a precis of the play or film and comments on all the actors. If a performance was marvellous, no problem, but if it was lousy what could you say? Jennifer Swallow was horrendous as Henry's mistress. Archie Starling can't act his way out of a paper bag. Madeleine Swift forgot all her lines and burst into tears. No, of course you can't say that if you have any heart at all. Somehow you had to find a way not to destroy the poor sod's chances of work at Yorkshire Television. After all they may have had flu or a run-in with the bailiffs or a row with the leading man. This could have been the one night when they weren't on form. However, though they were frequently difficult to write, the reports were useful as records. But, being subjective, they should've been for our eyes only and certainly we shouldn't have had to wait to be reimbursed.

The drama and comedy output at Yorkshire Television in the early seventies put a serious strain on the casting department. I was pushed to my limit when, during the casting of *Hadleigh*, a long-running series, I was given five comedy pilots and a dramatised documentary as well. There was a serious risk that I'd book someone for the wrong part in the wrong programme. Inevitably, there was soon a backlog of unwritten play reports and I was annoyingly out of pocket. I decided I'd had enough. So had the other two casting directors for that matter. With their support, I tackled Muriel. I told her politely that we wanted our expenses and our play reports could wait until we were less busy.

For a moment she was speechless but then she stood up from her desk and blew out her bosom like a

Christmas turkey. 'Nobody, but nobody, has ever had the audacity to question the way I run my department,' she spluttered.

'I'm not questioning your rules, I'm merely saying we're frequently out of pocket and could do with our money as soon as possible.' As she stood over me I could feel the challenge in her icy stare but I held my ground. 'We could scribble off a sub-standard report, but we don't. We try to write something helpful and that takes time.'

She moved slowly round her desk and sat down again. 'Hmph, well, I'll have to think about it,' she said coldly. 'You can go now.'

She did think about it and she acquiesced and, unexpectedly, treated us rather better from then on.

Not all our theatre-going was paid for by the company, often we were invited to go with an agent to see one of their clients, so they would pay for the tickets and dinner. Usually their actor would give a good performance and when we went backstage afterwards it was a pleasure to be able to congratulate them, but sometimes we were unimpressed. As the play progressed and the performance didn't improve, it was hard to concentrate knowing you would have to meet them after the show and be enthusiastic.

You'd be ushered into a stuffy little dressing-room, introduced and handed a glass of whisky—for some reason whisky was invariably the only refreshment on offer. You sipped it slowly, trying to put off the moment when you'd have to express an opinion. You could hardly tell them they were in the wrong profession, could you? No, you had to be polite but not insincere. And it was best not to use see-through

171

avoidance tactics: 'I thought your costume was splendid, your hair looked great, the sets were good weren't they? Your entrance from stage left in Act Two was most dramatic.' No, you'd cross your fingers and say something like this. 'What an interesting performance. I was particularly intrigued by the scene in the police station. How did you enjoy working with George Crane? Has it been a good experience?'

With luck that type of question could shift the emphasis and the client would then hold forth on the high and lows of the production. And actors usually have a lot to say about directors. By the time they'd finished it would be getting late and we'd all be ready to go home.

Mike and I

With Frankie and Madame

Canadian Pat and I

Terry

22

A BAD TRIP

One sunny Sunday afternoon Terry and I went up to Chanctonbury Ring, a site full of ancient magic and with an astonishing view from the top. It was a place of spiritual renewal, a launching pad to the heavens.

We reached the highest point and sat down on the grass gazing silently into the distance. I shut my eyes and pulled my hair back from my face. The wind on our cheeks was soft and warm.

'Fancy a trip?' Terry whispered in my ear.

'What?' I was irritated at the interruption. Why couldn't he just let me enjoy the moment?

'Well, do you?'

'Terry, we can't have a holiday yet. I'm in the middle of …'

'No, no, no. I don't mean that kind of trip. I mean acid. LSD trip.'

'Oh …' I hesitated; I'd wanted to try it because so many friends were tripping and swore it'd changed their lives forever. Annie had said it was like travelling into the heart of the atom and Nick was convinced he'd discovered a fundamental truth. It all sounded wildly over the top but I had to admit that the trippers I knew had clearly been somewhere the rest of us could never imagine and were all the richer for it. 'Yes, I do want to try it, I think. But we haven't got any.'

'We have,' he chuckled. 'A client slipped me a couple of tabs with my tip.'

That night we went round to Steve's. He and his wife knew about the acid and fancied trying it too, so we took half a tab each.

Sadly it wasn't the mind-expanding experience that I'd hoped. Yes, colours and textures took on a whole new dimension as did the body I was living in, but I could now see clearly into the minds of our companions. The sensation was terrifying; they were full of malice. I couldn't look them in the eye, I simply gazed at my feet desperately wanting to escape. But where to? The idea of going out into the night streets was scary, so I staggered into the bathroom and slid down onto the hair-cord carpet. There I stayed, moulding myself into its fibres and wishing things were different, longing to float away over woods and fields like the airy creature I was in my dreams. It was not to be. I felt glued to the carpet and there I stayed until Terry, without a word, pulled me up and took me home. The next evening I felt compelled to confront him. 'Something's wrong, horribly wrong, isn't it?'

'You could say. In fact I'm fucking pissed off.'

He spilled out the sorry truth. The partnership with Steve was getting no nearer. Terry felt he was being treated like just another stylist and they'd looked at no premises. It seemed Steve was stalling for some reason.

'But you're building up a good clientele. I don't understand,' I protested.

'I reckon it might be that although we worked well together as employees, being the boss has gone to his head. He keeps having a go about the way I talk to clients, says I'm not respectful. Bloody cheek!'

'Perhaps he can't cope with the fact you've come to Brighton from a top London salon and wants to put you in your place.'

'Huh! Tough. I'm not going to pretend I haven't been working in Belgravia.'

'He should see it as an asset,' I said crossly.

'Whatever, I've had enough.'

The next day the two men had a blazing row and Steve issued an ultimatum. If he wanted to keep his job, Terry had to change his attitude and behaviour.

Without a flicker of response, Terry gathered up his equipment and walked out of the salon and their relationship, forever.

For days he moped about the place in a fog of disillusionment. I was as supportive as I knew how. 'Terry, it has to be for the best. Obviously you two in partnership wouldn't have worked.' What could I do but trot out the usual sympathetic clichés? Although there was something else that was guaranteed to keep his spirits up. Sex. So, whether I wanted it or not, I pretended.

With all this activity in the bedroom I began to wonder if I'd been on the pill too long. When was Terry going to commit to the idea of having a family? Would he ever? Anyway, I'd heard that no more than five consecutive years on the pill are recommended and I'd been on it for seven. I went to the doctor to ask about the coil, a relatively new device that was becoming popular. I was shown a sample of the recent arrival from America. It was made of white plastic, flat and shaped like a fish with fins or spines down either side and a long thread like a tail. The doctor explained how it worked. 'It goes into your womb and embeds itself in the lining to prevent a fertilised egg from catching hold. Insertion is a little uncomfortable but quick and then it'll take about a couple of weeks to settle in. During that time you might have some bleeding and period-like pains.'

'It sounds pretty horrible to me.'

'It's harmless and very effective and the best method I can suggest for you at the moment. Unless you want to go back to the Dutch Cap.'

'No thanks. Okay, I'll give it a try.'

He was right, insertion was quick, but uncomfortable was absolutely not the right word. The pain was intense, as though a lighted match had been put up inside me. The tears poured involuntarily, I felt sick and faint and had to lie down for a while before feeling fit enough to walk home. At each step I was aware of something foreign inside my body. It was several days before I could bear intercourse, and soon after that I had a much heavier period than usual. It lasted for two weeks. Painkillers were useless. I resorted to whisky. The doctor assured me it would pass and I'd feel fine. I had two more dreadful periods before it began to ease up.

Terry, in the meantime, had signed on and joined the dole queue. There were no jobs for senior hairdressers. He soon became thoroughly despondent. 'It's hopeless,' he said. 'I'll just have to find something else.'

'Not necessarily, Terry. Why don't you open you own salon?'

'Be sensible, I don't have any capital.'

'Get a bank loan then.'

'Don't be ridiculous, I'm on the dole,'

'I'm sure something'll turn up, it usually does,' I said feebly.

'Huh!'

I was right. Within a month we'd heard that his brothers were thinking of selling a house in Fulham that the three of them jointly owned. They got the asking price and Terry got five grand – enough to buy a lease and equip a premises. It gave him something to aim for and lifted his spirits out of the quagmire.

There were plenty of possible premises but, after a couple of weeks intensive looking, he hadn't found anything he fancied. 'It's no good, I can't afford a place with a shop front,' he announced in the flat voice of dejection.

'What are you on about? Steve doesn't have a shop front. Why not look at ones that haven't. You could always move on later, when the business is up and running.'

'If it's up and running.'

'Don't be so bloody negative. You'll make it work.'

And so he broadened his brief and carried on with the search. A few days later I came home to find him in a state of excitement. 'Think I've found it. A prime site in the Western Road with a good-looking entrance hall. The rent's just about manageable.'

'Brilliant. Go for it.'

He did. The next day he negotiated the lease and started planning the redecoration and fitting.

For three months I hardly saw him. Apart from plumbing and electrics, he fitted and stocked his salon-to-be himself. He would stagger home late, collapse into a hot bath to soak away the paint stains then shovel down his dinner and fall into bed.

When the work was nearing completion, he contacted two of the stylists from Steve's. He knew they were unhappy and thinking of moving on. Both were highly experienced and would bring a good clientele with them. They liked Terry and agreed to join him. As he needed a book-keeper I said I would do it until he could afford to employ somebody else. Finally he was ready to contact his own clients to tell them the news.

On the 24th of June 1972, *Poynters* opened for business. The brightly painted scissors sign swung high above the beautiful wrought-iron gate entrance of 140 Western Road, Brighton. A weight was off my mind, or so I imagined. Terry was now his own boss.

PART THREE

DIVINE RETRIBUTION

23

I DO, I DO, ALREADY

By the Christmas of 1973, Terry's salon had begun to build up a reputation. It may not have had a shop front, but that didn't seem to matter, there were plenty of regular clients, so netting lots of casual trade wasn't hugely important. I believe the privacy was an advantage. Who wants to be seen stiff with rollers, bleached blue at the roots or with a headful of aluminium foil spikes?

Things were going well but Terry never seemed to be satisfied. If he'd had a busy day he'd stagger home knackered and irritable. If business was slack he moaned non-stop.

Most of the time we were bringing in good money, but, for me, that wasn't the point. I wanted us to enjoy life together. Weekends were neither restful nor fun. On Saturdays Terry worked while I had the shopping and housework to look after and on Sundays there was the boring task of keeping Terry's books. It took nearly all day and I hated it. Worst of all, our relationship seemed to be going absolutely nowhere; he couldn't even admit to loving me. My dream of marriage and a couple of kids was no nearer to coming true.

At the start of the January sales, Mother rang to say she would be up in London on a shopping trip and did I want to meet for lunch.

'Yes, yes please.'

I walked into the book club where she was a member. There she stood, all spruced up for her day in town. I gave her a big hug. She pulled away to study my face, she'd sensed something was wrong immediately. 'What is it? Terry?'

'Mother, I'm fed up.'

We went through into the dining-room and found a table. Out came my grievances. Being able to tell her was a big relief.

'Does he know you feel like this?'

'Does he care?'

'Oh come on, dear, he's devoted to you, even I can tell that.'

'He's got a funny way of showing it.'

'Well, things aren't going to change unless you try to find a solution together. Talk it through. That's my advice. Right, shall we order? My treat,' she added virtuously.

As I walked up Burlington Arcade on my way back to the office, it struck me that she'd been remarkably restrained. To her mind, Terry was hardly the ideal mate. A hairdresser, from a poor family, dear me. She could've wallowed in my discontent but she'd managed to hold back. Sometimes Mother could be great. I felt a lot better having shared my troubles with her.

That afternoon I was casting a television film adapted from *Joby,* a Stan Barstow novel. The leading character was a small boy around nine years old. It was our first session and I'd lined up a selection to meet the director.

Casting children can be pretty unrewarding. As a rule the best solution is to trawl the ordinary schools for natural talent. However, we tended to see stage school candidates first.

After a couple of uninspiring hours we had a short break and Em went off to organise teas. Suddenly, the door flew open and in swept Muriel. It was well-known she loved to poke her nose in. She flashed a coy smile at the director. 'Hello, Jimmy, dear. Do excuse my interruption, but I think the young man waiting outside is for you. Toodleloo.'

'I'll go and get him,' I said.

I went out to the waiting room and there he was perched on a chair swinging his legs and staring at his feet which didn't reach the ground. He was in school uniform and still wearing his cap. At a slightly cheeky angle, I noted.

'Hello, and who are you?' I asked him.

He looked up with a start, pulled off his cap and jumped to his feet. He had freckles, mud-brown hair and buck-teeth and was quite adorable. 'I'm Sebastian.'

I felt the goose-pimples springing up all over my body. He was just about the right age to be my son, my baby, who I'd lost all those years ago. 'Come with me, please.' He looked curiously at me. My voice had come out in a strange, hoarse whisper. I cleared my throat. 'This way.'

He wasn't right for the part, thank goodness. Seeing him had up-rooted the pain I'd buried and I couldn't wait for Em to show him out at the end of the interview. Would I ever get over my loss? Even if Terry and I got married and I had the babies I longed for, would the fact that I'd given my child away haunt me forever?

Thankfully a musical in the West End followed by dinner with an agent took my mind off the little boy. By the time I caught the last train, I was so tired, I slept all the way home. Not unusual.

With all the late nights, our sex life was suffering and, to make matters worse, the coil was giving me serious problems. I'd had another horrific period that had lasted two weeks and come on again a fortnight later. The pain was so bad I dragged myself to the doctor and begged him to take the wretched thing out. It was obvious my body was trying to reject it.

The removal was even worse than the insertion. The spines pointed downwards, it felt like I was being scraped by an internal knife. I passed out and it was an hour later before I had the strength to stagger home. I was shaken but sure I'd done the right thing in ridding myself of the intruder inside me.

There seemed no alternative but to go back on the pill although everything in me cried out against it. All this contraception when I wanted to become pregnant again, to finally be a mother. At night, in the sleepless hours, my head throbbed with questions. How long could I wait? And was Terry the right man for me anyway? Was I being unrealistic? Perhaps I should stop taking the pill and see what happened. But I couldn't do that without telling him. Yes, I would tell him, when the right moment came up.

That summer Terry refused to take time off from the salon. I just had to have a break so I accepted an invitation to go on holiday with my old friend, Carol Drinkwater. She and I planned to spend a week on a Greek island. Not only did I love the idea of the place, the sunshine, the food and the good company of my friend, but it would give me time to think about my relationship with Terry. And I would have to be brutally honest with myself. Did I want out or didn't I? I knew Carol would be loving and supportive and any advice she offered would be constructive. I was selfishly very disappointed when she rang to say she'd been offered a good part in a television series and couldn't turn it down.

Luckily, the tickets hadn't been booked. I could think of going somewhere else. Then cousin Beth's husband, Dave, from Dublin, who was pilot training in Algeria, came by for a night between flights and suggested an intriguing alternative. He had an apartment just outside Algiers. I was welcome to visit.

I had no idea what to expect but it would be an adventure and I hadn't had one for a long time.

Dave met me off the plane, led me round to the driver's side of his decrepit Renault and told me to drive to the compound where he lived.

'Me?'

'Yes, you!'

Typical Dave. I had to get on with it or be ridiculed. The roads were full of potholes, it was my first experience of left-hand drive and Algeria had no apparent highway code. You just pointed the car and went, dodging any other car that appeared. And they appeared from all sides at speed. At first I was terrified, but before long I adjusted. Where there are no rules, you expect everyone to be crazy and make allowances. Unlike Britain where you expected drivers to be sane and were unprepared for the occasional maniac.

I drove a lot that holiday, Dave delighted in taking me to risky places. I felt I was constantly being tested for nerve. A white girl with long blonde hair in Arab eating houses was a great novelty and the back streets of Algiers felt dangerous yet strangely enticing. I had to avert my eyes from the dark gazes that followed my every move. Still it was interesting and exciting. The evenings we weren't dining out, were spent with Dave's friends. It was a relief not to be stared at, well almost not.

One of the pilots was a dishy Frenchman, Serge, whose attentions were plainly intentions. He oozed charm and appeared to be bowled over by me. We went out to dinner, chatted for hours and finally, inevitably, I went to bed with him.

Wow, I'd never experienced lovemaking like it. This had to be what it was all about. A genuine rapport, complemented by sweet words, gentleness and warmth.

There followed three more days and nights of bliss. I was desolate when the time came to go home. Serge begged me to stay but I needed to sort out my life in England, tell Terry I was leaving, and that it was over between us. I left my work phone number so Serge could call me as soon as he landed after a long haul flight that would take him to the States for three days.

Dave was pilot on the way back and invited me into the cockpit. It was so distracting I was able to forget for a while what I was going home to. The plane landed at Heathrow in rain and drizzle. I said my thanks and goodbyes to Dave and joined the disembarking passengers. Unlike most of them, I had nobody waiting at the barrier to meet me. I made my way up to town and crossed to Victoria station where it was pelting down. Somehow the weather compounded my desolation—I'd left Serge in glorious sun. I sat on the train to Brighton holding my feelings in check. What was I doing here in this hateful place with an emotional cripple?

When I arrived at the salon, Terry was too busy to acknowledge me. I had to wait until the end of the afternoon, by which time I was in a desperate state and, as soon as we were on our own, burst into tears. We had an ugly row, I told him about Serge, packed my bags and left. It wasn't the civilised discussion I'd planned, but then had I really expected it to be?

Whilst waiting to hear from Algeria, I stayed with Gilli in Primrose Hill and went back to work. I allowed myself no respite, every moment had to be full. There had to be no time for reflection. I'd done the right thing and the practical side could be dealt with later. But by the end of the week, there'd been no word from Serge. Never mind, he must have been held up, I told myself. Anyway I was certainly not turning back. The following Saturday I drove down to Brighton to collect my stuff. Em came along for moral support.

Tiggles, our cat, came to welcome me, rubbing round my legs and purring ecstatically. Terry's socks and pants blew on the windy line and washing-up-for-one tore my heart out. I collapsed in tears of guilt, pity and sadness. Em had to drag me back to London.

By the end of the next week, I was forced to admit Serge wouldn't call, it had just been a holiday romance. What an idiot I'd been. At the weekend I had a message to call Terry. I steeled myself. Little was said but I agreed to meet him.

We sat on the grass in St. James's Park. He was shaking and had noticeably lost weight. He tentatively reached for my hand. I hadn't the heart to refuse him.

'I … love you,' he stuttered. 'Life's no good without you. Please marry me. And we can have … a family.'

He began to cry. And so did I. Fishing around in my bag for the tissues, I was able to look away from his tragic face and to find the strength to say, 'I have to have more time, time to think.'

'No, please just come home. It's your birthday on Friday, I want to be with you again.'

'Terry, I'm sorry. I don't know. But I'll call tomorrow. Let you know. I'm sorry.' I got up from the grass and brushed down my crumpled skirt. 'I have to get back to work. I will call, I promise. Bye.' And so I left him. Sitting alone on that big, empty patch of green, with the rumble of London life way off behind him. I couldn't look back, I would've caved in and rushed to hold him. I knew my weaknesses, but I also knew my needs and, if there were to be any chance of our relationship surviving, they would have to be met.

True to my word, I called the next day and told him if I agreed to come home, it was on the understanding we thrashed out our differences.

So, on my thirty-first birthday I returned home. Terry was wonderful. He did and said all the right things. We had a lovely evening and over the weekend agreed to sit down and work out terms for the future.

I returned to work on the Monday bursting with the news that I was getting married. We'd agreed we could have a great future together. Terry now had a staff of ten and had to admit the salon was doing really well and it was time to take on a book-keeper. I had my career and, when I got pregnant, could go back to freelancing, set up an office at home and combine work with looking after babies. We had a house we'd renovated to our mutual taste but were prepared to move onto something bigger if necessary. And, perhaps most importantly, now we really understood each other.

It was early September, 1975, five years since Terry and I first got together. He'd lost both parents and drifted apart from his brothers. We both wanted a simple marriage ceremony. Unsurprisingly, on a weekend visit, Mother announced she had other ideas or, at least, thought I didn't really know my own mind. Other girls might yearn to be a 'star' for a day, but for me stardom meant achieving much greater heights.

'Now, dear, are you sure this is all you want?'

'Mother,' I sighed with exasperation. 'Neither of us are into the full works. How many times do I have to say it?'

'Yes, but …'

I raised my hands to stop her. I would not be put off. Absolutely not. 'We both think it's an appalling waste of money. Why should you have to fork out thousands for what amounts to a commercial extravaganza of one-upmanship. Just because everyone else does?'

'That's not fair, dear.' Despite her protestation, I could tell Mother was relieved. Had we wanted a big do, she'd have got the money from somewhere. She'd have found the means to keep up appearances.

'We don't want the impersonal, registry office version either. We'll settle for a quiet church ceremony with you and Daddy and a couple of friends as witnesses. Okay? Now, I want to show you what I'll be wearing on the day.'

In the bedroom, as I pulled the long purple dress over my head, I realised it was going to cause comment. Some of the more conservative relatives would be bound to think it inappropriate. I brushed my hair into place and, smoothing the creases in the full-length skirt, returned to show Mother. I pushed open the dining-room door with a flourish. 'Da, da! What d'you think?'

'Oh, my God! Where did you get that?'

'Bought it from Richard La Plante, Lynda's husband. He imports from Mexico. This is a traditional Mexican wedding dress. Isn't it gorgeous?'

'Rather bright don't you think? And hardly a suitable colour for a young bride.'

'Mother, come on. Thirty-one isn't exactly young and white would be ridiculous, wouldn't it?'

She had to acquiesce. I twirled round to display the exquisite hand-embroidered gown. White leaves and flowers in panels down the front and back, under the arms, round the deep cuffs and covering the yoked top. A row of tiny people with coloured hats, held hands in a band across the chest. It was quite beautiful. My hair, now halfway down my back, complemented the dress perfectly. I knew that, for me, it was absolutely the right look.

'I have to admit it's very pretty,' said Mother. 'Now, what about Terry? Will he have a shave and trim those unfortunate side-boards, d'you think?'

I stayed at my parents the night before the wedding— for practical as well as traditional reasons; the latter to please Mother naturally. She was all of a dither and, like me, unable to sleep. When I heard footsteps around three in the morning, I went to investigate. She was boiling the kettle.

'Just what I could do with,' I said.

We sat at the kitchen table cradling our mugs. She reached across to take my hand. Her eyes were sparkling with the hint of tears. 'Are you sure about this? It's not too late to change your mind.'

'I am sure and I know, Mummy.'

'Oh, it's so nice to hear you call me that again. It seems years since I was Mummy. Perhaps my little girl's still in there somewhere.'

'Of course she is, and always will be.'

'You were such a happy child, always laughing.'

'I was happy. D'you know I can shut my eyes now and be four again. I'd be wearing a gingham smocked dress and a bow in my hair.'

'Come on, girls. Time you got to bed. Busy day tomorrow.' Daddy was standing in the doorway.

'Yes,' I sighed, getting up from the kitchen table. I kissed them both and went back to bed but I still couldn't sleep, couldn't get comfortable. I was getting married tomorrow. At least that was the plan. But now, at this very last minute, panic engulfed me. Oh God. Tomorrow was supposed to be the most important day in my life. The prospect was frightening. I was committing myself. I could back out now. I could. I wouldn't need excuses. We'd been living together for five years and for a while things had been great. Of course, we'd had our rough patches, like any other couple. But would we be happy? Would Terry change his mind about having a family? Did I really, really love him? By dawn, I'd convinced myself everything would be just fine.

So, on the fifteenth of September 1975, I became Mrs Susan Balfour.

After a liquid breakfast, Terry drove down to the church with our witness friends, Neil and Jane. He was wearing a suit for the occasion, but it wasn't a new one. And, glory be, he'd shaved and trimmed his sideburns.

During the service I got a sudden attack of nerves and lost my voice. This felt like very serious stuff I was promising. My responses were croaked or whispered. Terry managed well but couldn't resist saying in his best Jewish accent, 'I do. I do, already.'

The vicar's eyebrows shot up to meet his hairline. He coughed, glowered at Terry and finished us off quickly. In the vestry he apparently whispered to Mother he was glad 'that' was over with.

A glorious dawn broke beyond Limoges. We were more than half way to Souvic. Cousin Beth and Dave had an old farmhouse in this tiny village in the Dordogne and had agreed to let us spend our honeymoon there.

We arrived later that afternoon and soon found the house: yellowy-white Quercy stone and several hundred years old. The steep, slate roof rose up into a tall *pigeonnier*.

Terry unloaded the car while I went to pick up the key from Madame Arguelle, a neighbour. It was good to speak French again although I was bemused by her strangely nasal accent. She gave me a dozen eggs and a loaf. I thanked her profusely and excused myself for not staying to chat; we'd had a very long trip and Terry was waiting.

The key was enormous and clearly as old as the heavy wooden door which, after much wrenching, pulling and straining, we finally managed to open.

As there were no electrics, we had to grope our way through a dark windowless, dirt-floored entrance area and into the kitchen. The musty air was thick with the smell of wood smoke and the windows were closed and shuttered. We opened one and light poured in.

The oak-beamed room had a large central table with benches, a sideboard, an old gas-bottle cooker and a gigantic open fireplace stained with the soot of centuries. Terracotta pots, yellow enamel pans and a variety of interesting kitchen implements hung from every available hook. We opened the multi-paned French windows to discover a field that stretched way off down the most beautiful valley bordered by cliffs and tall poplars. An old tobacco barn was positioned neatly to one side of the picture-postcard view. Above the opening, small green grapes cascaded from the vine that ran the length of the back of the house. The place had a magical ambience; we knew already we'd want to come here again and again. Ah, France, another side of France, a side I hadn't seen before. It felt so good.

The kitchen was the only habitable downstairs room. Up the rickety wooden stairs were two bedrooms, also with blackened fireplaces. Tobacco wires still hung from the ancient wooden beams where swallows nested and spiders spun their webs undisturbed. The floorboards undulated like a slightly choppy sea. A small bathroom led off the landing. It was all we would need and it was lovely.

Our fortnight was spent exploring cliff-top castles, underground caves and picturesque villages. My French didn't fail me and everyone was most welcoming. Usually we took picnics on our expeditions but several times we ate set-menu lunches in smoky little restaurants abuzz with local workmen and farmers.

We walked all around the Souvic valley, paddled in the river and gathered bagfuls of walnuts and chestnuts.

The lazy autumn evenings were a little chilly so we'd build up a fire and eat by candlelight. It was a perfect honeymoon.

On the Channel crossing home, I left Terry nursing his seasickness and went out on deck. For a moment I was back on the ferry from Dun Laoghaire when, heavily pregnant, I'd run away to England. The wind whipped my face, the salty spray stung my lips. I was thirty-one and a married woman, I could hardly believe it.

24

FAMILY MATTERS

Glowing with newly-weddedness, I found myself pre-occupied at work. After all Terry and I had agreed we wanted a baby. I eagerly awaited the non-arrival of my next period. Nothing much else seemed to matter. 'I need a break from work,' I told him. 'I'm permanently tired and it's not going to help our chances of my getting pregnant.'

'S'pose so,' he said unenthusiastically.

I suspected he was thinking of the drop in income. 'Just for a while, then I can go freelance again. How about it?'

'Okay. If you think it'll help.'

The following Monday I handed in my notice. I'd been at Yorkshire Television for the best part of three years and learned a great deal. Muriel would have been well-cast as a school-ma'am; strict down to the last detail. Her methods were precise and systematic and she encouraged her staff to follow suit. Every performance I'd seen was recorded, I'd devised forms for each stage of the casting process and I was now able to come up with a ballpark figure for the actors' budget simply from reading a script. All this and being pushed to the limit had to be to my advantage when I became my own boss again. For all her pomposity, Muriel had been a terrific teacher but with broodiness now monopolising my consciousness, my drive was at an all time low. I left YTV just after Christmas 1975.

My first priority had been a visit to Dr Helena Wright, the gynaecologist who'd been so good to me before. She must now, I calculated, be approaching eighty, but being the pioneer she was, she would carry on to the death, literally. I was highly amused to see she still had the little paisley scarf but, as she probed around inside, a moment of *déjà vu* brought unwelcome tears to my eyes. I sniffed them away and sat up for her verdict. 'Splendid, dear, you're in good shape, if a little scarred around the cervix. How many stitches did you have?'

'Five,' I replied.

'Pooh, that's nothing. You shouldn't have any trouble.'

I thanked her and paid.

'Good luck this time, dear.' She shook my hand and winked.

One evening, a few weeks later, Mother rang me to say she'd seen Dr Wright's obituary in the Telegraph.

'Oh, no, that's really sad,' I said. 'She was great. She'll be missed, and not least by the Women's Movement.'

'And, guess what. Dossy's coming over at the end of the month and she's bringing little Geoff.'

'Hardly little, Mother. He must be thirteen by now.'

I was thrilled. It'd been such a long time since Dossy and I had seen each other and, although we'd corresponded, it had been hard to maintain the intimacy we'd achieved eleven years ago.

It was arranged they would come and spend a few days with us in Brighton. What would she make of Terry, I wondered. She was rather strait-laced and his conversation was peppered with swear words.

196

It was after midnight and we'd just dropped off when the phone rang again. I turned on the light and reached to answer it. 'Hello.'

'Sue, it's me, Dossy. I need to talk to you. Something's happened.'

'What? You're okay aren't you?' I was alarmed, she sounded so strange.

'I've had this letter. Sue, I have two brothers. My mother died six months ago and made them promise to find me. What shall I do?'

'Heavens, I don't know. Do you want to meet them? I mean, if they've found you, presumably they want to meet you.'

'Yes, they said they'd come to the States. But, I don't think I want that. Complete strangers, staying at our house. It could be very difficult. Oh, Sue, I sure am confused.'

'Look, why not arrange to meet them when you come over here. That's the obvious thing.'

'How can I? I'm staying with Mother and Daddy and they mustn't know. You won't tell them, will you? I trust you not to. Daddy'd be furious.'

'Of course I won't. We'll arrange something. And whatever you decide, I'll be right there beside you.'

She chose Windsor and persuaded Daddy to drop her and Geoff off for a day's sight-seeing on their own. I drove up from Brighton to join them. Dossy fair flew into my arms. I could feel her tension, tight as a coiled spring. 'Oh, Sue. I haven't slept a wink. What'll they be like? Will I like them? Will they like me?' she whispered. 'Geoff doesn't know what's happening.'

I glanced at my nephew, he stood apart, long-faced and morose. Hands in pockets, he shuffled his feet and stared at the ground. I gave Dossy a squeeze. 'It'll be okay, I can't imagine they're monsters. Just take things as they come,' I said quietly.

I disentangled myself to say hello to Geoff; expecting him not to remember me. He'd been four when I'd last seen him. 'Hi, Geoff. How're things?' I said awkwardly.

'Okay, I guess.'

'Geoffrey! Don't be so darned rude. You just give your Aunt Sue a kiss, now.'

Poor kid. It was the last thing he wanted to do. I put out my hand instead. He shook it limply. At that moment a car drew up and two men got out.

It was the weirdest of meetings, unreal, almost surreal. Dossy's brothers she'd never met. Blood relatives, yet complete strangers. She offered her hand solemnly. Well, what else could she do? Indeed what would I do if I ever got to meet my son, my Sebastian? Dear Dossy, my heart went out to her.

Larry and Martin were both big guys, warm and outspoken. Typical Yorkshiremen. We hired a boat and went on the river. Geoff wasn't in the least interested in what was going on; he sat in the bow and read his comic. I did the rowing while the others talked.

'Our Mam never got over losing you. There were only us boys after that. She mourned you right up to her death,' Martin said to Dossy.

She looked sceptical. 'I find that hard to believe. She never said a word when your father shut me in the cupboard under the stairs,' she said fiercely. 'All night, in the dark with nothing to eat. Or when I was locked in the front parlour with your grandfather, dead in his coffin. Or when …'

Martin raised his hand to stop her. 'Our Mam and Dad would never do them sort of things,' he said testily.

'Not likely. Mam was a right softie, and Dad wouldn't harm a fly,' Larry agreed.

'Why don't we change places, Martin. You row for a bit,' I suggested.

The atmosphere eased up a little as we swapped over. Dossy moved onto safer ground. 'Tell me about your families. Do I have nephews and nieces?'

Larry dug in his pocket and fished out a thick pack of photos of their wives and children. I watched as Dossy carefully studied each one, knowing she was thankful for a little respite from the frankness of their scrutiny.

Geoff, wanting a pee, began to fidget, so I suggested we turn back and go for tea somewhere. Larry took over the oars and Dossy talked distractedly about Jerzy, the kids and her life in the States until we pulled into the landing stage. After tea and cakes in the town, Larry and Martin left, promising they'd be in touch soon. Dossy, visibly shaking, reached across the table. I took her hand and held it still. We sat in silence, there seemed nothing appropriate to say. Geoff was buried in his comic and oblivious. Finally Dossy spoke. 'Now, Geoff. Listen to me. Meeting Larry and Martin was private, just between us. You understand? You're not to tell Granny and Grandad. Promise?'

'Yeah, if you like,' he said without glancing up. His disinterest was reassuring.

'I'll explain when we get home.'

'Okay.'

By the time Dossy came down to see us in Brighton, she'd decided she felt nothing for these two men, her brothers. Their lives had been so different, they had little in common, and it'd been forty years since she'd seen her mother. On the other hand, she did have feelings about Terry. She was not impressed and told me so. 'Sue, he swears. You know I don't like bad language. What have you done marrying this man?'

'He comes from a different background, that's all.' I sprang to his defence.

'He sure does.'

'But he's honest and reliable and he can be very nice, and funny. And he's not stupid either.'

'Do you love him?'

'Yes,' I said firmly. I'm not in love with him, but he's so much a part of my life now and I understand him. And when we have children, I know he'll be a great father.'

'Huh. We'll see,' she said.

Dossy wrote to me soon after they got home. She didn't mention Terry at all. Perhaps she thought she'd said enough. However, she had heard again from Larry and Martin who'd written to suggest they might visit her one day, with their wives. Time would tell if they were serious. She rather hoped they weren't.

For me the months passed, each one accompanied by a period. A hateful, rotten period. Why did I keep having them? I should've fallen pregnant pretty quickly. Now I began to dread that time of the month for other reasons than pain and discomfort, simply because it still was 'that time of the month'. Mid-cycle after ovulation time, I would be looking for signs, any sign, no matter how minute, that I might be pregnant. I bought a couple of books on infertility and read them start to finish and back. Terry was patient enough but irritated by my obsession. 'If you're that hung up about it, why don't you go see the doctor?'

I did. He examined me, could see nothing obviously wrong and gave me a temperature chart so I could work out when I was likely to ovulate. We were to lay off sex for three days beforehand to allow Terry's sperm to build up then do it on the dot. 'Try that for three months and if nothing happens, I'll refer you on to a local gynaecologist,' he added.

Nothing did happen and I got more and more depressed. Everywhere I looked evidence of procreation confronted me. So many women with prams or babies slung to their chests or backs and a proliferation of bulging bellies. I'd been like that once, hadn't I? I'd fallen pregnant with consummate ease. Where was my baby now? Little Sebastian, he wouldn't be little now—he'd be a teenager. Suddenly there were teenage boys round every corner. Any one of them could have been him. Now I was being denied for the second time. The tears bubbled up to the surface with alarming regularity. Terry became increasingly intolerant. The doctor referred me on.

The gynaecologist delved inside, prodded my stomach and asked a load of questions before saying he wanted to check Terry's sperm. 'I want to make sure they're up to strength and speed,' he said. 'Then we'll do a laparoscopy. It's a minor operation. Under general anaesthetic, a probe with a camera is pushed through the navel and into the womb. It'll show up any irregularities.'

I agreed. Of course I did. I'd have agreed to anything if it meant I could have a baby. He booked me into a local clinic and told me to drop a fresh sperm sample into his surgery as soon as possible.

Terry wasn't entranced at the idea of doing the biz to order and into a pot but, with help from me, he managed to capture his climax and I scooted round to the surgery.

The doctor rang me later. 'Your husband's sperms are a bit sluggish but they should still make it,' he told me. 'So the problem is likely to be with you. We shall see.'

The following week I had the laparoscopy and was pronounced clear.

'Nothing wrong with you. I suggest you stop trying so hard. Relax. The reasons are obviously psychological,' said the gynaecologist. 'Get a good night's sleep and try to forget about having babies. If you're meant to have one, you will. If not, you won't.' He departed leaving me feeling stupid and helpless.

Back at home I spent the day in a frantic round of chores, my thoughts drowned out by the radio. By the time Terry got home, I'd worn myself out. 'You won't believe this,' he said. 'That bloody Mrs Wolf got into an argument with another client. They were screaming at each other over the basins. Luckily Sally Grant shut them up. Told them the salon was hardly the place for a row and to take their quarrel elsewhere.'

'Oh really,' I said feebly.

Terry looked sharply at me. 'What's your problem?'

That was it. I burst into tears.

'Why the waterworks?'

'You haven't asked me how I am. How it went. You don't care do you? All you can think about is your bloody salon,' I wailed.

'I'm sorry, I forgot. Well?'

'There's nothing wrong with me.'

He burst out laughing. 'So what's to cry about?'

'You don't understand, do you? I'm not getting pregnant and there's no reason. He said it was psychological.'

'Then it probably is. I think you should stop crying and have a drink.'

I didn't just have one, I had several. Which made matters worse not better. I continued to agonise. Terry got fed up with me and marched out to make his own supper before going to bed and leaving me to it. I curled up on the sofa with my sodden hanky wondering if I was some sort of neurotic headcase.

It was well after midnight before I began to sober up, made a coffee and decided. No, I damn well wasn't neurotic and I wasn't going to accept the diagnosis, after all when I'd asked him to do a post-coital test, the gynaecologist had said there wasn't much point. I hadn't agreed, but he'd insisted. I'd read enough about the subject to know that it was important to check the vaginal fluids after sex to see how the sperm are faring. So, not prepared to take his word for it, I decided I'd go for a second opinion.

On a friend's recommendation, I took myself off to see another man in London. He didn't want to do the test either, but he did find a couple of cysts on my cervix which he removed there and then and told me to get on with my life.

I was now so low there was only one way to go—up. Like it or not, I would have to follow their advice, there was no other option. If it was going to happen, it would. To Terry's relief I stopped taking my temperature every day and made a determined effort to cheer up and felt better for it. I decided that maybe my failure to conceive had been psychological after all and this way my repro department might stand more chance.

By July I had a great tan—it was 1976 and the hottest summer since goodness knows when. I spent enough time on the beach to feel like it was becoming a habit. Day in, day out, meeting with a group of friends and roasting myself. I may have looked great but it did nothing for my intellectual health. The conversation was dominated by prices, clothes, men, kids and all the other stuff women can fill their heads with when they don't want to think of anything meaningful. It had only been six months and I was already missing the distraction of work.

That autumn my baby blues started crowding in again. I resolved to have another try. My broodiness just wasn't going to go away. I rang Dr Wright's old number to see if it was still a gynaecological practice. I was sure that if she'd handed it over herself it would have been to a woman. A woman with similar ideas to her own. I was right. I made an appointment to see a Dr Jean Infield.

She was just who I needed. Sympathetic, reassuring and bubbling with enthusiastic energy. She was sure it wasn't psychological and insisted the next step should be a post coital test, which should have been done before the laparoscopy. I knew I'd been right. I trudged up again a week later around ovulation time and she popped the phial contents under her microscope. 'Yoo, hoo! Well, there we are. The poor mites don't stand a chance,' she exclaimed. 'Have a look.'

She was right, the little tadpoles were trying to move but seemed glued down. She explained that I was, for some reason, not producing the right secretions to help them up into my womb and onwards to meet my eggs.

'Don't lose hope, dear. I can arrange for you to have a course of AIH – that's artificial insemination husband—where you have the sperm injected straight into your womb, bypassing the cervix. It should work.'

I went home jubilant. I wasn't neurotic or psychologically disturbed, I had a genuine problem and something could be done about it. Terry was very relieved too. I rang Dr Infield the next morning to say we wanted to take the AIH route.

'Very wise, very wise, dear,' she said. 'You'll see, you'll be pregnant in no time. I'll be in touch.'

Just before Christmas I got a phone call from Granada Television. They were short of casting directors and the workload was too heavy. It would only be for a couple of programmes. My spirits were instantly revived. I was out of the business but not forgotten. It was time to go back to casting for the money, the stimulation and, most of all, because I'd missed it. Here was an opportunity to establish myself as a television freelancer working from home.

So 1976 ended on a high note. Next year I had every chance of becoming a mother. A proper mother, who could keep her baby. Who could do all the things mothers do—change its nappy, rock it in her arms, cuddle and sing to it and slowly introduce it to all the wonders of living.

25

BABY BLUES

The following Spring, I got a call from my director friend, Jimmy Ormerod. He was working for Southern Television on *Spearhead*, a series about the troubles in Ulster, which were at their height. Could I come and cast it for him? Great, it would keep me busy for several months. When I got the first scripts I realised I'd be looking for an endless selection of soldier types. The series certainly didn't glamorise the army, far from it. In fact it probably undermined the recruitment drives of the day.

Whilst working for Southern, I made a good impression on the producer, Rex Firkin, and worked for him over several years on other series.

It's invariably the producer who will engage the crew. If the production involves freelancers, directors will probably and understandably, ask for people they've worked with before, but if not, the producer will bring in someone of their choice.

Whichever of the two ask for you, you then have to create a good relationship with the other one, at least for the duration of the job. I worked with some great teams, but not always.

Some directors are prima-donnas, some producers are a pain, poking their noses into the tiniest details of the creative process and constantly panicking about the budget. And God help us if the two don't agree about a particular piece of casting. Getting your own way whilst keeping both of them happy and without obviously taking sides, can be ultra tricky. It's vital to be diplomatic, it's not clever to trample in hob-nail boots over a director or producer's suggestion: 'Oh, I don't think he's right. He can't act to save his life and his breath smells. I saw him the other day at the Cottesloe and his leading lady had to hold him at arms length. No, we can do far better than that. I think we should have Antony Smotherby, now there's someone who can really act.'

The ideal, unneurotic producer will, quite naturally, want to be involved in choosing the leads, but will leave you and director alone to do the rest of the casting.

Some directors are very insecure and only want to cast actors they've used in the past. Then it's hard work steering them away from their usual little repertoire. Heaps of reassurance and the odd recommendation from another director might persuade them to be a bit more adventurous. Another annoying type is the director who can't decide who he wants.

You might say, 'I see the character as a big, beefy chap with twinkling eyes and a great smile. How do you see him?'

'Well, not like that,' says the director.

'Can you describe what you're looking for, so I can bring in the right types next time?'

'I'll know the right person when he walks in the door.'

Wonderful! You decide you're going to be busy if he asks for you again.

True to her word, Dr Infield arranged for me to start AIH, with a Dr Swyer in Hampstead. His surgery was in the basement of his home. It was welcoming and informal and he looked stereotypically more like a city gent than a gynaecologist. His manner was kindly but reserved. That was fine by me. All I wanted was to get on with the process. He examined me, studied Dr Infield's report and proclaimed me a suitable candidate. I was to start a course of AIH the following month.

It meant going back to temperature charts and regulated sex. As soon as my ovulation time could be ascertained with a reasonable degree of accuracy, a regular appointment could be arranged and Dr Swyer would wave his magic syringe and I'd be a mum-in-waiting within months. I left encouraged and elated and unconcerned that the procedure was not going to be cheap.

Spearhead turned out to be more fun than I'd anticipated and during my Southern stint I had time to contact heads of casting in all the television companies to let them know I was officially freelancing. I formed a company, set myself up with a PAYE scheme and designed my stationery. It was an exciting new development. I would be holding the reins of my life and it felt good. I realised I had a true freelance mentality. The idea of periods out of work didn't worry me, something would always come along. Within a few months I was established and more offers came in from Southern Television, then from Thames. Soon I was juggling jobs.

Once a month, on the day of my appointment with Dr Swyer, Terry and I would be woken early by the shrill of the alarm. Then I had to get him in the mood. It wasn't difficult but it was discomforting; not what making babies should be about. When he was ready I had to grab the plastic pot and catch the first spurt.

Apparently the second spurt is more diluted by seminal fluid. I would then quickly wrap the pot in cotton wool, grab my breakfast and run for the early train to town. The sooner I could get to Dr Swyer, the better. I'd arrive puffed and sweating after sprinting from the tube station clutching my hopes in my warm coat pocket.

The AIH process was extremely uncomfortable. The burning sensation inside resembled the pain of insertion I'd experienced with the coil. The syringe had to pass through the neck of my cervix and shoot the sperm straight up into my womb. I tried hard to relax but knowing the exact sensation that was coming, it was almost impossible not to tense up. But it was over soon enough and I was consoled by the idea that this time it could have taken. Within three weeks I'd know.

By the autumn I was exhausted from work and privately miserable. My trips to Dr Swyer had not been rewarded. Terry was worn out too. Poynters was doing well enough for him to take on more staff but frequently he'd arrive home late, legs buckling from the strain of standing up all day and declare himself brain-dead from being nice to all the clients. He was also becoming fed up with the sperms-to-order routine. We both needed a holiday. So did Terry's mate Neil and his wife, Jane, a zany redhead fondly known as Child-Bride—there being ten years between them.

I rang and asked Beth and Dave if we could go down to Souvic for a couple of weeks. With characteristic kindness they agreed to let us stay in the house again.

In the Dordogne the copper beauty and fragrance of autumn embraced us as before. Neil, ultra trendy art director in advertising and an ace photographer, captured misty mornings and shafts of evening sunlight. It was as perfect as we remembered and the house now had electricity and a terracotta tiled floor in the kitchen.

We felt the stress fall away as we strolled through fields, woods and village streets stopping only to collect walnuts or blackberries or to gaze wistfully into estate agents' windows. One day we resolved. One day.

Back home my spirits held up for a while, but I was beginning to lose hope of ever becoming pregnant again. Dr Swyer, however, was more optimistic and calmly reassured me. 'Sometimes it can take months before the moment is exactly right.'

'But it'll have been a year soon, and my husband's getting fed up. And every month hoping, praying, my period won't come, it's hard.'

Dr Swyer put a hand on my shoulder. 'I know. But I would recommend persevering. For some people it takes a little longer, you know. Don't give up hope yet.'

That night I dissolved into despairing tears. 'Why, why, why isn't it working?'

Terry passed me the tissue box. 'I feel like I'm being punished. Like it's some sort of divine retribution,' I sniffed. 'I should never have given him away. Now look what's happened.'

'You mean what's not happened. So stop crying and talking nonsense. If the doctor says we should persevere, then we should.'

I blew my nose and tried to think straight. 'I suppose so. As long as he thinks there's a chance, we ought to carry on.'

Nonetheless, although I was fine when distracted by work, I'd collapse in an unconsolable heap when I allowed myself time to think about the situation. I realised I needed a project and Terry needed a break from my long face. One Saturday night, I threw an idea his way. 'I'd like to look for a new house. With the salon doing well we can afford to move to somewhere bigger.' I refrained from saying that, with luck, we might need another bedroom. 'This place is looking pretty good now. It should fetch a reasonable price.'

We'd been at Westbourne Street for nearly seven years. Terry had spruced the place up considerably and I'd enjoyed what I called 'dressing the set'.

'Why don't you get an agent round,' he suggested. 'I'd be interested to hear what they think.'

The valuation took us both by surprise. We could ask over thirty thousand pounds. Wow! We could ask it but that didn't mean we'd get it, well not immediately anyway. We put it on the market straight away and went off looking. It wasn't long before we found a house and, again, we just knew it was right.

102 Stanford Avenue, a Victorian semi in need of complete restoration, was high on a hill overlooking Brighton and a wide expanse of sea. The agents' details had described it as 'bristling with original features'. For once they weren't exaggerating; we wandered round marvelling at the mosaic tiled floors, ornate cornices, extensive wood panelling and marble fireplaces. It would present a huge challenge, but we knew it could once again be a beautiful house.

Our offer was accepted, the bank agreed a bridging loan and two months later the keys were handed over. From then on every available moment was devoted to our new project. With a head teeming with design ideas, I had little time to feel sorry for myself and cheered up considerably. We might not be able to produce a family, so 102 would be our joint creation.

The restoration took up all of our spare time. Terry was doing most of the work himself and he proved to be dedicated and talented. I was relegated to labouring and paint stripping. That was okay. I'd listen to the radio and concentrate on peeling away the layers. Things were going well until Terry started sending me out to buy the materials. Saturday mornings were soon spent hanging around waiting to be served at trade counters. I came to resent every long drawn-out minute and builders' merchants shot to the top of my *bête noire* list. I'll swear they saw me coming. They never seemed to have what I asked for, insisted on a substitute and sent me home to an inevitable row with Terry when my repressed emotions would re-surface. Despite the transformation that was taking place at our lovely new house, all I really wanted was a baby and we were still trying. In fact we'd been trying for fifteen months. It was always a miserable experience but never worse than April 1978.

Dr Swyer's secretary had called to tell me my next AIH would be at his surgery at University College Hospital. As the appointment was on a Monday, we decided to stay over with Neil and Jane on the Sunday. Terry would drive me to UCH first thing. 'Don't ask me to come in with you. You know I can't stand hospitals,' he said.

'Oh, Terry, I wish you would. I could do with moral support for once.'

'You'll be okay. I'll park the car and wait for you outside.'

I was directed to the infertility clinic on the first floor. When I walked in, the hopelessness in the air was overwhelming. Couples sat around the walls in silent still-life, paced the floor or stood staring out of the window. One couple, hands tightly clasped, gazed unblinking at the wall. Two of the men sat slumped forward, elbows on knees, hands clasped. One woman sniffled into her hanky, another fiddled with her coat buttons. Everyone looked utterly dejected. I sat in a corner wishing myself a million miles away. After about ten minutes a nurse appeared with a clipboard. 'Mrs Balfour?'

I shot out of my seat. 'Yes.'

'This way please.'

As I followed her out of the room I could feel the resentment behind me. I was a private patient, they were probably National Health. It wasn't comfortable to be this privileged.

I was shown into a consulting room and told to remove my lower garments. Once naked from the waist down, I heaved myself up onto the bed and the nurse slipped my legs into stirrups. 'Dr Swyer will be along in a moment,' she said and bustled out.

And there I lay, genitals displayed, unable to sit up, waiting. I heard the sound of the door opening and two male voices. They took some papers from the desk and left. Then a nurse popped in with a pile of towels. As she opened the door the buzz in the corridor outside drifted in. I was a specimen on a slab, not a human being. Just like those sad little frogs in the science lab at school. I remembered that place with its nasty stink and the frog, sickly yellow, cut open down its tummy and pinned on a board. I remembered how we were supposed to find it interesting and to learn important things from the gruesome dissection of the tiny sacrifice. Like not being cruel to animals, perhaps? The door opened again. It was Dr Swyer.

As soon as he'd finished with me, I fled through the waiting room and down the stairs, two at a time. I was already sobbing. Terry was outside having a cigarette. 'What's the matter?' he said. I told him. 'Well, you're not coming here again. Fuck that. If he can't see you at his consulting rooms, you'll just have to skip it.'

Two months later Dr Swyer laid out our options. 'I'm sorry to say you're one of my disappointments,' he announced sadly.

'Isn't there something else we can try? I've heard about test-tube babies, couldn't we have a …?

Dr Swyer raised his hand. 'Hold on, hold on. That's still very much in the research stages. But anyway, even if it were to become available, and we're talking some years from now, you wouldn't qualify.'

'Why not?' I asked indignantly.

'You'd be too old. I'm sorry. Right now you have three choices—carry on, give up or take a break.'

These were the words I'd been dreading. As long as he wasn't admitting failure, I'd felt there was a chance. I grabbed my coat and handbag and made for the door, not wanting to break down in front of him. As I left I managed to say, 'Thank you. I'll let you know.'

That was it, I'd had enough. My emotions were in shreds, I just couldn't take any more. Neither could Terry. 'Look you're never going to be a mother. You've got to accept it,' he said.

Deep down, I knew he was right. I would have to accept it, I had no choice. As Daddy would say, 'You'll just have to get on with it.'

PART FOUR

TAKING OFF

26

CASTING ABOUT

Mother was a worrier. It was as though everyone else's problem was hers and we had to feel terribly sorry for her because she was so worried. Luckily this was a time when she wasn't getting in a tizz about me. In fact, she was wallowing vicariously. 'Of course, Sue got her love of the theatre and drama from me. I was a devoted theatregoer in my time. I've seen all the great names, Gielgud, Redgrave, Olivier. Seen them all.'

I cringed to hear her preening. But I supposed most mothers were like that. And my freelance career was going rather well although, despite what Mother might have imagined, it most certainly wasn't glamorous. My job was strictly behind the scenes, and like most of the backroom boys and girls, I looked on the actors as part of a big, though temporary, team. There was no drooling over them, they were there to do a job just like the rest of us.

Although I loved my work, I usually avoided telling people outside the business what I did, because they would invariably ask which famous people I knew or had met and my mental filing cabinet would instantly slam shut. Because, I suppose, I was concerned with acting ability not stardom. After all it was my job to spot talent and then to persuade a director to give them a break. Helping an actor on the road to success was far more rewarding than casting one who'd already made it.

How does anyone judge an actor's potential? Well, instinct is certainly involved but there are useful guidelines too. I would look for three major qualities—the skill to convince an audience of a character's psychology, the ability to engage them on an emotional level and the possession of a potent physical presence. If the camera loves them and their features can stand big close-ups (no tics, bad teeth, dodgy skins, casts in the eye etc.) then they have the potential to become a leading film or television actor. Of course, character roles are exempted from the 'no flaws' conditions and, sometimes, the quirkier they are, the better.

In our job clearly developed powers of observation are essential. Good casting directors will study every detail of an actor's facial animation, body language and deportment, their hands and how they use them, the tone of their voice, accent, diction and delivery, their smile, their laugh and their mannerisms. They will ask such questions as 'Am I looking into a warm soul or does this person appear shifty or to be hiding something? Do they make me feel comfortable? Are their features fine or coarse? Are they easy on the eye or would I rather not look at them?' No good casting someone who looks like a dog's breakfast unless it's a monster that's called for. 'Do bits of them wobble annoyingly or do their noses twitch when they talk? Can they take a close-up or would the audience be mesmerised by some strange feature or habit and stray from the plot …' The list is endless. A bit like psychiatrists, a casting director will glean a lot from the outer shell.

Most important is the ability to imagine an actor in a variety of guises and to gauge how believable he or she would be. Most actors think they have a far greater range than they are allowed to demonstrate, and, in many cases, they might well be right. However, few parts, aside from the leads, require a great deal of characterisation. Audiences tend to have preconceived stereotypical ideas of what a doctor, a policeman, an MP, a prostitute or a school teacher will look and sound like. Physical features, mannerisms and actions have to say it all, which is sad because casting against type can be much more fun. Of course, these days, it's perfectly feasible to cast the policeman as a heavy and the villain as a straight-looking guy.

The phone never stops, thank God for assistants. If the casting director were to answer every time, they'd get no work done at all.

It's an agent's job to ring round to find out what's being cast, if possible to get a breakdown of the characters and then to suggest those clients they think are suitable. Sounds simple, doesn't it? Far from it.

A busy casting director rarely has time to compile a detailed breakdown. If you do have time and decide agent input would be helpful, you will be inundated with mail.

Some of their clients will be right for the part and included for consideration, but the majority probably won't be. So really the whole exercise will have been time-consuming for everyone concerned. Anyway, most agents send out availability lists so you can see at a glance who's free and add them to your list if you think they'd be good.

With the top agents whose clients are mostly big names, the balance of power tips the other way. You ring them to discuss the leading roles and hope to get some good ideas.

As for actors ringing, you can only say you'll remember them if the right part comes up. You can't help feeling sorry for them; they're desperate for work and get nothing but a load of fob-offs. I guess that applies to any business but somehow it seems more personal in ours. The process of casting a prestige television film, for example, is no doubt similar to the workings of the average personnel department. It goes something like this:

I've read the script, done a budget, talked to the producer about it and been asked to cut back, as usual. I'd allowed for that and with luck this is not one of the many low budget pieces that can only be made if everyone works for nuppence. Increasingly, that's what's expected. Now the moneymen are getting their nasty little toes in the studio doors, 'Cheap, cheap, cheap,' is all that can be heard. Like a flock of cuckoos they're pushing quality out of the nest.

So on to the creative part, which I'll enjoy despite having to spend days wading through Spotlight, the actors' directories. I like to be sure I've thought of every possible actor for each part and then whittled it down to a good list, ready to present to the director. Hopefully he or she won't be indecisive, inexperienced, insecure or nursing an inflated ego. Of course, there are some who are absolutely great to work with. The ones that trust casting directors' opinions and knowledge, respect their intuition, on which many choices are made, and are secure enough to make up their minds from the first, and usually the best, bunch of suggestions. Most women directors come under this category. The other types come out with such lulus as:

'I'd like to see more people,' when I've brought in dozens.

'But she was so sympathetic in … do you really think she could play nasty?'

Good actors are versatile for heaven's sake. And anyway, why would I have suggested her if I weren't sure of her ability?

'See if you can get Judi Dench to come in for an interview.' Sub-text: 'Surely she would for me?' Who are you kidding?

'I'll have to sleep on it.' Meaning 'I have to ask my wife what she thinks.'

'He looks too old (when it doesn't matter), too tall (when the part is played sitting down) too pretty (she's caked in make-up) or (my favourite) his hair's too long!'

Ad infinitum and nauseam. Often these are the types who, against all advice, insist on casting someone unsuitable then blame the casting director when the performance is a disaster. Or, at the other end of the scale, after hours of persuasion, they finally agree to cast an actor then take all the credit when the performance is brilliant. It seems to me that if you can't give credit where credit's due you must be short of it yourself.

Another stumbling block with certain male directors is that they have trouble with their lower deck when it comes to casting pretty ladies. They simply can't be objective. If they don't fancy the woman, nobody else will either. This fact, incidentally, explains why so few successful casting directors are heterosexual men. The casting couch, by the way, has little to do with casting directors, it's a reputation that comes from lecherous producers and directors who just can't keep their hands to themselves.

Next a meeting is arranged with the director and producer to discuss the lead roles. They nearly always want a star name—prestige for them and satisfaction for the co-producers. And God help us if they're American. This is what casting directors might expect if there's a trans-Atlantic connection:

American producers think any actor, regardless of status, will be available, jump at the chance to be in their film and will do it for a special low fee. Because they don't know many English actors, they'll probably ask you to go for the 'flavour of the month' whose movie was up for an Oscar. Or they'll want you to set up meetings with a long list of top British names, at their smart hotel (which is swallowing budget money by the bucket-load, of course) and even if you can get any to agree, you'll find yourself in a Whitehall farce of front, back and side entrances trying to prevent said names from bumping into each other. The so-called meeting will turn into an interview when Jeremy Irons (who?) will be expected to produce a CV and (heaven forbid) read a few pages of script. When it gets this bad, and it can, you'll be trying to melt through the wall into the next room with the most acute embarrassment you can remember. Then when you finally arrive home exhausted, they'll ring to discuss who else they want to subject to humiliation. They won't care what time it is, they'll ring at all hours of the night and day, so it's best not to let them have your home phone number—they live and breathe their jobs and expect everyone else does too. They can't make decisions for fear of making the wrong ones and being given the boot by the big boss, so those conference calls will last forever and get absolutely nowhere, The final week before the cameras are due to roll will be panicsville. No, it's not fun and every time you swear you'll never do another one.

At the initial meeting, if there are no Americans involved, the usual starry names come up, are chewed over and discarded. Not available, too expensive, getting on a bit now, was lousy in his last play/film, losing her looks or is 'Difficult'. (And they sure can be, especially if they believe their own publicity, or are drunks). A short-list is finally agreed on and a script will go out to the first name with a plea for an answer soon. That out of the way, the producer departs and the director and I discuss the support roles. Hopefully, although by no means usually, he'll have a reasonable knowledge of actors and know who I'm talking about. If not, I have to produce CVs and possibly videos. The trawl can be lengthy. Finally we bring the meeting to a close having agreed a date for the first casting session when the director will be meeting actors he doesn't know or hasn't met.

The list is full. I've allocated a quarter of an hour per person and pray the director isn't too keen on the sound of his own voice. The first hopefuls have arrived and are eyeing one another to try and decide if they're up for the same part. Often they know each other and are relieved to have someone to chat to whilst they wait. I like to have a few words with each one before they meet the director, give them an idea of what's required and what to expect and what not to do or say. I want them to feel I'm on their side, illogically as I have to bring in at least two actors for each part and naturally only one can get it.

225

There is no doubt casting directors have power, which is not something I feel particularly comfortable about. A few commendatory words from us can set an actor on the road to stardom. Their ability to pay the mortgage or the school fees or replace the old banger can rest with us. That part in a long-running series can solve their money worries for years. We can open the door for them and push them through or we can shut it firmly in their face. This power is part of the job and unavoidable so it is up to us to deal with it honourably and honestly. To remember actors are people with families, feelings and the same needs as the rest of humankind. Courtesy, kindness and consideration are essential if we are to maintain our integrity.

If I'm lucky the director is the only person present at the casting session, but sometimes we have to put up with a producer or producers, then you know you're in for casting by committee. That can take forever and is often a gigantic bore. Today I'm lucky and so are the actors. The director is the only person they have to impress.

So we wade through the afternoon, sometimes getting horribly behind, with an embarrassing build-up in the waiting room, or the director has them in and out in a trice. I hate that. They've often come miles to this interview; to be given a measly two minutes is an insult. Some directors are pretty gauche and I have to do the talking, some get the actor to read a script extract, cold and with me, poor sods. Some witter on and on about the show and the part when they have absolutely no intention of casting the person. Nerves I suppose. Some are absolutely great, they give the actor a general idea of the piece and the part, ask him enough relevant questions to get him to relax and, at the end of the interview, thank him for his time.

After the session we have the post mortem. Who to cast? Endless discussion can ensue, him or him, her or her? I wish I hadn't brought in such strong contenders. Or the director wants to go again on some of the parts. I sigh inwardly knowing they've seen the best available, in my opinion anyway, and no matter how many others they meet, they'll probably come back to the first lot anyway. Or, on the whole, it has been a grand success, everyone was interesting but the best are … and we have the kernel of a good cast coming together. I'm happy. I trundle home, awash from teas and coffees and thoroughly exhausted. If the director's a smoker, I'll stink as well. Tomorrow I'll tackle negotiations—another matter entirely.

It's best to get the tricky ones out of the way first. Research needs to be done, so I look through any available records so see what each one was paid last time, ring other casting people, compare the figure to my budget and hope for the best.

Some agents are a dream, some a nightmare. Most know me well enough to believe me when I say this is all I have. If it's low I wouldn't insult the actor by trying to negotiate. In those cases I promise to up the fee if I can when everyone else is on board. I leave the agents who are unpleasant to deal with until I have spoken to some of the nicer ones.

I believe it's essential to spend all the allocated budget, unless the producer is begging you to cut down where you can. To get clever and come in way under by squeezing the actors, is not only mean but can make problems for the future. If you did it for less this time, you're expected to do it for even less next time.

Budgets go down and down and the actors pay the price. Only the stars are well paid because of their audience-pulling power. The rest of the profession are lucky to achieve a decent living.

In television and film, actors are paid in different ways. They might get paid for days or weeks according to the schedule, or they might get a fee for the job and small payments for each day worked, either rehearsing or filming. They might be 'bought out' or get repeats and residuals, a percentage of profit (points) or deferred fees. They might be paid for certain territories—countries where the programme or film may be shown—and not others. There are percentages of fee for all countries with an established television network or cinema industry. Points are complicated to negotiate, based on the pecking order and whether it's net or gross. Deferred fees are for very low budget movies only where profit is expected but the kitty is too small to pay normal fees at the outset.

On top of fee negotiation, there are goodies like overtime, overnights and expenses—often standard but, in the case of a big name, negotiable, as are billing, location rest rooms, accommodation (Winnebegos) and transport. Is there an exclusive car or is it shared? Is there a car at all? Most actors have to get to location or studio under their own steam. With major stars the fun really starts. They have their own entourage and will expect them to be paid and accommodated by the company. And these details by no means complete the operation. You may have a great cast lined up but sorting out their billing can bring the house of cards tumbling down. Or the schedule might change and you have to adjust everyone's contracts to accommodate it. It can even change several times and then you might be in for payments for cancelled days. The computations are tricky and endless.

Finally, fees and conditions have been agreed, contracts have gone out and those who were not chosen have been thanked. We have a cast and it's time for the read-through.

Once the script is read, frocks and make-up are discussed, fittings arranged and rehearsal schedules handed out, my job is over. It's been a challenge and mostly enjoyable, or quite the reverse. If the experience has been good I will get out to location or go to the studio recording. I like to see how things are going. It's usually fascinating and a pleasant change to get a break before the next project begins and the procedure starts all over again.

~

After a stint at Thames Television, it was suggested I might like to join the casting staff. No, I wouldn't, thank you, but I would be happy to work on a renewable yearly contract. It would mean the security of regular money but I'd still be freelance. Autonomy had become all important to me. I'd made some good friends and contacts at Thames and had the chance of working on a series that was to become a household favourite—*Rumpole of the Bailey*. Some of the main cast had appeared in the BBC play that preceded the series, but there were to be a host of interesting characters, both regular and one-off, to stretch my ingenuity. I got on well with John Mortimer and made a lasting friend of the producer, Jacqueline Davis, who was to take the series forward through several years.

At the first read-through I introduced myself to Leo McKern. 'I'm Sue, the casting director. I don't imagine you'll remember, but we've met before,' I said.

'Frankly, my dear, I don't. Tell me.'

'You were playing Peer Gynt at the Old Vic, way back in 1963. I was relief stage door keeper.'

'Well, well. Not the little girl with the pixie haircut and the big smile.'

'That was me. And I want to thank you for your kindness and courtesy. They meant a lot to me, our little chats.'

'I'm glad. It's good to see you again and I can tell you've done us proud. We have a fine cast. Thank you.' And off he went leaving me rather flushed.

In between series of *Rumpole,* I cast one-off plays and a couple of drama documentaries. One in particular brought me in contact with a very special man.

Frank Cvitanovich was already known, principally for a wonderful documentary about shire horses and a most moving piece about his brain-damaged son Bunny. Now he was to direct a dramatised version of a betting coup where a group of punters from Ireland had diddled the bookies. *Murphy's Stroke* was a fascinating real-life story. As Frank hadn't worked with actors before he could have been very insecure over the casting. But he wasn't. He assumed I knew what I was doing and if he liked the look of the actor he was happy. So was I. We'd cast the piece within a week and were really pleased to have assembled a smashing group of actors, including an unknown whose screen presence was to take him to Hollywood, Pierce Brosnan.

27

FLYING HIGH

It was summer 1978 and Terry and I had decided to visit our friends Chris and Andie in San Francisco.

Chris, a man of enormous energy and enthusiasm, was an independent documentary film maker who worked from home with Andie as his equally energetic assistant. His projects occasionally took him on location to far-off places, and such was his success, he'd been able to afford his own plane, a Piper Cherokee. He had an English PPL (Private Pilots Licence) which passed in America. He was now into training for an instrument rating, so flying was taking up most of his spare time. Andie often went with him on business trips and had begun to seriously worry what she would do if, for instance, Chris had a heart attack or other serious health problem during a flight. She didn't have a clue how to fly an aeroplane. She'd better learn. We arrived to find them both knee-deep in charts and instruction manuals. The Hayden household was taking off in a big way.

As they were busy and we had our own transport, we chose to go off exploring most days but on the first weekend Chris suggested we fly out to the Nut-Tree restaurant for breakfast. It had its own airstrip. I was entranced at the idea, Terry not so; he didn't like flying very much. However he was persuaded.

Chris invited me to sit up front with him. I waited until we had climbed high enough to level off before speaking. 'Is it difficult?' I asked him.

'Not at all, d'you want to take the controls?'

I'd hoped he might say that. 'Yes, please.'

I grasped the U-shaped handles and held the plane straight and level. As we slid smoothly through the morning skies, I experienced a unique and exhilarating sense of power.

On our return to Brighton I drove west down the coast road as soon as I quietly could. I hadn't mentioned my intention to Terry, he would've been very negative and anyway I didn't know if anything would come of the idea. I'd noticed several small aircraft parked at Shoreham airfield so I figured there might well be a flying school.

I parked outside the terminal, a beautiful Art Deco building that had once handled a lot of small passenger flights, and went into the lofty foyer. There was nobody around and no obvious signs of a flying school office but there was a buzz of conversation and peals of laughter coming from the snack bar. I went in.

A group of young men and an older woman were drinking coffee and apparently swapping hilarious stories. They looked like they belonged and might be able to help. I approached them. 'Excuse me. Could you tell me who I can talk to about learning to fly.' I blushed, it sounded rather silly.

'Look no further, me dear,' said the woman. She was brisk and jolly, smartly dressed and wore a lot of make-up. 'D'you want to start now?'

This was Jenny, flying instructress, supremely confident in manner, thoroughly down-to-earth and yet intensely feminine in the unfrilly sense of the word. She was thrilled at the idea of having a female in her thirties to train. That first flight was free and I was given the opportunity to change my mind if I hadn't enjoyed it. No way, it was great.

Since we'd bought the new house my Saturdays had been taken up with fruitless trips to builders' merchants, shopping for the week and trivia domestica. Life was all work. We weren't going to have a family after all and, with the restoration of 102 going well, I needed a new challenge; anything to help get over the biggest disappointment. Learning to fly could be it. Perhaps perversely I needed to push myself to some sort of brink. But was I really clever enough, adventurous enough, rich and brave enough to take to the air?

Well, I'd just have to do my best to absorb the endless theory that went towards gaining a licence, I was unquestionably adventurous and my contract with Thames meant I could afford the sixteen pounds an hour charged by Jenny's club, Air South. They were considerably cheaper than the other flying school that operated out of Shoreham and I rather fancied I would be getting the best possible training from the remarkable Jenny—it was a bargain. As for bravery, we would see.

'Why do you want to learn to fly? What for?'

Typical. Trust Terry to ask such a stupid question. Nonetheless, I couldn't think of a good answer. 'I fancy it, that's why.'

'You're mad. It sounds like a bloody waste of money to me.'

'I don't have any hobbies, Terry. I want to see if I can get my licence. I know you don't like going up in aeroplanes, but you don't have to come with me, do you?'

'Huh, not likely.'

'Jenny says I can go on Saturday mornings, then I can shop in the afternoon and do the salon books in the evening.'

'Got it all figured out, haven't you?'

'Of course.'

'What about 102?'

'We can work there together on Sundays. And as for the builders' merchants, it's better if you go anyway, on Mondays. I never get the right thing and I'm fed up with trying.'

'Well, I don't like the idea. But you'll go ahead whatever I think, so there's no point in arguing.'

'Thanks T. It won't get in the way of things, I promise.'

Phew, thank God that's sorted, I thought. It never entered my head that he might worry about my safety.

The following Saturday crawled slowly towards me, I could think of little else but the air. I passed a restless night but awoke refreshed. On that early June morning around nine I zoomed up the hill that would reveal at its crest a stunning view of Lancing College, the sea and the flat greenness of all grass runways. I was burning with anticipation and enthusiasm. But the view wasn't there—sea mist had wrapped it in grey denseness. The rest of the morning was spent drinking coffee and trying not to feel as downcast as the weather. My first lesson was moved forward a week. I bought the manuals, a log-book and other necessary paraphernalia. At least I would be fully equipped. The following Saturday the weather smiled and training began.

Over the next few months I had to master straight and level flight, stalls, slow flying, and glide descents. Jenny's patience was admirable, but I suspect she was glad of a break from the endless trail of adolescent males she normally had to control. They were usually full of bravado, not desirable when newly in control of a flying machine, whereas I was more likely to be precise, cautious and understanding of the concept of danger.

Spiral diving, akin to spinning, was a terrifying experience the first time. My instructor that day was Alex, a young man who, like me, was in his early thirties. He took the controls and told me to hang on. He pulled us back into a stall and dropped the wing. All effect of controls was lost and we twisted round into a spiral dive. I lost my centre of gravity and immediately felt sick; the ground spinning ever larger and larger towards us was too frightening to behold. Desperately I reached across to bury my face in Alex's shoulder. I felt him pull back on the controls and apply full opposite rudder. We swooped out of the dive and back to straight and level. I emerged red-faced. I knew who'd be the joke of the evening.

'Your turn?' He smiled at me. I shook my head firmly but, knowing I had to rescue my reputation, suggested maybe I'd be alright if I followed through on the controls. 'Okay, go for it,' he said.

Miraculously I'd been right—it was a bit like getting back on the horse after a fall—this time I didn't have to shut my eyes and found the experience almost exhilarating. After a couple of follow-throughs I took complete control and, despite the surprising amount of strength needed, managed to pull us out. Alex congratulated me and, with a certain amount of honour restored, I headed us back to Shoreham.

28

AN IRISH STRIPPER

After six months on the bridging loan, we sold our house in Westbourne Street for the asking price. We'd finished the kitchen and first floor bathroom at 102, but there was still a long way to go. We would have to live in the chaos of renovation for a good while to come. I said I didn't mind, after all I was flying high.

Terry, who was obsessive about getting the best deal, was happy to take on a very economical worker to help strip the wood panelling of its coats of many colours.

Paddy, who'd been recommended by a painter-decorator friend, was a case. He was a hard worker: thorough, fussy and certainly very cheap, but he had a problem of course. Paddy, a redheaded, red-faced Irishman with several missing teeth, was an alcoholic of no fixed abode. He slept wherever he found himself and carried his possessions in a plastic bag that doubled as a pillow. Not surprisingly his lifestyle meant he smelt horrific. One morning he was particularly unsavoury.

'Paddy. D'you ever get the chance to take a bath?' I asked.

'Well indeed, I'll be stinking, I suppose. I can't remember the last time, to be honest with you.'

'Would you like to have one now, here?'

'Well, that'll be very kind of you. But I have no towel, nor no soap.'

'I think I can provide those. And if you want to put your clothes in the machine, I'll wash them for you. I can find you some other stuff to wear.'

Paddy's leathery face crinkled even more. In fact, I thought he was going to burst into tears.

'Go on then, use the top bathroom. There's a towel in there. I'll sort you out some gear and then when you're done we'll have a cuppa. Okay?'

'Thank you, thank you. Very kind you are.'

After that he was happy to take a bath or shower whenever I insisted, which was often. What he saved us in wages he probably cost us in soap and water.

Naturally Paddy had a tale to tell and of course it was tragic. One of a large brood of Catholic children, he'd come over from Ireland in his twenties, apprenticed as a carpenter and done well for himself. The grubby photos he carried around showed him as smart and attractive when he married and later as the proud father of a couple of children. But he simply couldn't resist a drink and often became violent. His wife finally threw him out, penniless. Since then he'd lived in doss houses, boxes, people's sheds and other hell-holes. At weekends I'd work alongside him whilst he recalled better days and his slide down into destitution with an almost detached wry humour as if he were talking about someone else. I liked him immensely and felt really rather motherly towards him. He was a wreck but he carried on. I fed him and, at his request, we held back all but a few pounds of his wages. 'Well, I'll be drinking it all away at once. So it'd be better. I'll only be needing me baccy and papers.'

'Whatever you say, Paddy.'

Terry was quite happy about the arrangement, it meant that Paddy would turn up for work and keep away from the pubs, mostly. Sadly, the need to go on a binge would build up and then he would beg for enough to drink himself senseless for a few days. We learnt pretty quickly not to argue and resigned ourselves.

Paddy was with us for several months, during which he revealed the wood panelling and skirting in all its glory. With a coat or two of satin varnish, it looked magnificent. Sadly, because of a misunderstanding, he left us. The work was nearly completed and he'd agreed to help with the decorating next, but it was not to be. During a discussion about women's rights, Terry called him a chauvinist and Paddy, not wishing to admit he didn't know what the word meant, decided to interpret it as a huge insult and stormed out of our lives. We never saw him and his plastic bag again even though I trudged round Preston Park on several summer's evenings inspecting the occupants of the benches.

For my thirty-seventh birthday, Terry and I spent the day down at Yateley with Mother and Daddy. The weather was perfect, which was just as well, they were in the midst of packing. The Triangle had been sold and they'd found South Cottage, a small converted coach house in Midhurst. There they were planning to end their days. Daddy had retired and now had a consultancy contract with a small engineering company.

We left early the following morning, but not as early as Daddy. I'd seen his Rover 2000 disappearing through the gate in painful slow motion as I made our cups of tea. 'T, I know you'll say I'm being neurotic, but I think Daddy's driving must be getting slower and slower,' I said as we drove out of the lane and up the hill to the A30.

'What d'you mean?'

'Well, he always was ultra-cautious, but he said it took him over an hour to get to Reading the other day. When I asked whether there'd been lots of traffic, he said no more than normal. He can't have got out of third gear.'

'He probably forgot to say there were road-works or something.'

'Yes, maybe. But nonetheless I have this feeling he's going to have a prang. Or at least cause one.'

'For fuck's sake, now you really are being neurotic.'

'It's not neurosis, I comes from my gut. It's as if I know,' I insisted.

'Don't be ridiculous. Start thinking like that and you'll drive yourself potty.'

'Sorry, Terry, but you just don't understand, do you? I pray I'm wrong, that's all.'

'All right, all right, forget it. Over, done, finished.' And with that he put his foot down and I shut up.

That night Mother rang to say Daddy had crashed the Rover and been taken into Frimley hospital. He'd swerved to avoid an overtaking car on the other side of the road and driven into a tree. Nothing was broken, but the pedals had been pushed upwards and jarred his whole body. He was still in shock but would be coming home the next day provided nothing sinister showed up in the routine tests.

I was in shock too, and so was Terry, although he tried his best not to show it. He certainly wasn't prepared to concede I'd been right. Premonitions are scary, there's such a fine line between a gut feeling and a genuine worry.

Within a week Daddy appeared to be back to normal, it seemed the only remaining symptom was anger. But the accident had taken more out of him than we'd realised; over the next year his general health deteriorated.

29

PUT TO THE TEST

The salon was booming and Terry was thinking of looking for other premises, this time with a shop front. 'I'm sure we could do even better if the salon was visible from the road,' he told me.

'Yes, possibly. You could be right.' I tried to be supportive but was mostly distracted by work and flying.

'If I can find the right place and then maybe a corner in a department store, well, we could expand. You could run that part of the business, couldn't you?'

'Terry, have you gone bonkers? Hairdressing! It's the last thing I want to do. Why the hell would I want to give up a successful career? I'd be hopeless as an ever-smiling manageress pandering to the clients. Yuck!'

'Your trouble is you only think of yourself. You're no support at all.'

'Charming! Who does the books? Who steps in as shampooist if one of the juniors is off sick? Who helps clear up the salon on Saturday evenings?'

'When you're not at that fucking airport.'

'That's unfair. How often am I there on Saturday afternoons? Virtually never.'

Not able to argue with that one, he slunk off.

Sadly, our rows were becoming more and more frequent. But at least I could escape. Flying took me up and away from our arguments; their importance diminishing the higher I flew.

Training was advancing well and the time had come to tackle the circuit, a roughly rectangular flight pattern for take-offs and landings a thousand feet over the runway. These were known as Touch-and-Go's. I would need ten hours practice before being ready to go solo. Round and round we went, Saturday in and Saturday out. After eight or nine hours my confidence had grown, and almost eliminated the butterflies in my stomach. You see, I knew Jenny would soon be aborting a Touch-and-Go, jumping out and telling me to go it alone.

My first solo was in September, three and a half months or nineteen hours flying time from my first lesson. Jenny said nothing until we'd touched down. 'Right, brake and pull over.' I did and she got out. 'You're on your own matey.' She waved and walked away without a backward glance.

'Oh my God, she's right, I muttered to myself and, with a deep breath, called the tower and asked for permission to take off again.

Somewhere around the edge of my concentration, I heard the triumphant and probably misogynistic note in Whiskers' voice—Whiskers being the controller in the tower and the image of James Robertson Justice. I knew not only his, but many other eyes were on me. I reined my thoughts in tight and off I went, down the runway gathering enough speed to pull back on the controls and take off. On the climb-out I kept checking the instruments and talking myself through the procedure. Balance and angle of ascent were all important. At a thousand feet I turned neatly downwind and headed towards the crosswind leg with ever-increasing awareness that I was, for the first time in my life, in very real danger. I couldn't just pull into a lay-by for a few minutes of nerve restoration. I had to get this right or end up on the ground in a heap of metal.

On final approach, the grass grew greener and greener as I descended, but I quickly realised I'd misjudged my approach, and would be landing too far down the runway. Oh shit! I'd made a balls-up, I'd have to go round again. I wasn't landing and bugger what anyone thought. Even Jenny, who'd been pleased with my progress. Now I was letting her down. Asking for clearance to abort, I deliberately didn't hear Whisker's tone. The circuit went well. This time my approach was just right so I landed and taxied from the runway ready to face Jenny's disappointment. I told myself I'd done right and didn't care what the reactions might be. I went through the post-flight procedures and walked towards the terminal with my head held high. Then I saw the crowd of faces at the window and … they were all smiling. As I came into the snack bar a cheer went up.

'Bravo, well done, I'm proud of you.' Jenny gave me a hug.

I wondered if everyone got this treatment. 'I'm sorry I had to go round again.'

Jenny waved her arms about. 'No, no, you were brilliant. I haven't seen such a splendid first solo in ages. You showed your competence and judgement and even Whiskers was impressed.'

That seemed the greatest accolade. We all had a drink to celebrate and I went home in euphoria. Typically, Terry couldn't share my delight. He blanched at the whole idea and wittered on about somebody he'd had an argument with at the salon. In a fit of pique I went off to concentrate on getting the dinner. In the kitchen I could dwell on my deflation in private. After eating, Terry made straight for the television so I went to bed.

The next morning he told me one of his staff was pregnant and a junior had left in a huff. I felt rotten and selfish. I'd been too wrapped up in my own glory to take any notice of what he'd been trying to tell me.

Flying instruction continued through instrument approach, cross-country, steep turns, forced and crosswind landings.

After the dual-control cross-country with away landings, I was ready to go it alone. Rain eased up obligingly but not early enough to prevent me getting stuck in the mud at Thruxton airport. But I extricated myself unaided and set off back towards Goodwood with a sense of relief and pride. Then, after changing radio frequency, I found I was off course; I'd strayed into military airspace north of Southampton. A tired 'Oh God, not a woman' voice told me to descend to a couple of thousand feet and, though not in so many words, to get the hell out of it. I was terrified. Not until Goodwood came in sight did I feel safe again.

Map reading, more than just the basics of radio telephony, navigation and meteorology, air law and the literal nuts and bolts of airframes and engines had to be learned and understood for the exams which were all part of gaining a licence. It was a slog but I was ready with the necessary passes when GFT (General Flying Test) day arrived. It was February 1981 and fifty-nine and a half hours flying time from my first lesson. Not amazing, but not bad.

I was extremely nervous. Jenny's husband, John, a commercial pilots instructor at Gatwick, was the examiner. Luckily I'd met him before and liked him (this, of course, would have nothing to do with his judgement of my ability). I decided I'd better calm down. If I failed I was meant to, if I passed I'd still have massive amounts to learn before feeling totally at ease at the controls, so it was all the same. Getting my licence was simply a stepping-stone along the way.

I passed. I'd done it. I was qualified, at least on paper, to take passengers. I could offer joyrides to friends and potter about the sky simply for the pleasure of it. Up there I'd be gloriously out of reach. No phones, no nagging, no bustling humanity. I could soar in my element and gain from the new perspectives of the earth beneath.

Despite being qualified to take passengers I was amazed and happy that several friends had enough confidence in me and the craft I flew to want to come up and share the experience. Most particularly, Jane and Neil entrusted their daughters, Selena and Melanie, eleven and eight respectively, to my captaincy. Wow, that was a huge responsibility. So too was the flight with friend, Lynda Bellingham. The insurance would have soared had I mentioned I was taking her up. Her Italian husband, Nunzio, refused my offer to come with us. I didn't ask why, I knew better than to challenge his bravery. As for Terry, he maintained a determined distance from my dangerous hobby and I doubted his attitude would ever change. So I was astonished at his suggestion when, one Sunday afternoon, Mother invited us to tea in Midhurst. 'You could fly us there, it'd be quicker, wouldn't it?'

'Sure. But we'd need to get them to pick us … ' I said automatically. Then my mouth dropped open. 'Did you really mean that?'

'Well, might as well get it over with.'

Daddy was away on business and Aunt Tillie was keeping Mother company. I rang to ask if they could pick us up from Goodwood airfield.

'Of course, dear. But, for heaven's sake, be careful. I don't like to think of you floating around up there.'

'Mother please, don't worry. It's only a twenty minute flight.'

As I didn't want Terry to change his mind, I drove us to Shoreham as fast as I dared and literally ran into the snack bar to ask Jenny if there was a plane free? Yes, there was. Could I land at Goodwood that afternoon? Yes, I could. So we went out onto the field and I ran through the checks without catching Terry's eye once. I knew if I did and he was looking frightened, consideration would force me to forget flying and drive us all the way.

We got into the plane. I strapped us in and started the engine. More checks before taxiing to the runway. Bumping over the grass rattles the bones and I could sense that wasn't all that was rattling in Terry's case. Then the engine started missing. It coughed and it spluttered most alarmingly.

'Oh no!' I called the tower and told them I was aborting the flight. 'Looks like Fru-Fru's (G-FRU) available. Er, I always preferred her anyway,' I said to Terry, managing somehow to sound confident.

Through all of this, Terry hadn't spoken. Fear must have got his tongue.

Fru-Fru was indeed free, so, after going through the check procedures on her, we taxied without coughing to the runway and took off. On the gentle climbing turn, Terry found his voice. 'Oh God, do we have to lean over like this?' He clung on. His knuckles were as white as his face.

'It's okay, we'll be round in a moment then it's straight and level to Goodwood.'

A bit of his colour returned.

As we neared Goodwood airport I noticed heavy traffic and hordes of Sunday motor-racing freaks at the nearby track, where cars were speeding round and round with regular monotony. I wondered if the drivers would get the same kick out of pottering around the sky in a flying lawnmower. My thoughts came back to concentrate on our approach as we had to bank again to come round to land into wind. I warned Terry. He shut his eyes. We came down gently enough and he let out a huge whoosh of breath, as if he'd been holding it all the way. I was proud of him. I knew he'd done it for me and how much courage he'd needed to summon.

Mother and Aunt Tillie were considerably delayed by the activity around the racetrack and we'd almost begun to wonder if they'd forgotten. I rang South Cottage. No reply. They must be on their way.

They finally managed to get into the terminal forecourt, ruffled but jolly enough. We were all dying for a cuppa by this time. Terry and I got in the back of Aunt Tillie's Renault 4. She started the engine and slam-crashed the gears into reverse. With a huge amount of over revving and huffing and puffing as she turned the wheel, she manoeuvred out of the parking space narrowly missing the car alongside. Once out we were jolted into first gear and promptly stalled.

'Whoops,' she cried gaily and started us up again.

Luckily the way out didn't involve going by the racetrack. We were very grateful. By the time we reached South Cottage, Terry and I were clinging onto each other's hands. Auntie in charge of a car was terrifying. We felt lucky to have arrived intact. The cuppa was a lifesaver.

'That was even worse than the flying bit,' Terry whispered.

'And there's the return drive,' I reminded him.

After a very pleasant tea and lots of giggles we were ready for the trip back. By then Auntie, full of Mother's sponge cake, was a lot steadier, or was it that our expectation of hell-on-wheels had increased during our visit?

The flight back was fine too. The wind was against us and Shoreham was in that direction, so it was straight out and straight in. After landing I gave Terry a hug and thanked him.

'First and last,' he said. 'Not my cup of tea.'

30

OVER AND OUT

One morning in June the phone rang very early. It was Mother. She was calling from the Isle of Man where she and Daddy were holidaying with friends. 'Darling, it's Mother. Daddy's in hospital. He's had a mild heart attack, but he's okay. We're coming home as soon as he's up to it.'

My Daddy? He didn't seem the sort of person to have a heart attack, mild or otherwise. 'Why? Did they say why? What was wrong or anything?'

'No, dear. But he's seventy-five now. He's not a young man any more. But I can't stop now, there's someone waiting to use this phone.'

Sod them, they can wait, I thought. 'Mother, for goodness sake.'

'Must go, dear, must go.'

'Alright, but give him a big kiss from me and ring as soon as you get back. Promise?'

'Of course I will. And you're not to worry. Bye.'

That was rich coming from her. There was no way I wouldn't worry. The idea was inconceivable. My Daddy was immortal.

'Your Dad's not been himself since that accident,' Terry reminded me later.

Not long after the attack, Daddy was allowed home to Midhurst. I drove over as soon as I could. It was a shock; he looked really old. 'How are you feeling?' I asked him.

'Like I've had a heart attack,' he said testily. 'Time to go, as far as I'm concerned.'

'John, please, do stop talking like that,' Mother pleaded.

'Well, look at me, shaking like a dratted leaf, my writing looks like a drunken spider.'

'They said at the hospital that your father's got Parkinson's, the early stages that is.'

'Hmph! On top of stomach trouble and shingles. A bloody wreck I am. Life's not worth living in this state.'

Mother was close to tears. 'I'll make us all a nice cup of tea,' she sniffed and fled to the kitchen.

I decided to tackle Daddy head on. 'So what do we do with you when you've gone? Cremation or burial?'

'Chuck me on the rubbish dump,' he said.

'Seriously, Daddy.'

'Cremation, I suppose.'

And that was the end of it. Mother came back with the tea-tray and we small-talked for the rest of the afternoon. Daddy drank several cups and brooded.

Over the washing up Mother told me. 'Your father's a member of the Euthanasia Society,' she said flatly.

'God, how morbid. Er … you don't think he's planning anything, do you?'

'Of course not, dear.'

'Well, I wouldn't put it past him. He's so damned practical.'

'Susan, I will not have you talking like that about your father. Now do you mind if we drop the subject.'

'You started it, Mother.'

'Enough, no more!' She wrenched off her rubber gloves and marched out.

Instantly I realised how horribly insensitive I'd been, but I knew that if I ran after her to give her a hug and said I was sorry, she'd burst into tears, then so would I and Daddy would want to know why and things would go from bad to worse. So I finished the wiping up, said I had to get home and left.

That autumn Daddy died. A pulmonary embolism took him from us. Our phone had been out of order over the weekend and it wasn't until I arrived at work on the Monday morning that the news reached me. Immediately I drove back home, picked up a few clothes and hurried over to Midhurst. Dossy was already there. She'd caught the first available plane to be with us. Both she and Mother were in helpless shock and there was the funeral to arrange. In a way I was grateful to take over the organising and allowed myself to believe Daddy was there with us, directing the proceedings. I could hear his voice. Particularly when Mother declared she wanted him buried. 'Chuck me on the rubbish dump.'

'Don't be ridiculous, Daddy,' I replied out loud

Neither of them noticed; Dossy was wailing into a sodden hanky while Mother was wallowing in morbidity. 'I'm going to be buried with him so I can't have him being … burned,' she declared.

'Mother, he said he wanted to be cremated, surely we must respect that,' I insisted.

'No, no, no!'

From then on I stopped trying to reason with her. Then Dossy announced she wanted to see Daddy one last time.

'For God's sake, girl, what on earth for?' His voice echoed in my head as I tried to dissuade her. 'Dossy, I'm sure he'd want you to remember him fit and well.'

'Sue, don't tell me what I should and shouldn't do. It's my right. And I'm going.'

'In that case I will too,' I said. I couldn't let her go alone.

So it was arranged and we walked down to Eddie Lintott's funeral parlour hand-in-hand. In truth I was terrified at the prospect. It would be the first time I'd seen a dead body and I wasn't ready for it, wasn't ready to confront the dreadful reality that my father no longer existed. Such an idea was inconceivable. He would always be with us even if we couldn't see him.

There he was, still as still in his coffin. Like he was set in stone. I held back as Dossy collapsed onto his chest in tears. From the eerie pallor of his face it was hard to believe there'd ever been life inside. I just couldn't relate this replica to the Daddy I'd known all my life.

After that I carried on with the miserable ritual arrangements in a state of emotional suspension. However I was determined Daddy's service should somehow, if only momentarily, transcend conformity. It wasn't easy but I finally managed to persuade Mother's brother, Uncle Donald, who was suspicious of anything he suspected to be either unconventional, or even worse, unchristian, to read a passage from Kahlil Gibran's *The Prophet*.

For what is it to die but to stand naked in the wind and melt into the sun
And what is it to cease breathing but to free the breath from its restless tides, that it may rise and expand to seek God unencumbered?

Only when you drink from the river of silence shall you

indeed sing.
And when you have reached the mountain top, then
you shall begin to climb.
And when the earth shall claim your limbs, then shall
you truly dance.

To me, words far more beautiful and uplifting than the ' … ashes to ashes, dust to dust …' of the Anglican burial service. But then my faith is my own.

After the funeral Terry took me home. I was totally drained. Every fibre of my body taut, every emotion strait-jacketed. I sat gazing out at the passing countryside like a zombie. That night, as my head hit the pillow I finally gave in. As Terry put his arms round me the dam broke. All my regrets for the past and the future crowded in on me, even though it seemed pointless thinking about what might have been because I had to admit that the physical being who had been my Daddy had irrevocably, irretrievably gone, forever.

31

CHEATED

Soon after the funeral and in a complete daze, Mother flew off to America with Dossy. I felt so alone in my grief; Daddy was permanently in my thoughts. Mother had asked me to pop over to Midhurst to water her plants whilst she was away. I knew the house would seem horribly empty.

I did the watering and put the kettle on. Then I saw them. There on the dining room table. Three spiral bound notebooks. I knew at once they were Daddy's diaries. I made myself a cup of tea and settled down to read.

I remembered the first entry from way back—January 17th 1939, bought engagement ring for Joyce. I read on—September 3rd 1939, war declared. September 14th 1940, wedding day, what a day! They'd told me about that.

Daddy had arrived late, on his bike, there being some trouble with public transport. The marriage had been at St. Botolph's in Aldgate, which was considered to be the family church, Jenkins that is—Mother's side. Grandpa had been born next door to the royal mint and was very much a man of the city. There were a couple of photos of the event in the album; Mother had worn a blue crepe ensemble, a feathered hat at a rakish angle and the most hideous high-heels you can imagine. I knew the ensemble was blue because she'd shown it to me.

On July 18th 1940, strange names started to appear—Tetrarch, Valentine, D.D., Bren. These mysterious objects were transported, floated and sometimes sank at places such as Brent Reservoir, the Welsh Harp, R.M.F.U., Sandy Point. I deduced it must have been something to do with the war effort, but what, I had no idea. When, as a child, I'd asked why Daddy hadn't been a soldier, Mother had said he'd been involved in very important but secret work and that she was sure he'd tell me one day, but I wasn't to ask. And I never did. Now, reading these enigmatic entries, I tried to figure out what he'd been doing.

November 18th 1942, first shoot at Val D.D. December 30th, five Brens at Welsh Harp. February 19th 1943, eight-day struggle with dud prop unit. March 14th, launches from LCT, ramp angle decided. June 23rd, Sherman first floated. Then—on September 29th— tank loading test at Portsmouth. I shot out of the chair. This had to be it—my Daddy had been working on amphibious tanks, getting them ready for the D-Day landings.

At the end of 1943, the V.I.P's started making appearances, and on December 18th, Daddy was vaccinated to go to America to demonstrate the capabilities of these extraordinary craft. He set sail on the Queen Mary on January 3rd, arriving in New York on the 9th. His travels took him on to Akron, Fort Storey, Washington (to meet Generals Barnes and Gatehouse), to Cleveland, Chicago, and Minneapolis, by road, rail and air. He returned to the UK on February 28th. Just over three months to D-Day.

The last days of May and the first days of June were spent rushing round the departure ports and completing final checks on the craft. June 6th 1944 read, quite simply—D-Day.

Then June 13th—Joyce getting restless. June 14th—Susan Mary born. It seemed an appropriate place to stop.

That night Terry and I tried to figure out why Daddy had never told me, why it had been a big secret even after the war. I remembered Mother saying he wouldn't want to talk about it and that's often how it was with war work. 'People didn't like to be reminded.'

'Well, if you want to find out you'll have to admit you read the diaries,' said Terry.

'And why shouldn't I? Daddy's gone, his diaries are surely a legacy for his children as well as his wife. No, I don't think I did anything wrong and I'm going to find out what happened when Mother gets back.'

Suddenly I felt dreadful. Dossy and I had agreed that a short holiday in America would be the best thing for Mother but, in retrospect, I was sure she'd be lost and miserable away from her home and I should never have let her go.

When, three weeks later, I picked her up from Gatwick, she seemed calmer and more together, but there was a flatness I hadn't known before. It wouldn't have been kind to broach the subject of Daddy's wartime activities immediately so I waited until she'd settled back at Midhurst and we'd sorted out his stuff and rearranged the house. 'Mother, I have a confession to make; I started reading Daddy's diaries. I'm sorry if you think I had no business to, but it somehow brought him closer,' I said.

'No, dear, I don't mind. I understand. He kept track of everything for all those years. You know how methodical he was.'

'So now will you please tell me what he was doing during the war and why he would never talk about it.'

'Let me make a cup of tea first,' she said in a croaky voice and shot off to the kitchen.

This is bound to be difficult for her, I thought. Was I premature in asking her to dig up such memories? Fortunately, when she reappeared she seemed more composed and, taking a deep breath, she began.

'For three years Daddy worked for the Straussler company on the designs for the amphibious tanks which were used on D-Day. I never knew what time he'd be home, often he'd be at his drawing board all night. Then there were the tests, here and in America. They involved endless travelling. He was permanently exhausted, poor man. But we were at war and winning was all that mattered. Anyway, after D-Day he continued on tank projects and went back to America in March of '45 for more meetings and tests. He was away for nearly six months.'

'He must have missed V.E. Day.'

'Yes, and then the projects were cancelled. He carried on at Straussler's for another couple of years even after they cut his salary by 30%.'

'Why did he put up with it? Surely, with a track record like his, he could've got another job with better money.'

'Your father was a very loyal man and, in some ways, not very worldly. Here, look at the entry for May 25th, 1948.' It read: NS dispenses with my services. After that Daddy went to work for the Ministry of Defence as Principle Scientific Officer on fighting vehicles research and development.' Suddenly she became very agitated. 'Your father was cheated. His contribution to the war effort, his major contribution, was never recognised. The company took all the credit.'

'But that's unbelievable,' I spluttered.

'Well, it's what happened. And it's not the end of the story. About nine months later he received a cheque for a thousand pounds. Approximately one and a half percent of Straussler's D-Day award. And in all the publicity, his name was never mentioned once.'

'The shits. How dare they treat him like that! It's obvious from the entries who did all the work. Why didn't he say something, put the record straight?'

'Your father wasn't like that. He didn't say a word. I was so angry and hurt for him, but he told me to shut up and from that day on the subject wasn't allowed to be mentioned. But I do have a couple of photos you might like to see.'

The first was of Daddy sitting on an amphibious tank, the other was a newspaper cutting.

'He had to take Field Marshal Montgomery to see it.'

And there he was walking into the sea piggy-backing a man wearing a hat like a black pancake. It looked so comical we had to laugh.

'Your father never got over what they did to him,' Mother said, her lips quivering. 'We must pray, for his sake, that … one day the truth … will be told.' And she burst into tears. I did too and we fell into each other's arms to cry our hearts out.

In the weeks that followed, on the way to work, I managed to keep my emotions under control. It wouldn't have done to turn up at meetings looking red-eyed and puffy. Driving home was another matter. On more than one occasion I arrived at 102 in tears. Terry got fed up with it and, one evening, he told me he'd had enough. 'Sue, you've got to get a hold of yourself. You can't mourn forever,' he said.

I clutched my hanky to my nose and ran up to the spare room to get away from him. How could he be so callous? He may have had no respect for his own father but mine had been a truly remarkable man, and, as so often happens, you don't fully appreciate a person you love until they're gone.

How many times had he fixed my cars for me? Not just cars, anything electrical that went wrong. And what about all the furniture that needed making, painting or repairing? He'd done it for me and anyone else who asked, particularly the local widows. Daddy was known for his kindness, capability and willingness. Mother hadn't always been supportive. 'John, you can't fix Margaret's fridge, we're going out to dinner.' Or, 'I want to go shopping, surely Elaine's compost box can wait until tomorrow.'

Actually, she may have complained but she was also immensely proud of him and loved to bask in the light of his popularity. And she knew how lucky she'd been to have shared her life with such a remarkable man—man of ideas, projects and amazing foresight.

In 1971, after he'd retired from the Ministry of Defence and in between doing up the house, Daddy had decided to pursue an idea that had been germinating for some time.

He was not just practical, he was an eco-fanatic. Everything was recycled, nothing was wasted and he treated nature with respect. He foresaw where the modern world was heading. 'Drat it, the planet's overpopulated. There should be legislation if the human race is to survive. People can't go on breeding. At this rate by the year 2000 resources will have run out.'

'John, you're exaggerating, and anyway you can't dictate such things,' Mother argued.

'Huh, if I were in charge …'

'Well, you're not, dear.'

In the '70's pollution was becoming an issue, the public were hearing more and more about the lead our cars were chucking out into the atmosphere. Daddy could see a solution. He designed a dual-combustion engine that could recycle the exhaust emissions without losing performance and thereby improve mileage to the gallon. Mother thought it sounded wonderful until he announced he was going to build it and had his eye on not just one car, but two. 'John dear, where are you going to put them? The garage only has room for the Wolseley.'

'She can stay outside and I'll make a hard standing by the vegetable patch. Don't worry, they won't be an eyesore. Even if they were, this is important. It's a question of priorities. The earth's atmosphere or our front drive.'

That shut her up. So Daddy went ahead and bought a 1935 Triumph Gloria with a longitudinal transverse engine and a Humber Sceptre MK1 for its chassis.

Over several years he slaved in the garage and finally produced a workable model which he took to Brunel University to be tested. The results were so spectacular that they insisted on repeating them in case there'd been a mistake. There hadn't.

It was time to hawk the idea around the motor manufacturers. Daddy, being a boffin and not tuned into matters commercial, was in the process of applying for a provisional patent, which was all he could afford at the time, so was unwilling to show his blueprints to the research and development people he approached. He had the test results and needed the money to finance a modern prototype. If a company was interested, a deal in principle had to be on the table before he would divulge the details of his design. None of them wanted to know. Daddy became more and more frustrated and disillusioned. Finally he gave up, choosing to put their disinterest down to the 'Not Invented Here' syndrome.

When Daddy died, I was thirty-eight. Most people in our society are in their fifties or sixties when they lose their parents, so they have many more years together. I felt cheated as well as bereft. But I bottled my tears and by the following summer had developed a stomach ulcer.

The doctor quizzed me. 'What have you been doing? Are you under particular stress? Has something traumatic happened to you?'

'My father died.' I burst into uncontrollable tears. The doctor handed me a tissue. I finally sniffled myself back under control. 'I'm sorry. I haven't cried for ages'.

'Well, it's time you did. Organs weep for tears unshed.'

I have kept those wise words in my mind ever since.

32

FEARLESS FRANK

Verity Lambert, head of drama at Thames Television, commissioned a daring new series from writer Howard Shulman of *Rock Follies* fame. Called *The Ann Lovington Hour*, it was about a young girl living in a fantasy world. The series was to be shot in black and white for the reality sequences, and colour for the fantasies, which were quaint, outlandish and full of eccentric characters. It promised to be one of the most exciting shows I'd ever cast. But I had yet to meet the director and it was essential that we saw the piece through similar eyes.

Verity chose a relatively inexperienced man, Roger Bamford. She'd seen a BBC play he'd directed, been very impressed, and decided he had just the right touch for *Ann Lovington*. He was a solid, uncomplicated character who you instinctively knew could hold a boat steady, which was just as well as he was into sailing. We hit if off immediately and were both extremely enthusiastic about the project. We soon had ideas for the leading roles and planned to offer to Rowan Atkinson, Pamela Stephenson and Tracy Ulman, all of whom were on the brink of success. I also brought Pierce Brosnan in to meet Roger who agreed he'd be great as the boyfriend. We were buzzing and it looked as though *Ann Lovington* could create a new genre. But it was not to be because there was a regime change at the top. Verity left to set up her own company and the new head of drama didn't like the project. It was scrapped. We were bitterly disappointed. Roger was offered, as consolation, a play about delinquent youngsters, so we started interviewing London teenagers for the lead roles. *Jimmy Skin* was a raw little story but it had potential, or at least we thought so. Then it too was pulled, for reasons unknown.

'There has to be a jinx on us,' I said.

Roger and I, wondering what bad energy was in the air, had gone off to the pub to get plastered.

'Well, I find it all most strange. I suppose it's a case of the new broom,' he said miserably.

'Just when we were getting a good cast together. It makes you lose heart, doesn't it? Still, we were a good team, while we lasted, weren't we?' I said.

'Yes, and I expect we will be again.'

'Sooner rather than later, hopefully.'

Roger and I had become friends. He was an untypical television director who possessed a calmness I found both refreshing and reassuring. A man of strong opinions who didn't come on strong, Roger said little, but what he did say, he meant. We'd already developed a great rapport and working with him had been fun. The fact that it had all been for nothing was particularly galling. I decided that, if I had any say in the matter, we would work together again. One day.

My next few projects did come to fruition. One was a new series of stories about an inept reporter—*Bognor,* a comedy half-hour with a cast of unconventional characters in far-fetched situations. It was to be recorded without an audience—a daring idea really. The producer, Bernard Krichefski, was all energy, fun and enthusiasm, and being newly drafted in from radio, had a good knowledge of actors. We were on the same wavelength and got on well, so *Bognor* was a pleasure to work on.

I was also busy on a series of Agatha Christie stories. The scripts were superb, the quality actors we approached were keen to be involved and there were some very interesting newcomers around—three in particular were being introduced to all the casting directors and it was obvious they were going places.

I met Gabriel Byrne over lunch with his agent, Caroline, and was bowled over. Those eyes! And the Irish lilt. I could feel my knees shaking under the table, which was really unusual because, having met loads of good-looking actors, I'd become a bit blasé.

Then Daniel Day Lewis came to see me for a general interview. He was charming, a little shy and with that certain impenetrable mystery. An actor whose versatility was soon to be demonstrated in *My Beautiful Launderette* and *My Left Foot*.

I was able to cast one of these exciting new faces, Rupert Everett, in the role of a wayward 'young thing' in a '20's episode of *The Agatha Christie Hour*. He had all the makings of a star: good looks, a zany personality and screen presence.

So life at Thames Television perked up again. The new head of drama was a director I'd worked with in Yorkshire Television days. John Frankau knew what he wanted, who he liked and respected and said so. He gave me the pick of the programmes. My popularity with John bred unpopularity with the rest of the casting department. It was most unpleasant to catch the shifty looks or to stop a conversation just by coming into a room. Their attitude was getting to me and I was ready for a holiday. Terry and I booked a flight to the States to see Dossy and Jerzy.

When we arrived, they announced they'd organised a treat for me. They had a flying chum called Frank who instructed from time to time. He'd agreed to take me through a safety course. It was a sensible idea and Dossy mysteriously assured me I'd be in for some fun.

I met Frank at the local airfield. I was expecting an ordinary sort of chap, not a chunky type who looked as though he'd been drawn in Pentel by a four-year-old. He had a gleaming shaved head and a mesmerising mouthful of capped teeth and gold fillings which caught the light when he smiled. He was wearing hob-nailed boots, army trousers and a very tight short-sleeved shirt from which emerged various crops of black hair. He grabbed my hand and shook it vigorously. 'Hi Sue, it's real good to meet ya. Right, let's get to it.'

I followed him over to the other side of the field. The runways were tarmac, nice and flat with no potholes. I was used to the unevenness of grass. This'll feel quite different, I thought, there'll be no bones rattling.

The Cessna Frank had chosen looked okay, until we got close up. It was extremely uncared for: chipping paint, rusty bits and a bird's nest in the tail plane. Crikey. I wondered if it would get off the ground.

We finished the outside checks and climbed in. She refused to start. Frank jumped out, lifted the cowling and fiddled around underneath. He emerged some minutes later with black oil on his face, hands and shirt. He closed the cowling, wiped his hands on his trousers and got back in. 'Sure as heck she's gonna go now.' He sounded pretty confident.

He was right. The old crate spluttered into life. The tick-over was choppy but she didn't cut out. We did the

266

instrument and engine checks then I took control and, following instructions, taxied to the runway.

We'd hardly lifted off the ground when Frank reached over to nudge me into the climbing turn. I nudged us back. 'We need more airspeed,' I insisted.

'Don't worry about that,' he said. 'Go on, bring her round.'

He's the instructor, I thought, and this is a safety course. If I was being tested at least I'd objected, which had to count in my favour.

We climbed to about three thousand feet and levelled off, heading North East to float over the lush wooded countryside which once had been inhabited by Mohawk Indians. The names of places were romantic and evocative: Ticondaroga, Niskaioona, Sacandaya. There was history laid out below me, a bird, soaring over time.

Frank's instruction technique was unconventional and full of naïve bravado. He was full of letch too; my thigh became red from the frequent slappings. He tested me on stalling and spinning, steep climbing turns and glide descents. I followed through each manoeuvre exactly as I'd been taught. When he asked me to go too near cloud, descend too low over houses or go into a spin at barely two thousand feet over the local shopping mall, I'd object and he'd say, 'You're in control.'

I suspected the big test was yet to come, but couldn't imagine what it might be until he told me to head south and keep going. The instruction so far had been to the north and east of the airport. And there, ahead of us, was the reason. Stretching away into the distance was Albany International Airport. It looked huge and terrifying.

'Time to call 'em up, I guess,' said Frank. 'I could do with a coke.'

He wanted me to land the tiny Cessna down there among the passenger aircraft. I was glad at least the air was empty—as far as I could see.

Cleared for landing, I started on the descent and headed towards finals. Knuckles white and breath held. The ground rose up to meet us and I realised it was going to be easy. The runway had a centre line and lights and almost disappeared over the horizon. It felt like second nature as we came closer and closer to touch down. Jenny's words rang in my head, as they always did, 'Indian elephant height. Time to flare.' Actually I'd always meant to ask her if she'd ever ridden one.

We were down. It was smooth and I felt quite chuffed with myself. Frank flashed all his teeth at me as we taxied towards the small flying club where we could leave the plane to go and check in. After I'd had my temporary licence stamped I went off to find the 'powder room'. I was rather hot and keen to remove some clothing.

I'd been wearing a light cotton flying suit, zipped up the front, under the armpits and over the shoulders and round mid-thigh. It was comfortable and practical, but at that moment, too hot. I unzipped and removed the arms and then the legs. The cold zips were like icy needles on my hot skin. I stuffed the unwanted bits in my bag and went to join Frank in the coffee bar. Well, he was dumbstuck, you'd have thought I'd done a striptease. His lascivious stare brought out goosebumps of embarrassment. I was glad to sit down and hide my legs under the table.

When we walked back to the plane half an hour or so later, I was feeling more relaxed and ready. Take off ought to be a doddle. But … I hadn't reckoned on becoming a very inadequate sandwich filling. A jumbo in front and a jumbo behind and too close to be ignored. When the first one took off I thought we'd be blown back to Schenectady by the force of the slipstream. Then it was our turn. I applied full power, unsure we'd make any headway at all. Luckily the Jumbo lost no time in his climb out and we steadied up pretty quickly. Now I had to get on with it, the other Jumbo was right behind and likely his style was somewhat cramped by having such small fry take off before him.

We climbed out and, this time, I banked early, I had to get out of the way of that roaring monster. The noise of the engines behind was deafening, the jitters returned. But up and up and round we went to set a course for Schenectady and as the jumbo was going South that awful roar receded quickly enough.

'Phew!' I let out a long-held breath.

'Good gal.' Frank slapped my knee for the nth time. 'You done okay, for the first day.'

By the end of the three-day course, I'd figured out that Frank hadn't been winding me up for a giggle—his cavalier suggestions had been deliberate; intended to test how safe a pilot I was. It was a huge boost to my flying confidence when he marked up my log book and handed me a certificate to say I was safe. I gave him a big bottle of Jim Beam as a thank-you.

'Gee, thanks. Wish all my students were like you,' he said fruitily grabbing me in a gorilla hug.

'You just get your mits off my sister,' said Dossy fiercely. She told me later Frank had a reputation for groping the ladies.

'I had noticed. But not to worry, I survived. And the course was brilliant experience.'

'I know,' said Jerzy. 'I did it last year.'

That summer he hadn't been flying quite so often—he'd acquired a new toy; a personal computer. It was the first time I'd seen one in operation and I was fascinated. It could do all sorts of extraordinary things and summon up information in a trice. The storage potential with instant cross-referencing capabilities gave me a great idea. I couldn't wait to get home to test it out.

15th September 1975
Wedding day (with Jane)

Pre-flight with Lynda Bellingham
and Nunzio

Christmas party with Em,
Kathleen and Steve

Posing with Fearless Frank

33

RISKY BUSINESS

My brainchild was soon taking shape. I'd found two partners; an agent, Hugh, who wanted to try something different and an entrepreneurial friend of his, Marilyn.

The Role Call Company Ltd. was designed to help directors and casting directors looking for actors with special skills or physical characteristics. When faced with casting briefs such as—very tall, black, able to play the banjo and sing, or Italian, mid-thirties, a whizz at tennis and a good dancer, one's heart sank. It meant a trawl round all the agents, many of whom would send people in for interview who weren't right 'just in case'. Role Call would do the trawl for them. Actors' details would be recorded on computer and lists of appropriate names could be accessed immediately.

At Thames my unpopularity in the casting department had increased. My ever-loyal secretary, Vicky, told me tongues were wagging. 'They think you suck up to John Frankau to get all the best programmes,' she said.

'That's ridiculous, I knew him from Yorkshire Television days, that's all. He doesn't suffer fools and says so. Some people find him scary. I don't, I rather like him. And if that gets up their noses, then tough.'

'And … well, they think you're having an affair.'

I couldn't help giggling. 'Who with for goodness sake? Not John surely.'

'Hugh, of course. They've seen him arriving and the two of you going off together.'

'Christ, they are pathetic. What they don't know …'

' … they make up,' we said in unison.

Initially I found the idea hilarious, but then it pissed me off. I couldn't wait to get out of the place.

So not long after, I slipped quietly away from Thames. No fuss, no bother, no hypocritical leaving party.

Marilyn, Hugh and I drew up our business plan and got a bank loan to buy the necessary equipment. We rented an office in Finchley Road and persuaded Equity, the Actors' Union, to send out our application forms with their next newsletter. They agreed. The forms started coming back and soon we were up and running, with a skeleton list at first, but with more names every day.

At the same time as manning the office, alongside Hugh and Marilyn, my freelance casting was going well. A drama documentary was followed by a Sherlock Holmes movie and a series about Northern Ireland. Not only that, I was working again with Frank Cvitanovich on a film about the Kray Brothers. Whilst the Irish series and Sherlock Holmes were relatively straightforward, researching lookalikes for Frank was taking up much of my time. I needed an assistant. Hugh persuaded his cousin, Tricia, who'd been doing agency work, to join us at Finchley Road.

Like a snowball, the projects increased. I was introduced to Mike Leigh and his unique style of film-making. He would start with the kernel of a theme to be followed by a preparation period during which the chosen actors would immerse themselves in the lifestyle of the characters they were going to portray. They would live those lives for some weeks before everyone would gather to pull their experiences into the storyline and start rehearsal. To accommodate this unusual schedule and a very low budget, contracts had to be devised and agents persuaded. It presented a new challenge from which I learned contracts can say pretty much anything, as long as both parties agree. Over the years I worked on three of Mike's films; *Meantime, High Hopes* and *Life is Sweet*. They were all extraordinary.

My job was certainly diverse. You never knew what project would come along next. Like the light-hearted piece I was offered by a director I hadn't seen since MGM days. Fine and fun, I thought, but had yet to meet the producer, Harry Alan Towers, who, I soon realised, operated outside all the rules and regs of decent film making. He was the archetypal dirty old producer. His films were bawdy period romps with inserted scenes using strippers and sex performers as body-doubles for the main cast. Young actresses in the running for a part had to be warned to turn down his offers to dine. Being fairly elderly, he probably wasn't capable of sex Olympics himself, but letching and groping would certainly be on the menu.

Harry did his own contracting, I'm glad to say. He never had enough money, although I imagine his colourful renditions of such classics as *Fanny Hill* and *The Amorous Adventures of Moll Flanders* probably bought in a good few bob. So it fell to me to set up casting sessions and to tell agents and actors what to expect. After that they were on their own. For all this I couldn't help sort of liking Harry, or Hat, as I came to call him, and I cast for him whenever I could fit it in and his project wasn't too outrageous. It's funny to think his films would be considered pretty tame by today's standards.

At Elstree Studios a new series was being created with Roger Bamford directing every other programme. He invited me to join him and the cast for lunch during filming—for the fun of it and because Jimmy Nail, who was playing a character called Oz, was looking for an agent. Perhaps I could help. No problem.

The lunch was a laugh; the cast were a jokey lot who got on really well. Roger told me the scripts were excellent and he was delighted with his actors. *Auf Wiedersehn Pet* promised to be a success.

After eating, Jimmy and I left the group and went off for a quiet coffee. I gave him a list of appropriate agents suggesting he mention my name when contacting them. He gave me a couple of photos—one was of him at the Elstree bar with his trousers round his ankles! That was Jimmy.

A week or so later, a knock on the office door. In he staggered carrying a heavy cardboard box marked Grants of St. James's. 'It's a thank-you, like.' He plonked it down in front of me. 'I've got myself an agent!'

He'd been taken on by Pippa Markham, one of the top agents for up-and-coming talent. She'd already sent him up for a new BBC series to start after *Auf Wiedersehen Pet* and he was dead chuffed. So was I, not just for the excellent wine but because he'd thanked me. A rare thing with actors. Occasionally a card or some flowers would arrive from someone who was grateful you'd cast them in a part that would keep them and their family alive for the time being or longer. But usually they believed they'd been offered the part because they were extraordinarily talented and nobody else could possibly play it as they could. That was rarely true. The job of a casting director is to persuade the director, and producers too, that the person they are suggesting is the best out of many strong possibilities. It's a selling job, much as the agents are selling to the casting directors. Sometimes we had to fight really hard to get the actor we wanted for the part.

Role Call didn't really take off. There's no use pretending. It was ahead of its time and we found after a few months that we weren't attracting enough actors or subscribers. People were suspicious of computers. Hugh went back to agenting and Marilyn, who was in the middle of a divorce, got frustrated. Tricia and I were left holding the feeble baby. It limped along for a few more months and I thanked God I'd carried on casting. So did Tricia.

At weekends during the summer months I fitted in as much pottering about the local skies as I could. The South Downs are even more stunning from the air. Then, mostly for the hell of it, I wrote to Capital Radio, saying I'd just got my licence and would like to go up with the Flying Eye. I fancied the chance to see London from a couple of thousand feet, but imagined they'd be unlikely to agree. To my amazement they did and, after take off from Elstree at first light, I was able to spend an hour or two aloft identifying streets and even houses. It was a particularly powerful experience—seeing so far and so much all in a glance.

Not long after my London flight, Pippa, the agent, rang to say she and her boyfriend were spending the weekend with Frances Tomelty, Sting's wife, in nearby Hurstpierpoint. 'If you're flying this weekend, will you take Davey up with you? He's mad keen on the idea.'

'Of course,' I said.

He was ready and waiting when I arrived.

'We can fly over the house and I'll cough the engine, so you know it's us,' I called back to the others as we left.

'Yes, great,' they chorused.

It was a calm day and completely cloudless. We worked out a wee flight plan, taking in the house flyover and as much interesting countryside as possible. Over the downs, inland a bit and out over the sea. It was blissful and I could tell Davey was catching the flying bug. I wondered if Pippa would thank me for that. When our hour was nearly up I headed back to the airfield, called Whiskers for instructions and was cleared to land.

The descent was smooth and the approach just right. We sank to Indian elephant height, flared and flew parallel with the runway as the speed dropped off and we sank to touchdown. Only... when we hit the ground, the plane lurched to left then to right and bounced back into the air.

'Christ, what's happening? Hold on, Davey, hold on!' I shouted as I tried to steady the controls.

We balloon bounced several times. There wasn't enough speed to try and take off again. Then we pitched forward. The propeller gouged into the ground and we found ourselves hanging upside down in the cockpit. God, we could explode, I thought frantically. 'Get out. Quick! And run,' I shouted.

We managed to get our seatbelts off and scramble out. By this time the fire-engine was on its way. I grabbed Davey's hand and we ran for the terminal. Jenny hurried out to meet us. 'My God, are you okay?' she said breathlessly.

'Yes, yes. I think so.' I glanced at Davey who nodded firmly.

Jenny was furious. 'I told them. I bloody well told them. That's the third nose-wheel this week.' She led us into the terminal foyer. 'Look.' There, perched on a makeshift stand, was a huge bomb. 'Second World War. Unexploded!'

'Jenny, what are you saying?'

'Dug it out, they did, out of two-five. And they didn't fill in the hole properly, did they? Stupid buggers.'

Davey and I, already in shock, were transfixed. This whacking great thing had been found under the runway! It was unbelievable. And to think how many times we'd all landed on it. I backed away. Jenny took hold of my arm. 'It's okay. It's been defused. Just in case,' she laughed.

Then someone came by to take us up again—back on the horse after a fall sort of style. Throughout the flight we sat dazed, unseeing. We knew how lucky we were.

'Some joy ride,' I said to Davey in the car later. 'But at least we're okay.'

'And I'll have a great story to dine out on,' he laughed. What a star!

The following weekend, I went down to Shoreham for the verdict. Was I in deep trouble? I couldn't think it was my fault. I soon learned that the plane was a write-off but the owner didn't mind. He would get the insurance and she'd been due for an expensive overhaul anyway. I stopped worrying.

Despite getting back on the horse, the crash had unnerved me more than I cared to admit. The light of my enthusiasm dimmed. Then a major move meant I would no longer be able to afford to fly.

34

INNOVATIONS

Whilst at Finchley Road I'd reverted to commuting and had forgotten how tedious it could be. Trains frequently held up or cancelled and cold windy platforms in winter. Sometimes standing room only.

'T, d'you miss living in London?' I asked one night.

'Yeah, I do sometimes,' he said.

'How about moving back up to town and you doing the commuting?' I asked tentatively.

'I don't mind as long as it's by car.'

'So we'd need to find somewhere in the Richmond, Twickenham area. About an hour from here.'

4 Kingston Lane, Teddington, was in a dreadful mess and needed completely gutting. Were we masochists or what? No. We were told we could expect to have doubled our money on 102 in four short years. The house market was becoming more and more buoyant. Anyway, Terry enjoyed renovation; it was a hobby to him.

We bridge-loaned again to give us time to make No 4 habitable before putting 102 on the market. Luckily we sold pretty quickly to an architect. A compliment to our conversion we thought.

That spring Tricia and I quit Finchley Road, sold off the computing equipment and set up office in the front room at Kingston Lane. It was hell working in the middle of a building site.

Having been in casting for fifteen years, I fancied the idea of producing so I joined the AIP, Association of Independent Producers, to take their course in film production. It fired me with enthusiasm and I began searching for a project.

Mainly as light relief, I was into reading Tom Sharpe and, on my way to casting sessions, joined the ranks of chucklers on the tube. He was very much in vogue and it seemed as though the whole world must be in a state of amused outrage at the antics of his characters. I'd read *Wilt* and bought a copy for Daddy, which he'd taken on holiday just three months before he died. He'd pronounced it the funniest book he'd ever read.

Blott on the Landscape fair leapt off the page as a proposition for a television serial. A six-parter. I decided to ring Tom Sharpe's agent to find out if the rights were available. But, as he was a best-selling author, I didn't expect they would be and, if they were, it would be amazing if he and his agent would consider giving Mrs No-Producing-Track-Record a look-in. However I had to try. I rang his agent at Curtis Brown. The deep, dark-brown voice of Dick Odgers came on the line. 'As a matter of fact, the rights are available. But who are you?'

I was ready for this and reeled off a list of what I hoped sounded impressive credits. I stressed my management skills and that I'd trained in film production.

'Well you'd better come in and see me.'

We made a date for the following week. He'd given me no reason to hope but at least he was prepared to talk. I hadn't botched up yet.

On the day I dressed in my most successful-looking executive gear and set off. It had snowed heavily the night before and I made sure to leave plenty of time to get there. I couldn't be late for such an important meeting, no matter what excuse I might have.

The journey was slow and difficult but I made it to Queensway and found the Curtis Brown offices where I was greeted by a smart young secretary. I could almost feel her pricing up my outfit and was glad I'd made an effort. She showed me into Mr. Odger's office. He hadn't yet arrived. 'He has to come up from the country,' she said. 'I imagine you'd like a coffee.'

'Thank you, yes.'

Half an hour later I was beginning to wonder whether I'd made a mistake. No of course I hadn't, the secretary had clearly been expecting me. Then she waltzed in, picked up the phone on the desk, handed it at me and departed.

'Hello,' I said tentatively.

It was Dick Odgers. He apologised profusely. He'd had to turn back the weather had been so bad. He was deeply sorry and would I mind discussing the deal on the phone?'

Within ten minutes a year's option had been agreed and I could afford it, just about. On the way home I couldn't help looking to see if anyone was reading *Blott on the Landscape,* the book I was going to bring to life. No one was. Because of the lousy weather the train was virtually empty.

It was good to be back in London. The only blight was that Terry was now having to commute. He didn't complain but I worried when the weather was bad.

Around that time Tricia decided to move on so I had to find another assistant. Luckily, Em, my secretary from Yorkshire Television days, had been working in an agency and wanted to get back into casting again. I'd missed her forthright humour and refreshing earthiness. We agreed it would be good to work together again.

35

ONE BIG BLOTT

Doing a synopsis of *Blott on the Landscape* proved a daunting task, but I managed to capture the spirit of the piece. I now felt it needed a heavyweight writer to do the script adaptation and the excellent and popular Malcolm Bradbury seemed a pretty good choice. I contacted him and he agreed to meet. A week later we got together for lunch.

Malcolm, diffident, intellectual and eccentric, had an appetite belied by his slight frame. He ate a lusty meal washed down by wine and in between mouthfuls gave me his ideas of how best the book could translate. He was enthusiastic but reserved, probably wondering how on earth I expected to get a television company interested in such an outrageous piece. I suspected he'd also been a bit curious about me and that a good lunch was always an irresistible lure. I paid the not insubstantial bill and went home on a wave of wine-induced euphoria.

I knew who I wanted to direct *Blott* from the beginning. I rang Roger Bamford for a general chat and 'just happened to mention' I was reading the funniest book. He hadn't read it so I sent him a copy. A couple of weeks later we met for a drink.

'Did you enjoy *Blott on the Landscape*?' I ventured.

'Loved it.'

'I think it would make a brilliant six-parter. Is it the sort of thing you'd like to direct?'

He nodded emphatically. 'I most certainly would.'

I told him I had the option, had written a synopsis and also had provisional interest from Malcolm. And what did he think about coming in as potential director?

'You crafty thing. Of course I'd like to,' he laughed. 'Let's hope *Auf Weidersehen's* a hit.' I was sure it would be.

So now there were three names to offer. Tom Sharpe, Malcolm Bradbury and Roger Bamford. I had put the first creative elements together. That felt very good. I hoped their reputations would gloss over the fact I had no producing experience.

I touted the project round the companies and got a mixed but not entirely unpredictable response: 'I liked it but our schedule is full for the moment.' 'It's far too risqué for us.' 'Come back to us in a year's time.' 'You're mad.' But I didn't lose hope. It helped that Em and I were pretty busy in the office. In fact so much so I decided we needed more staff. I could take on two part-timers, who could be self-employed, like us. It would save me the whole caboodle of PAYE and the like. I'd had enough of that with Terry's lot.

I advertised and interviewed several possibles. One was a young Irish lad, Steve. He was obviously very bright and could make a go of it. I felt we'd all get on and took him on part-time. I was wrong about his suitability as a potential casting director. I'd forgotten, or had not yet noticed, that many heterosexual men have a problem disassociating themselves from their sexual proclivities. I soon became aware that he showed little interest when we were casting men and lots when it was young girls. Luckily, the new part-timer, Kathleen, an ex-dancer who wanted to move on, showed no preferences. We decided to cope with the Irish hots for the moment.

Time was passing and my *Blott* option was running out. Roger, who had a hit on his hands with *Auf Weidersehen, Pet* and was full of the beans of success, suggested we bring in some extra muscle; a production company he had associations with. They could act as co-producers. Going round their contacts they met with much the same response as I had so they decided to finance a first script from Malcolm which would give the project more weight.

Then it happened. Jonathan Powell at the BBC, who'd particularly liked the idea but had had no room in his schedule, decided to postpone a pricey production of *Middlemarch* and was interested in discussing *Blott* as a possible replacement. With this news we were able to renew the option.

Malcolm's Episode One script was terrific. Contracts were drawn up and shooting dates agreed. It was going to happen!

By this time we'd met up with Tom who, although initially a little apprehensive, was pretty pleased that one of his books was going to find its way onto the screen. We discovered he was as entertaining as his writing, a man who obviously enjoyed mayhem.

My idea of being sole producer was unacceptable to the Beeb, they had specific methods of working and always used staff. I would have to be creative producer. I was pissed off at first but then realised it was a good start and as I would be working predominantly with Roger, I'd be happy.

Naturally we didn't need to take on a casting director and had soon assembled a great group of actors. Most accepted immediately on the strength of the parts and Malcolm's brilliant scripts. Our main team consisted of George Cole, Geraldine James, Simon Cadell and David Suchet, who was going to play Blott. A strong support cast was easy to attract and good old Jimmy Nail, now a known face, agreed to play a drunken crane driver running amok with a demolishing ball.

That summer of 1983 Ludlow town centre was invaded by the film crew. A mansion on the Welsh border was dressed up to look like the pile of a place owned by Sir Giles and Lady Maud, employers of Blott, the gardener and handyman. A gigantic *arc de triomphe* rose up across a track amongst the treetops of a deserted Shropshire wood. This was to be Blott's gatehouse home and the scene of his last stand. Arrangements were made to borrow a variety of ferocious animals for Lady Maud's wildlife park and Deddington, a village near Banbury, was cajoled into allowing wild scenes of destruction to take place on the green. The wheels of production were well greased and moved smoothly along on schedule.

By the autumn all six parts were in the can and the task of editing and music dubbing had begun. Jonathan Powell wanted to air the serial the following February.

Over the shooting period I'd carried on casting—my BBC fee was derisory and I had to be content with a buy-out, besides during filming there was little I could usefully do except make encouraging noises around the place.

February came soon enough and, in a state of high excitement, I sat down with Terry to watch the series on actual air. My first project, my baby, had made it to the screen.

I've never been a fan of television critics, or any critics for that matter. Their subjectivity seems inappropriate. Audiences, I believe, are quite capable of deciding for themselves if they want to watch something and continue watching. *Blott* proved this point admirably. Comments in the press swung from ecstatic to appalled: ' … a hallucinogenic Keystone Cops version of *Brideshead Revisited* … I found it cruelly funny' from the Sunday Times had to be my favourite. ' … the actors were required to go over the top … and died a death'—Mail on Sunday. And the Express: 'It's completely over the top, of course, but somehow manages to attain a level of farce quite sublimely surreal … ' 'Blott may earn a black mark for all concerned'—Daily Mirror.

It didn't. The ratings were the highest ever for a BBC 2 drama and *Blott* became cult viewing. The title was used in part or entirety in a multitude of headlines. The serial was repeated in the autumn due to popular demand and again not so many years later. How I wished I'd insisted on repeats and residuals on my fee! But it didn't matter, I was just happy that, despite the mixed reviews, *Blott* had been ground-breaking.

Poor Mother had not been on good form. Glaucoma having taken the sight from one eye, she'd developed a cataract in the remaining one, and was unable to risk going out until it'd been removed. She'd seen *Blott* through a hazy film. But as soon as she'd had the operation she sped round Midhurst in a whirl of pride visiting her lady friends who said they'd enjoyed it, despite (or perhaps secretly because of) the *risqué* element. I gathered they were all subjected to lots of

'My daughter, you know'. I could just imagine their indulgent smiles.

Having gained some confidence and a little credibility, I wanted to move on to a different type of project and was optimistically enthusiastic about a little-known R.F. Delderfield novel I'd read. It would make a super three-parter, I thought. It was called *Come Home Charlie and Face Them*. Another memorable title, which had to be a good omen. I acquired the rights and started thinking about who could adapt the book.

Charlie wasn't the only project I was working on. Robin, an old mate from Young & Rubicam days, and I, had decided to form our own production company and develop some ideas. Our first proposal was to be called *The House Programme* and was all about house renovation. We felt we'd had sufficient experience and could pull together a small team to take people through the minefield of house purchase, architects, builders and decorators. There would be demonstrations for D-I-Y devotees too.

Alongside this idea was *The Health and Beauty Programme*—a series about healthy eating, exercise, alternative medicine and beauty advice.

Before long we were ready to show our presentation documents to the television companies. We were optimistic; both were innovative concepts and we felt audiences would enjoy them. Not so the television executives we approached. They just couldn't see it – 'No. We don't think there's the audience for that sort of thing.'

'Too specialised for us.' 'Sorry our schedules are full for the next couple of years.'

We were disappointed but undaunted. We knew that in the television business you just have to keep throwing stuff at the wall and hoping one day something sticks. We put the projects to the back of the shelf and looked around for other possibilities. Robin was keen to investigate a documentary about the life of H.G.Wells and went off to do some research. I fancied the film industry.

I'd read an extraordinary book that I thought would make a brilliant film and decided to contact the author to see if the rights were available. The book was called *Genesis* and the author, Allen Harbinson from Northern Ireland, was a hyperactive man full to bursting with ingenious ideas. One got the feeling he couldn't write fast enough to keep up. It seemed he only took time off from writing to catch the latest movies. He'd a long list of books to his name, most of which I read and enjoyed. The rights to *Genesis* were available and I negotiated an affordable option to buy. After that Allen and I met up a lot and, when we weren't cinema-going, we'd be deep in discussion about how best to adapt the book. We'd agreed I should write a first-draft script and how much artistic licence it would involve. So, evenings and weekends, whenever I could sneak away from helping with the work on the house, I'd be huddled over my typewriter.

It was extremely difficult and I was sure, when I finally decided it was okay to show my first draft to Allen, that he'd wonder what the hell I'd done to his book. To check out how it read, I asked a group of actor friends round. The story came to life and was pronounced acceptable for a first draft.

Allen was as excited as I was to hear that I'd produced something he could look at. I posted it to him the next day. He wasn't slow in getting back to me but it was with good and bad news. The good was that he really liked what I'd done, the bad (for me that is) was that his American agent had commissioned him to write a prequel and a sequel. This would entail a re-write of *Genesis* if the trilogy was to work. There was nothing further I could do. I was bitterly disappointed but glad I'd written my first script and anyway, I was now in discussion with Paula Milne, a possible adapter for *Come Home Charlie*.

For tax, image and reliability purposes, I changed my car every couple of years. Two Alphasuds had been followed by a row of Hondas. That year I acquired a CRX, a sporty two-seater convertible that nipped neatly in and out of tight spaces with ease. Although it was by no means top of the posing range, it was just the sort of car to try out in the South of France and that summer, we'd had an invitation.

One of my most recent projects had been an Australian film that called for an English actress. My old friend, Carol Drinkwater, was perfect for the part and had been chosen with no competition. And when she'd met the French producer, Michel, there'd been no competition there either. After many years of travelling and a conviction that she'd most likely never meet her ideal man, this was love at first sight. And now they'd bought a crumbling villa with a magnificent view over the azure sea that gives the Cote D'Azur its name. Terry and I couldn't wait to see the place and speculated wildly as we sped down the *Autoroutes* into hotter and hotter weather.

We had trouble finding the villa, in fact it took us all day; French road names and directions rarely seem to correspond to reality. We were suffering from heat exhaustion and highly relieved to flop down in the shade of a giant magnolia tree with glasses of chilled wine. Carol had been filling the ancient swimming pool, which had just about enough water to cool us off before dinner.

We ate outside and I gazed around at the unkempt garden. The terraced slopes were overgrown but Carol and Michel had been tidying up round the house where climbing roses draped themselves up the crumbling pillars that supported the long first-floor balcony. Having been empty and neglected for some time, their new home would clearly take many years and thousands of francs to put right, but it had a magical ambience and that was all that mattered.

Driving home to England, through ever-deteriorating weather, we fantasised about the house we were determined, one day, to buy. 'Not in the South of France, it's too hot for me, and too expensive. I fancy somewhere like Beth's in the Dordogne,' said Terry.

'Yes, me too. A stone farmhouse in wooded countryside would be great. Somewhere to escape to whenever life gets too stressful.'

We knew it was just a dream, but then, dreams can come true.

We got Kingston Lane straight just in time for the Christmas of 1985 and, by way of celebration or as further torture depending on which way things were going, it became a big family and friends affair including, of course, Mother. She was a handful most of the time having apparently lost her sense of humour. Although she said she enjoyed herself she was constantly on the defensive and complained whenever meals weren't on time. She moaned about her eyes too, but seemed able to read the smallest dice—games kept everyone entertained. I was as sympathetic as I could be but Mother was well known for playing up, self-pity and endless talk of illness. Had I realised it was only to be expected at her age and in her state of health, I would've been kinder, but I hadn't yet reached the stage where friends all around are having problems with decrepit parents and I thought it was just Mother being Mother. Terry was halfway up the nearest wall by the time she left and naturally it was my fault for having a mum who could be such an effing pain. 'You're really mean sometimes,' I told him. 'We'll probably be a bit like that one day.'

'I don't know about you, but I bloody well won't,' he said aggressively.

'Okay, you won't.' It was easier to agree and move on, but I was thinking he was unwise to tempt fate. His time could come sooner than he might imagine.

36

HURRICANE

Zapping between TV channels as I tried to cram yet more actors' performances into my personal encyclopaedia, I caught one word. It echoed round the room, round my brain. I went back—Dalkon. It was a documentary about the Dalkon shield, the intra-uterine device I'd endured for eighteen months. The report revealed that there was now court action in America— the shield was being withdrawn; it had fatal flaws and it was estimated that thousands of women, worldwide, might have been affected. The fibres of the tail which hung down through the cervix into the vagina like the fibres of a rope, allowed infection to creep into the womb with disastrous results. Damage ranged from discharge to death, from infection to infertility. Women were seeking recompense and a firm of solicitors in England had been appointed to handle the UK claims.

I was stunned at the sinister personal implications. I'd wondered more than once if it had harmed me or could even have accounted for my failure to re-conceive. At the end of the programme a phone number was given out. Any woman who had worn or was still wearing a Dalkon Shield was asked to call. I agonised. Did I want to become involved? A prolonged court case was not to my taste—after all money could never make up for the sadness, distress and discomfort I had borne whilst trying for a family. No. I didn't want to become involved.

I switched over to watch a video. Louis Marks, a producer at the BBC, had employed me to cast a period drama called *The Day after the Fair*. It had gone really well and he had another project for me. The director was to be Giles Foster and the video showed two of his most prestigious credits to date—*Hotel du Lac* and *Silas Marner*.

Both films were ultra classy and highly enjoyable. I looked forward to meeting Giles. The play we would be working on was an adaptation of the Gothic classic *Northanger Abbey*. It was the first of several films we were to tackle together.

Mother had been suffering. Her good eye was now deteriorating. She'd had to have an operation to try to relieve the Glaucoma pressure. It was successful, her spirits soared and she became far more positive. She was even able to express approval when I announced our latest intentions.

It was time to move—again. My little attic office was full to bursting with three assistants in a space four metres by four metres. They could have taken me to an industrial tribunal for contravening some act or other. It was casting by sardines. Kingston Lane had tripled in value so Terry didn't need much persuading. Off we went house-hunting.

It didn't take long to find our next home, near the Thames in Surbiton. It had a basement which was ideal for offices and very little renovation was needed. A buyer for Kingston Lane came, conveniently, just in time for us to put in an offer. It was accepted. I started packing again.

A few months later another report on the Dalkon Shield jolted me onto a new level of consciousness. Apparently the company who made the thing, A.H. Robbins, and their insurers, had concealed vital information about the dangers of the device. I was incensed. In some cases, this surely amounted to manslaughter. I decided the surviving victims had to stand up and be counted, and that included me. I rang the solicitors and was sent a complex form to complete—pages and pages of questions about the history of my reproductive system and where the shield fitted into the story. Filling it in was not only laborious but painful. All the old memories had to be dredged up and committed to paper.

I received a quick reply. I was considered to have a case. More forms to complete. The questions were agonisingly probing. The pages became dimpled with tears as I wrote out my pain. The form about emotional injury was the worst. I had to keep reminding myself I had chosen to be counted with all the others who'd suffered. I had to carry it through. Then I'd think of the women in the third world who wouldn't even get to hear of the court action; who wouldn't be able to claim even if they did. Some would still be wearing the device. God knows what damage it could already have done, be doing or had yet to do. Even after the shield had been withdrawn there was still the possibility it was being fitted in some remote corner of the earth. Surely my tears would be more appropriate for these women. I replied as requested to every letter and tried to forget about it in between. Our move demanded most of my time and energy. We took up residence in 34 Cadogan Road in February 1987.

The house was Georgian and in immaculate condition. Even Terry had to admit we'd made a good choice. Dressing the set and a few minor alterations didn't take long. There was a small garden in the front and a manageable one at the back. Terry was pleased to find a secluded and sunny corner to plant out the pot plants he'd been nurturing from seed. It was the first time he'd attempted home-growing and he'd achieved ten sturdy little plants. There was virtually no good grass to be found and he didn't like the impure, over-priced resin that was around at the time. Having given up cigarettes some years before I wouldn't touch it anyway, but neat grass might be a different matter.

Down at Poynters things were deteriorating. The salon was now on a downward slide. Several staff had moved on after their apprenticeships were over and they'd established a clientele. Terry couldn't make up his mind what he wanted to do about it. So he took out his discontent on me, criticising every single thing I did, screeching like a cat on curry and turning 34 into the noisiest house in the road. I was embarrassed to step outside some days in case I saw the neighbours. I was miserable and Terry was oblivious. It wasn't that I hadn't tried to cook decent meals, iron his shirts *comme il faut,* buy the right presents for Christmas and birthdays and, most important of all, come across with the bedtime goodies on a regular basis. I truly had, after all I wanted us to be happy.

That dreaded word happy. What did it mean? Even contented would have done. Even just a quiet life. It seemed as though these states were totally elusive. I felt bad that Terry's business was on the slippery slope but naturally I couldn't resolve the situation. He had to find a way himself. He'd always been a procrastinator. He'd seen the way things were going a year or two before and had hung on in moaning. I'd made endless suggestions and he'd had a million reasons why they were impractical. In the end, exhausted and bored with the whole issue, I gave up. But then I felt guilty and wondered if I couldn't have been more supportive. It was a muddling time as well as an unsatisfactory one. What could I do?

Get help maybe. Yes, get help. Ask an expert where I, if it were I, was going wrong in our marriage. I rang Victor Meier, who'd helped my Role Call partner, Marilyn, see her failing marriage for what it had become. I made an appointment.

Victor was different from any psychiatrist I'd ever heard about. Actually he was a behavioural psychologist. His consulting room was the front room at his house in Hampstead where he lived alone with the occasional lengthy visit between homes of one or both of his two young sons. His marriage had gone wrong years before. He must have been in his sixties. A pioneer of a school of psychiatry and head of department at the Middlesex Hospital, he had recently retired and now practised privately. I felt instantly comfortable with him. During our sessions he had plenty to say, no lying the patient on a couch, getting them to talk out their problems then asking them to pay for the privilege. No, Victor made you see things from a variety of points of view whilst making no actual judgements.

So out it all poured: my disillusionment with my marriage, how at work my self-confidence held together but crumpled into a heap of uselessness at home, how I found the least little task difficult to get right in Terry's eyes and how that very fact auto-suggested itself to me so I made constant mess-ups. How I wanted affection as well as sex. In fact affection rather than sex would have suited me most of the time. Was I living in a dream world of expectation of the ideal states I'd read about in women's magazines or was I just asking for something reasonable out of marriage?

I spilled out my unhappiness and Victor wrote copious notes before commenting. When he did, I was shocked. He was careful to preface what he said. 'Of course, I can't be sure until I've had a chance to talk to your husband, but ... ' He had the impression, only an impression, mind you, that I was married to an insecure perfectionist. From all I had told him of our backgrounds, Terry would be constantly wondering what on earth I was doing with him. What could a middle-class, well-educated, successful career woman see in a working-class, dyslexic, shorter-than-her hairdresser who didn't consider himself in the least attractive? She was either nuts or not so great after all. Subconsciously he just had to reconcile the fact of our marriage by putting me down in an effort to prove the latter. Then he asked me why I'd married Terry in the first place.

'Well, I suppose I just did. Maybe because he was there and wanted to and I wanted babies and we had our house and we'd been together for five years. Lots of reasons.'

'What about love?' Whoops! I knew what Victor was asking and the answer he needed, but ...

'Of course I love him. I'm not in love with him and quite honestly I don't like him very much. I mean I do like him but I don't like the way he's behaving.'

'You feel you can separate the two?'

'Yes.'

'Can you come and see me together?'

I told him I would try and arrange it but wasn't optimistic.

'Call me.'

And that was it. No answers, no reassurance, nothing to cling onto. Just possible reasons. Well, I supposed it was a start.

That night I decided to come straight out with it. 'Terry, I've been to see a psychiatrist.'

'What the fuck for? What's the matter with you?'

'I've told you often enough. I'm not happy.'

He exploded. Accused me of being unrealistic, unreasonable and a stupid romantic. There was nothing wrong with our marriage and he had no intention of seeing some shrink or other. It wasn't his scene and he thought I knew that. I burst into tears. 'Not the bloody waterworks again!' He stormed off leaving me to sob myself into a blotchy, swollen mess.

By the time I was all cried out, I'd decided. I would keep my distance for a while and hope he'd change his mind. I'd be polite but cold and certainly not available.

We'd planned a two-week visit to cousin Beth in France at the end of that summer. There, Terry was bound to be more relaxed. Perhaps I could bring up the Victor suggestion again. Until then, I was determined to enjoy the break.

It was a good holiday with gorgeous weather and Beth was just the company we needed. We had time to talk and I decided to ask Beth her opinion on the salon problem. 'I think he should accept it's the end of an era and maybe try doing something different. House renovation for example,' I said. I didn't see the point of pretending.

Beth hit back sharply. 'It's Terry's business. He's built it up from nothing. It's not as straightforward as you seem to think. You might be able to take decisions easily, but we're not all like you.'

'But surely if the business isn't doing well any more, he should seriously think about getting out before there's no good will to sell on.'

Terry, for once, sat and listened as the ball spun back and forth across the net.

'You're very dismissive. And don't forget, it's harder to start afresh when you're not so young any more.'

'He's only forty-five! Hardly ancient.'

Terry spoke up at last. 'I'm not sure I want to get into house renovation for a living."

So the conversation went round in circles. Every suggestion I made was useless so I eventually gave up.

The subject, by mutual agreement, was dropped for the rest of the holiday, which culminated in a wine buying excursion to the St. Emilion region. There it wasn't difficult to immerse ourselves in the processes of the *vendage* and the inevitable tastings. We drove back to Souvic loaded down with cases. At least we'd be able to drown our sorrows in good wine. And, of course, Terry's dope plants would soon be ready for harvesting. I thought wryly that giggling would be preferable to screaming matches until he could decide which direction to take.

Back in Surbiton, despite a good stock of booze and four pot plants hanging in the attic to dry, the prospects appeared gloomy. I threw myself into a frenzy of domestic activity as if change was looming and I should be prepared. I made huge pots of chicken casserole, beef stew, curry and kedgeree and filled the freezer. Then I dived into the mountain of personal filing that had built up. It was about time our paperwork was well organised with everything immediately accessible. Terry, on the other hand, did nothing, as if he thought events would rescue him at the last moment. I could stand his apathy no longer and steamed in. 'For Christ's sake, just cut your losses and sell up. With some time to yourself maybe you'd see things more clearly.'

'No way. No way. No fucking way!' It looked like he could nail me to the wall with the anger in his eyes.

I backed away. I didn't care what happened now. I'd had enough. 'You can't go on like this and neither can we as a couple. I want us to go and see Victor. He'd help, I know he would.'

'Fuck off! I'm not going and that's the end of it.'

'And us!' I grabbed my coat and slammed out of the house.

Down by the river all was calm. I found a deserted bench and sat oblivious of the late October chill, gazing at reflected lights gently bobbing along with the breeze on the water. My marriage was over. Where had I gone wrong? Had it been me? Let's face it, I thought, I've never been great at relationships. Perhaps I'd be better on my own. Other people seemed to get it right, well not everyone, but our friends' marriages were nearly all intact. They'd made the right choice, I hadn't. Oops, I'd admitted it. I should never have married Terry. We weren't suited, we were opposites in so many ways. They say opposites attract, but we had almost nothing in common. What had I been thinking when I said 'yes'? Now, at forty-three, I had to face the truth or write off my life. I thought of our cats, the house, the garden, our things. It would all have to change. There'd be a horrible divorce and I'd probably wish myself back in the lesser of two horrors. But I had to do it, or lose my integrity, deny my real needs and be a desolate doormat for the rest of my life. I thought of the past and all we'd experienced together, the good things we'd shared and the disappointment we'd suffered about not being able to have children. It was as well we hadn't—now.

The thought of living alone for possibly another thirty years was daunting to say the least. How would I cope? I didn't think I'd either want another man or meet one I fancied anyway. No, I'd concentrate on producing and writing and that would be my fulfilment. I'd have nobody screaming at me about dinner, the laundry, the finances. Nobody to tell me what to do. Nobody constantly bugging me to 'get my knickers down'. I'd be free. Yes, free … but wouldn't I be lonely? A lonely, sad, wrinkled failure? I'd have my friends of course and with my half of our assets I'd maybe find a little terraced house somewhere. I'd enjoy doing it up, but I'd have to pay for any renovation work. I could afford it, I was doing well at work. It'd be fun. I could have a mini-garden and potter in it at weekends. I might even be able to afford to take up flying again. Or something else, if I fancied it. There were lots of plusses. What Terry would do, I couldn't allow myself to think. Now there was a true stumbling block. He'd be devastated. Either that or he'd set his jaw hard, close off and survive. I had to assume he'd survive. Of course he would. He wasn't dependent on me, was he? Oh God, I hoped not. No, he'd be alright and it was definitely the best thing. Our marriage had to be over. Totally resolved I went home. The house was in darkness.

That night I slept in the spare room and, strangely, I slept well. When I woke the next morning and went down to make a cuppa, Terry had gone to work. The electricity was off for some reason. I popped the spare kettle on the gas and was about to check out the power cut when the front door opened. It was Terry.

'Got to the end of the motorway and the road was blocked. There are trees down everywhere, fences blown over, roof slates on the road. We've had a hurricane.'

I stood open-mouthed. 'I didn't hear a thing!'

'Oh, Christ. My dope plants,' cried Terry frantically. He flew out to the garden. All but one had gone. Blown away to God knew where. He'd probably supplied most of the neighbours!

For days the country was in a state of shock and it was clear nothing resembling normality would return for some weeks. We, like everyone else, were affected by the aftermath and I was reluctant to bring up the subject of our crumbling marriage for one last time before packing and leaving? But I hadn't changed my mind, it was time to move on.

Two weeks later, on the 15th November 1987, our lives, like the stricken countryside, were devastated.

PART FIVE

A TERRIBLE TWIST OF FATE

37

INTENSIVE CARE

Saturday mornings meant breakfast in bed with the Guardian crossword. This Saturday found me caught in the prickly branches of compiler, Araucaria. Outside the sun was shining. The phone rang. It was Mother. 'Hello, dear. I'm sorry to ring you this early but I've just had a phone call. From Cuckfield Hospital. Terry's there, he's had an accident.'

My face tightened, this was something I'd dreaded; Terry was, true to character, rather an aggressive driver. She continued. 'He's unconscious but nothing's broken, just a few ribs cracked. You must call them.' She gave me the number. 'Now dear. Don't worry. I'm sure he's going to be okay. Please ring me when you can. Good luck.'

My hands shook so much I could hardly dial the number. I felt sure Mother was under-playing the situation. It took an eternity to locate the casualty doctor I was to speak to. She told me the car had skidded, swerved off the road, hit a lamp-post and somersaulted. Terry had been knocked out on impact and thereby been saved from multiple injuries. The car was a write-off. He'd had some tests and a brain scan and was now in Intensive Care.

'Don't come alone,' she said. 'Bring a friend or relative, for moral support. It's always a good idea.'

What was I to think? Was she under-playing the situation too? Why had he had a brain scan? Of course if he'd hit his head and was still unconscious that'd be routine. I relaxed for a moment. But what if he didn't wake up? What if he had internal injuries they hadn't discovered yet? What if he'd been blinded? All the what-ifs jostled for most likelihood. Then I stopped. I had to find someone to come with me. Who lived nearest? Robin. I rang him and got the answer machine. Saturday morning most people are out shopping these days. Jane? Another answer machine. Oh God would anyone be in? I was getting further away now. What about Em? Chiswick wasn't too far—maybe a quarter of an hour if the Twickenham by-pass wasn't blocked with shopping traffic. I dialled. Mercifully she picked up the phone. 'Em – it's me. I've got a big favour to ask you. It's Terry, he's had an accident. He's in Cuckfield Hospital. In Intensive Care. He's unconscious. They don't want me to go on my own. Can you come? Please … ' my voice broke up, ' … please Em, could you?'

'Wattage, don't be daft. Of course. Stuart's got the car, he's gone to Sainsbury's but it's only down the High Road. I'll run and get him. Make yourself a strong coffee and I'll ring again when we're on our way. And don't worry.' Her reassuring tone, her instant reaction, her taking charge of the situation was typical and I thanked God for her.

I had a bath, dressed in heaven knows what and made several cups of very strong coffee. I was soon caffeine racing. I called the salon to say Terry wouldn't be in that day and I'd let them know as soon as I had any news. Em was with me by 11 o'clock, by which time I was pacing the floor, but I knew she'd come as quickly as she could. We took my car and I insisted on driving; it would keep me concentrating and I felt somehow safer that way.

It took about an hour to get to Cuckfield, not far from Haywards Heath. As we drove through the Sussex woods we were shocked and sad to see how many trees had been uprooted and stripped of their golden leaves. The hurricane had left them lying in a mess of broken trunks and branches. It was like driving through a deserted battleground.

Cuckfield Hospital was rather primitive. We were directed to a Nissan hut building that housed the Intensive Care Unit. Inside a small lobby then through swing doors with rubber skirts which swooshed liquidly across the lino as we passed. Down a corridor with numbered doors and taped lines on the floor towards the unit. We entered and, unwilling to walk straight into the ward, thought we should stand by the waiting room door until someone appeared. Inside a man sat hunched forward and sobbing into a hankie. The tiny room had faded mustard walls, a bathroom glass window, half a dozen uncomfortable-looking chairs and a Formica table with magazines. Hardly a reassuring ambience. It felt more immediate, more in touch with the outside world, not to go in. A nurse finally pushed through the ward doors.

'I'm Mrs. Balfour. My husband's … '

'Terry's wife. Good.' Brisk, businesslike but not unfriendly. 'But I'll have to ask you to wait. We're busy at the moment.' She gestured towards the miserable little room. 'Please, in there.'

Reluctantly we went in. The weeping man didn't look up. We were glad. After all, what could we have said? In deference to his distress and because we couldn't think of anything to say anyway, we didn't talk at all, just leafed through the ancient magazines and waited, and waited. The corridor was quiet, everywhere was quiet. I tried to imagine the ward. Terry was in there, I just wanted to see him and … I wanted to wee but feared that if I went to the loo they might come, so I crossed my legs tightly and hung on.

At the end of a long dark tunnel of time, the nurse came to take us to Terry. But first we were ushered into the consulting room outside the ward. A tall, thin man in a tweed suit was standing by the window. He turned. 'Mrs Balfour?' I shook his outstretched hand and introduced Em. He gestured to us to sit. 'I'm Dr Byrne. Now, before you see Terry you need to understand what's happened. He's sustained a serious head injury and, frankly, we're unable to predict the outcome.' He paused for this to sink in. What the hell did he mean, did he really have absolutely no idea? 'According to the CAT scan, there has been bleeding in the left ventricle of the brain causing paralysis to the right side. Rather like a stroke.' Again he paused. To give me time to question anything I didn't understand I supposed. But I most certainly did understand. 'And he's in coma.'

I sat dazed, suspended in time.

He went on, it registered somewhere in my head. Finally he handed me a booklet and got up, ' … and most importantly, make sure you keep up your own strength. This way.'

The Intensive Care Ward, which housed three beds, was extremely hot and brightly lit. One bed, near the door, was apparently for post-op people, the other two for the serious cases a woman, who lay conscious but immobile, and Terry. Only it didn't look like him— round-faced, sallow, oriental and, above all, expressionless. As Dr Byrne slipped quietly away, snippets of what he'd said flooded into my consciousness; ' … we hope his coma may begin to lighten … only time will tell … he's cracked a couple of ribs and punctured his lung … the lump on his head is pressing on the optic nerve. It will go down … Headway is the National Head Injury Association.'

Em and I held hands and stared. Terry's inert body, naked but for a thin sheet covering from the waist down, was a mass of bruises. A fan whirred above the bed. A spaghetti of tubes and wires came out of machines and went into him. The machines flashed and blipped. His ventilator breathed heavily and he had a nasal tube from the drip feed. Was this really my Terry? He looked like an alien.

We watched for an indefinable time. A young nurse came and sat on the other side of the bed. She took his right hand. It was completely limp. 'Terry, Terry wake up. Your wife's here to see you. Wake up.' She stroked the dead hand gently, repeatedly. Chanted her words again and again. No reaction. 'He'll come round. Just you see. I'm sure of it.' She gently placed the limp hand in mine and smiled. Immediately I warmed to her. She personified the best of the nursing profession; the backbone of invalid care.

'Thank you,' I said as she left.

It was time to go. We could do nothing except stare. There was no point in staying. Tomorrow would come more quickly if we left. Tomorrow he might …

On the way home we stopped at the police station and picked up Terry's briefcase. The sergeant at the desk could tell us nothing, he'd only just come on duty. He suggested I ring in the morning and gave me the name of the person to ask for. 'The car'll be at the breakers. It's on the right just before you get onto the motorway.'

Breakers? It sounded so final, so destructive. I knew where he meant. 'We'd better go,' I said to Em.

The man in the little hut that served as an office licked an oily finger and scanned the list of cars in his grubby exercise book. He found Terry's Vauxhall Astra and told us where she was. A depressing drizzle was now falling all around us, accentuating this metal graveyard, where the wrecks were piled up against and sometimes on top of each other. How many people had died, or at least been seriously injured, in these mangled carcasses? How many families had been shattered in a moment? It was hard to imagine the scale of the carnage represented here. Then we saw her. What was left of her. She was almost unrecognisable—the engine had collapsed forward over the front bumper and the crumpled chassis has shifted almost off the wheels over to the passenger side. The back seats had completely caved in. Miraculously the capsule of the driver and front passenger part were recognisable, although the roof was deeply dented on the driver's side. It was a horrific sight. I looked inside. There was Terry's little lunch box sitting on the front passenger seat. It looked so forlorn, so pathetic, so reminiscent of hours before. Before this dreadful thing had happened. I retrieved it and we left, silent, stunned, mechanical. It was time to go home.

Em and family were going out to eat so I phoned Kip, my friend from Young & Rubicam days, who insisted I spend the evening with him and his girlfriend, Liz, at their flat. I had to force myself to eat dinner. Later they refused to let me go home alone and suggested they could stay the night in Surbiton. I gratefully accepted.

It was nearly midnight and I was beyond exhaustion. Would I ever be able to sleep? Our bed was cold and empty. For once I longed for that hot figure to be lying alongside me, longed for yesterday again. Twisting and turning, this way then that, trying to settle, I searched my mind for a comforting image, something to help me get to sleep. None would come. In the half-light of the room, I stared at the black plastic bag on the floor in the corner. It beckoned ominously. I couldn't ignore it. I hauled it up onto the bed. It contained Terry's clothes and 'effects'. It had to be opened.

Inside I found his leather jacket, both sleeves slashed to the shoulder. His shirt, similarly slashed and with blood on the collar. His sweater cut up the front. His trousers, underpants and shoes were all intact. A small plastic bag contained his watch with the glass smashed, his reading glasses, both lenses broken, his wallet and keys. It felt like he was dead. Perhaps he's as good as dead, I thought. I could stand the sight of the signs no more and, sweeping the desperate pile to the floor, collapsed onto the bed and cried my eyes out. I let the tears go until I could hardly see out my eyes and my cheeks were raw from the salt of them. Finally I drifted into oblivion.

38

A LONG DARK TUNNEL

Kip and Liz left in the morning after I promised I'd be okay on my own. I had to be. I had to take on the day.

First I rang the police station and was glad to get a coherent and detailed report. Terry had been involved in a multiple pile-up. Miraculously, under the circumstances, he'd been the only one seriously injured. A patch of black ice had been the cause of the trouble. Placing itself strategically only a few hundred yards beyond the end of the M23 motorway, it had successfully caught fourteen cars. Terry had been number five. The police, an ambulance and a breakdown truck were already at the scene. The Astra had somersaulted into the truck, bounced off it and landed back on all four wheels. The truck was a write-off. Terry had been cut out of the wreckage of the Astra, bundled into the ambulance and rushed to Cuckfield Hospital.

I didn't question, I didn't analyse, I didn't wonder why there'd been no police 'accident' sign at the end of the motorway. They'd had time to get there, so surely … ? No, all of these thoughts came to me years later. For now there were only facts, facts that would have to be relayed to the insurance companies.

Major catastrophes hurl us into disorder, but, as if to take our minds off the shock, we are thrown into a frenzy of activity and there is little time to dwell on the significance of the situation confronting us. So much to do, so much to organise, so many people to contact, phone calls to make and letters to write. Through all of this I wasn't me; I was someone else—arranging, recounting and re-recounting.

With Terry's salon staff I played down the severity of the situation, calmly said he'd be back soon and made sure they knew what they were to do. Tomorrow I would have to tell the insurance companies—car, personal injury and private medical. And, of course, there were friends and family to inform.

In the afternoon I went down to see Terry. He was still a mass of tubes and wires. The nurse explained how antibiotics, to combat infection or malevolent bacteria and prevent him getting stomach ulcers, were being fed into his system. The accident and his condition would have put him into a state of extreme stress. I sat by his inert body stroking his hand and begging him repeatedly to wake up. For a brief moment there was hope, his hand twitched. I jumped up and ran for a nurse. She guided me back to the bedside. 'Only a reflex, I'm afraid. But keep talking, keep trying. He'll come round.'

Will he? Will he ever? And if he does, what will he be? I'd read as much of the Headway leaflet as I could manage. He could come back as anything.

Which would be worse? In coma for years to come, maybe the rest of his life, or to come back as a vegetable—incapable, wrecked, useless and incurable. My thoughts plunged me deeper and deeper into the abyss of my fear and despair. It took a gigantic effort to lift them back out and up towards optimism.

Each dawn heralds the rest of our lives. Mine was now on a track I could never have foreseen, even in my worst nightmares. But I got on with it. You do. You have to.

Somehow I held things together, my job, the salon, the house and the situation. Gradually Terry's coma began to lighten. Every day tiny progresses were made: a leg moved, an arm raised, a yawn, a hiccup. Each one was greeted with delight. Except when his eyes opened; they were dull, unseeing. I was devastated, the accident had blinded him. It was such a relief when he began to focus as the swelling went down in his brain. Next he sat up, but fell over then sat up again, steadying himself with his left hand. His right side was completely paralysed. The drip was removed and he began to take food in his mouth—mostly mush as chewing was difficult. Inevitably a lot ended up on the T-shirt he was now able to wear. He was still without speech and, to look into his eyes, seemed to be without thought too, although I fancied I could see hurt and suspicion in them. His mouth was open most of the time making him look vacant and baby-like. Yes, he was just like a baby; I fed him orange juice from a baby cup. I put his left hand round it with my own over it as we raised and tipped it to his mouth. He didn't resist.

I felt his loss of dignity so strangely and strongly, and his bewilderment and pain. I was a traitor leaving him every day to go back to the real world. The world in which he was no longer a normal, operating entity.

'He'll be suffering from post traumatic amnesia,' the doctor told me. 'He won't remember any of this. And the length of the PTA period gives a good indication of the extent of the brain damage.'

'Will he remember the accident?'

'No. Nor the period leading up to it.'

'How long a period?' I dared to ask.

They didn't know. It could be days or years; retrograde amnesia can stretch back over a very long period. It would be some time before we would be able to ascertain. But he did seem to recognise me, 'Or does he put his arm round the necks of the nurses too?' I asked myself and had to smile. Yes, I had to smile. You have to laugh as well as cry. You must be normal, even though you feel quite the opposite inside.

The salon was an extra strain. Somehow it had to be picked up from the doldrums, kept afloat. With a certain awareness of irony, I remembered Beth's words of not so many weeks before. 'It's Terry's business. He's built it up from nothing.'

I couldn't let it just fizzle out. When the time came to decide about the future of the business, Terry should be involved. I had to keep that foremost in my mind. When he recovered, there had to be a business.

I decided we needed another stylist to look after his clientele and started asking around. Anxious to hang onto as many of his regulars for as long as possible, I wrote letters to them all saying what had happened and that he was making a good recovery and would be back soon. Oh God, how I prayed for that to be true. And then, as if on cue, something happened. Terry smiled. The biggest smile, a smile that stretched across his face. And I smiled back, the biggest smile I'd ever smiled.

On day twelve he was moved out of the Intensive Care Unit and into a general ward. Terry's best mate, Neil, became my mainstay. Although a busy man running his own design company, he frequently took time off to drive me down to Cuckfield and, despite a deep dislike of hospitals, helped all he could. Apart from constant chatter, bed-tidying and massage, we spoon-fed Terry, thick vegetable soups, eggs and mash, liquidised dinners of spaghetti bolognaise, cauliflower cheese and the like, followed by yoghurts and fruit mousses. How the old Terry would've complained had he been served up any of these, although maybe, in some deepest corner of whatever consciousness he still had, he knew. Occasionally, he would raise an eyebrow and stare straight into my eyes as if to say. 'What's going on? Get me out of here!'

I tried to tell him, keep him up to date, explain about the accident, hoping something would register. I imagined it like a sort of hell in his head, a Bosch painting, all falling, mangled, sharp-clawed and thunderous. But it could've just been a fog with the occasional penetrating light. I realised all my visions would be far from the truth, but trying to empathise was important to me, however uselessly. I convinced myself he was desperate to communicate something, particularly when he put his arm round me and stroked my hair. Oh yes, he knew I was someone special in his life.

Throughout I was enveloped in a warm blanket of support. If it wasn't Neil driving me down to the hospital, it was Em, Jane, Kip and Liz or another friend or someone from the family. They were all great, particularly at cheering me up when I plunged into despair— usually directly after a visit. The strain of an hour with him, the false jollity, lifting him, not just his dead weight when he slipped down in the bed, but spiritually, with jokes, pictures, cassettes of friends' voices and his favourite music. Trying, trying, trying to bring him back, to get some sign of recognition from him. But there was nothing, just a smiling, burping shell that responded to some simple requests but had no apparent will. At least his expression was becoming a little less moronic. Or was it?

But then I'd think, I must pray that my words of reassurance are getting through and meaning something. My tears were always so near the surface but I couldn't let him see them, couldn't let him imagine he must be in a grim state. Then I'd worry—if he does have any idea of what is happening, he must think I'm taking it all very lightly. It was so difficult to find a balance, so tiring. Waves of helplessness would wash over me and crazy questions would plague me if, for one tiny moment, I let them surface. 'Where's Terry? Why isn't he here? He should be helping me through all of this. How could he leave me to cope on my own? Leave me with this stranger, this damaged clone?' I had to shake them out of my brain. Deliberately slam the door on their clamouring voices. There was no way I could crack. Then, as if she sensed my need from her haven in Souvic, cousin Beth came to stay. Only for a few days but so well-timed. She was such a comfort, seeming to know instinctively what to do and say.

Gradually a new routine became established and I allowed myself a little time to reflect. To realise that all being hangs on a thread—not just life. And in Terry's case that thread had broken and it was going to take one hell of a knot to bring him back to anything resembling his former self. It was strange to think that the man who'd made me so unhappy that I'd been on the point of leaving, now lay in a hospital bed in pathetic suspension. But my role was clear and although my thread was thoroughly frayed, I would splice it together so you wouldn't see the join. Whatever happened, I would no longer look back at the marriage we'd had, I would only look forward. The husband I'd been with for seventeen years might not return and whoever did emerge I would have to treat as a new person, someone I'd never known before.

39

A SLIP OF A GIRL AND A SOLDIER

Mother called me daily and, although still lost in the fog of her own health problems, she managed to pull herself into shape enough to insist on coming to stay for a few days.

I resisted at first, not needing what I assumed would be an extra headache, but then I felt mean and ungrateful; she wanted, no needed, to do something useful. 'Now dear, I'm coming. I can look after the house, wash up, get the dinner and so on. Please don't try to cope with this on your own. I'm your old Mummy, don't forget.'

'Yes, thank you. That would be wonderful.' It was hard to disguise the choke in my voice. 'Will you come by train? Let me know when you'll be arriving and I'll pick you up.'

I had to hand it to her, she fought off her usual self-pitying instincts and, as she stepped off the train, hauled herself up into purposeful mode. She knew she was needed, not as the ailing Mother she had recently become, but as the caring, supporting person she felt she had been, once upon a time. I almost fell into her arms, but, knowing that she might crumble under such emotion, forced my mouth into a smile and pulled back. 'Thank you. It's good to see you.'

That evening we sat opposite one another at the dining room table forking our half-hearted way through one of my defrosted chicken casseroles. We were mindless of the taste, each of us was elsewhere. We didn't talk until Mother put down her knife and fork and cleared her throat to speak. 'Dear, I do know, you know.'

'Know what?'

'That things weren't good between you and Terry. I've known for some time you weren't happy. He's not who I would have chosen for you.'

'Mother, please!' God, could she be tactless! I didn't want to discuss the state of my marriage. Not now. Not under such circumstances.

'Darling, I've been through an unhappy relationship. It can be hell. Your father wasn't the only man in my life, you know. There was Tom.'

I did know. Well, not much; Mother had sometimes talked about her first love, her Tom, but never in detail. He'd been a shadowy figure somewhere in her past, someone she very nearly married. Now it seemed she wanted to talk about it. In her own way she must have thought it could create some kind of a bond, or at least be a distraction. She was right. I needed to hear her story as much as she needed to tell me.

~

Joyce was just twenty when she met Tom in 1930. Her younger sister, Tillie, was being courted by Cyril, a good fifteen years her senior, dashing and with prospects. At seventeen Tillie was peaches and cream, white-blonde, pert and vivacious. Joyce, tall, skinny and rather buck-toothed, felt the disadvantage of comparison on the rare occasions the sisters were allowed out beyond parental surveillance. When Cyril proposed a trip to Ascot races it was considered permissible. The girls spent days trimming and re-trimming their hats for this grand event.

Cyril picked up his charges from their home in Pinner in his brand new Mercedes Roadster, promising their father, Frederick, he'd look after them carefully and deliver them home by nine p.m. at the latest.

Round the corner in West End Lane another car was waiting. In convoy they drove to the course. The girls whispered and giggled, as young girls do, and took it in turns to glance behind to see who their companions were.

Cyril and the mysterious driver parked side by side in a field reserved for privileged ticket holders and the girls' curiosity was pleasantly satisfied when another couple and a single man jumped gaily out of the other car eager to be introduced.

Joyce was instantly smitten. Tom, clearly invited along to make up the sixsome, was quite gorgeous. In fact, he could have been mistaken for a young Clark Gable, and, oh joy of joys, he took on the role of third escort with a heady mixture of glamour and gusto. By the time Cyril gathered his two charges to ferry them back to Pinner, it had become clear that Tom was entranced by the tall, shy, slip of a girl who hid her toothy smile behind an elegantly gloved hand. Thin she may have been but she had an ethereal quality. She was to become his angel, a wispy being in his dreams, complete with the whitest of gossamer gowns, delicate wings and a harp. Tom's taste for the romantic was truly Byronic and Joyce was overwhelmed.

She had recently graduated from secretarial college and had been taken on as a junior secretary in a local engineering company. In those days a secretarial training was considered just about respectable, after all, it could tide a gal over until a suitable young man took her off the hands of her middle-class parents—those whose pretensions were not supported by wealth, that is. When she was not working, Joyce attended to the needs of her asthmatic mother, Nora, and the pernickety Frederick, a man whose life still firmly adhered to Victorian values, behaviour and hypocrisy. In family portraits he was stereotypical; rod up his back, not a crease in his dress, nor an unruly hair on his head or upper-lip. He terrified both Joyce and little Donald, the youngest. Only Tillie took no notice. She was going to marry Cyril even if it meant eloping.

Understandably Joyce was aquiver with apprehension when finally obliged to introduce Tom to her parents. Luckily Tom knew exactly how to charm. A young officer in the British Army with an upright stance and a veneer of confidence was bound to impress. Sure enough Frederick acquiesced; Tom would be permitted to see Joyce no more than twice a week and then she had to be home by ten o'clock at the latest. Joyce was thrilled; her very own boyfriend just when she'd given up hoping for a suitor.

Through her teens she'd spent what little spare time she was afforded awash in the slush of romantic novels. Tom was full of grand plans for the future and the epitome of the heroes she had sighed over. Soon she was whisked and whirled from picnics on the banks of the Thames, afternoons heavy with modern art and musty history in galleries and museums, to summer balls and moonlit strolls. Love was not letting her down. Well, not at first.

Then, for no reason she could fathom, Tom's behaviour changed. On several occasions, at the very last moment and with no excuse, he backed out of a dinner date, a concert or a picture show. Joyce was devastated. What had she done? Had she not measured up? All her insecurities rose up to torment her. Sometimes when he did arrive as arranged, she would wish he hadn't, if all he could be was sullen or argumentative, critical or just plain silent. Once she was particularly down herself and just couldn't cope, so she left, there and then and got a taxi home. Two days a letter arrived. *'My dear angel (for I presume it was upwards you went after your sudden departure from our midst), no wonder I haven't heard anything from you ...'*

On another occasion he tried to appease her with a gift, couched as a favour. He said he'd never once intentionally hurt her and would have given anything to spare her. Then he asked if she would do one little thing for him, would she accept Peter as a belated birthday gift because ' ... *he's terribly fond of you and doesn't really give two hoots about me.'* She had to admit she was disarmed but distressed too. Peter was Tom's dog. He must've known she couldn't take him because of her Mother's asthma.

At other times, Tom would ring, apologising profusely, 'It's all my fault, dearest. I promise it will never, ever happen again. Just suddenly, I felt dreadful, suicidal almost, and couldn't face leaving the barracks.'

'Tom, dear Tom, I do understand. It's the political situation. I read the papers, I know about that Hitler person. He seems to be very dangerous. And you being in the army.' So she forgave him, time after time, grateful for the days he was once again the charmer she loved, who, when he was up, was everything she needed, for life at home could be very difficult. To Frederick, the sound of Nora's coughing and wheezing was unbearable. So he would drown it out. He'd disappear into the sitting room, set himself firmly down at his grand piano and play, for hours. Tillie was useless and Donald was too young, but Joyce could cope. If necessary, she would sit all night by her mother's bedside in the spare room at the end of the corridor where Nora slept during her attacks.

When, through sheer exhaustion, Joyce couldn't manage to dress up for a date, Tom would insist on driving down to Pinner. If the weather was fine, they would go to the summer house at the end of the garden. There she would collapse onto the day bed whilst he would gently stroke her hair, her cheeks and the dark circles under her eyes. He could even persuade her to sip from his hip flask. The brandy burned her throat but she didn't care. It revived her enough to face the possibility of another night of vigil.

For all his moods swings, Tom could be strongly supportive, sympathetic and understanding. After one attack and when Nora felt better, he encouraged Joyce to take a break, to go and stay with her Uncle Bertram, Frederick's brother, and his wife, Beatrice. They were a warm, kindly couple.

'*Darling,*' Tom wrote after visiting them over the weekend, '*You're looking tons better since seeing your aunt and uncle. I'm so awfully glad. Very soon now, I hope, I'll have you looking like that all the time … it is comforting to know that others are happy in our happiness. You do believe I love you very, very much, darling, don't you, though I never seem able to say it.*'

And so their relationship pitched and rolled on the breakers of the years until one Monday morning, a strange young man came to work at the engineering company where Joyce was a secretary.

He looked at her over his glasses and winked. She didn't know what to make of him. He had the highest of foreheads filled with brains, a twinkle in his bright blue eyes and a soft Northern accent. His name was John. And before long he asked her out. 'I see you aren't wearing an engagement or wedding ring,' said John. 'Does this mean you might agree to join me for lunch one day?'

Joyce blushed and muttered 'I ... don't know. Well ...'

'Let that mean yes, please.'

'Yes. Thank you. Why not.'

And so Joyce found herself torn between two men.

Soon Tom began to feel neglected. He was barracked near Liverpool at the time, so they weren't seeing much of each other anyway.

Darling Joyce, I have been rather foolishly clearing the letter box two or three times a day, just in case there should be a word from you to me, so far there has not been. Why don't you write to me darling? ... I have loved you all along and now after our vicissitudes I am absolutely certain ... will you marry me please?'

Joyce was cornered. She had to choose. Although John cut nowhere near the same dash, he was reliable, honest and never moody. He was always kind, down to earth, romantic in a rather corny way, and he had a practical approach to the future that was a blessed change from Tom's crazy dreams and schemes. On the other hand, she truly loved Tom. Or at least she thought she did, but maybe she just felt sorry for him. He was a lost soul, she'd come to see that. She decided she couldn't marry someone she pitied, no matter how much she loved him.

She tried to tell Tom she was exhausted by the ups and downs of their relationship and just needed calm and mental relaxation. She was tired of being on her toes all the time, watching what effect whatever she did was going to have on him, wondering what he was going to serve up next. When things had been good she'd been deliriously happy, but they had gradually become more and more rocky and she'd had enough. She couldn't accept his proposal.

Her rejection plunged Tom into a crazy downward spiral. He deluged her with letters, pages and pages of typewritten nonsense. Joyce waded through incomprehensible muddles of diagrams, jokes, accusations, apologies and declarations of undying devotion, which were immediately wiped out by 'goodbye forever' as if it were he doing the ditching. She sensed he was becoming seriously unhinged and asked John, who was under the impression she and Tom had split up some time before, for advice.

'You have to tell the poor man the truth, for goodness sake. Put him out of his misery,' he said. The cold edge to his voice frightened Joyce into the realisation that she'd been dishonest.

She wrote to Tom the night of the 24th June 1937. He wrote back four days later. His reaction to her admission was bizarre and unnerving. It was formal, worded as a business letter and ended—*'signing off for a long time. Yours faithfully.'*

~

'Not long after that your father proposed to me and I accepted.'

'What happened to Tom?' I asked.

'He died in a riding accident,' she muttered, hurriedly jumping up from the table. 'I'm going to make some tea.'

'How dreadful,' I said to her retreating back.

Her words jerked a memory back into my conscious mind. I had an uncomfortable feeling I'd already known he was dead. Yes, that was it. Dossy had mentioned Tom's death, but she'd said he'd committed suicide. Oh well, I thought sadly, if that were really the case, Mother is in denial and what good would it do to force the truth out of her? Best to accept her version and to be glad she'd tried to tell me, in an oblique way, that I wasn't the only one to have made wrong choices.

40

WARDS AND ALL

Terry was off the danger list and taking up a bed in Intensive Care, but he obviously couldn't go home. Unlike brain disease, brain damage isn't illness, though the patient can recover, over days, weeks and even years. Rehabilitation offers the best hope and Cuckfield had no such facility. So they decided, for the moment, to put him in Men's Medical. Poor love, what a place that was.

The myriad of smells invaded your nostrils from many paces away—mixture of stale sweat, urine, farts, sick, over-cooked food and disinfectant. All this drenched in the mustiness of old men. It was quite foul. I noticed the nurses kept their glass-walled office door firmly shut even though they must've been well used to it. It was a place of no dignity—place where anything went. There was every excuse here to make a variety of unpleasant noises and, what a blessing, no wife to tell you off. In some ways it was merciful that Terry was so unaware.

However, the aim was to get him back to awareness. Every day presented a new challenge, every day there'd be a tiny step forward. He learned to chew properly, lick his lips, hold his cup, tip it and drain it, keep his head up when eating, learned to sit properly and to attract the nurses' attention by some odd gesture or other. Sometimes he would go a little too far. On one occasion he picked up his water jug and poured the contents up and down his body until he was thoroughly soaked.

Then he began to laugh a lot. And we laughed with him. He touched his head and laughed—no hair. He studied his left hand and laughed. Stared at other patients and laughed. The sound was cackly, cracked, gurgly and, to those on the receiving end, a little disconcerting, but it was so infectious, he soon had the nurses laughing with him. His bed was next door to their office. That way they could keep an eye on him. But when he fell out of bed, they were too late; he bruised himself quite badly and chipped his front tooth. After that his exaggerated smile looked even more comical.

Although the ward had no television, there was enough entertainment to keep him amused. People moving back and forth, chat, bed changing, food arriving, visitors arriving, doctors' rounds and so on. Compared to the quiet of Intensive, here was Piccadilly Circus and I was glad. The watchword now was 'stimulation'.

At home Mother was true to her word, popping up the road for essential shopping, tidying round, organising the dinner and washing up. I think she was glad she didn't have to cook, merely to delve into the freezer and boil up a few vegetables. Except on one occasion when Neil and I arrived back to find her in a real state. 'Whatever's the matter, Mother?'

'Oh dear, dear. I couldn't help it. I never thought, well, it never occurred to me,' she wailed.

'For heaven's sake, what's happened?'

'It's that cat. Whilst I was watching the news he jumped up on the side and ate all the kedgeree I was going to give you for dinner. Oh dear, I'm sorry, I'm so sorry!' She looked really distraught. Neil and I couldn't contain our laughter.

'Mother, it doesn't matter,' I spluttered, 'I'll make us some omelettes.'

'Yes, yes, dear. But it gets worse. He sicked most of it up on the sitting room carpet. I've cleaned it as best I can.'

'Yuck! Thank you for sparing me that. Now, please let's forget it ever happened. Hopefully the little bugger's learnt a lesson.'

A few days later Mother went home, having made sure to err on the safe side by never again leaving the dinner within jumping range of the cat.

In Men's Medical, across the ward from Terry, old George sat propped up like a puppet. A wrinkled prune of a man with an obscure incurable disease, he wasn't quite all there, but his son insisted on surrounding him with gadgetry. A Sony Walkman with tapes, a radio, cards, solitaire and a variety of books and magazines, plus a bowl of fruit, full of equally wrinkled apples, pears, grapes and brown bananas and several vases of flowers. It was the saddest sight. All old George seemed capable of was farting and coughing up phlegm. I thought the nurses should give the fruit to other patients who had none, but they must have had some rule, or were worried the son could arrive at any moment and might complain.

Then there were the smokers. Four old chaps who appeared after lunch and before dinner. They would shuffle down the ward to the day-room where there were several armchairs, a table and a telly. The stink of stale smoke often drifted out into the corridor. They all wore woolly dressing gowns with silk, tasselled cord belts, striped pyjamas and comfy slippers. The leader, a chubby chap with a thatch of tatty hair and a tobacco-stained moustache, led his friends with head held high. Number two was terribly bent and bony with little hair and glasses anchored to his face by elastic, presumably to stop them from falling off. Three looked distinctly wobbly and were it not for the drip stand that went everywhere with him, would probably have toppled over. His jaw was so stiff with determination, the sinews in his neck seemed in danger of tearing. Finally, a smiley old gentleman in a wheelchair. He must have been in it for some time, he manoeuvred with ease and dexterity and his arms gave the impression of being well muscled. You could have set your watch by the appearance of this quaint quartet. Terry was always fascinated and would smile hugely as they went by. They nodded back, almost in perfect synch.

The nurses were angels in Men's Medical; jolly, patient and very grateful for all the help Neil and I and other friends could offer. Although we didn't give him bed-baths or deal with his incontinence, we continued to feed Terry, lift him up, massage his feet, sponge him down and slather him with moisturiser. We brought in small portable items for him to study and hold and, through it all, we would talk.

Before long he began to react to simple requests—to raise his hand, to smile, to shut his eyes, but not to speak. Until one day our old friend Lynda's husband, Dick La Plante, came down to the hospital with me. And boy, he was adamant (as only Dick could be) that he could get Terry to speak.

He closed the curtain around the bed and I was banished. I stood outside and waited. Dick had a bunch of Muscat grapes—the bait. I heard his American drawl 'Terry, d'you wanna grape?'

No response. He repeated the question. Still no response. He continued to ask, time and time again. Then suddenly, 'Es!' A strangled little voice spat the word out with effort.

'Again!' Dick ordered.

'Es, es, es!'

A loud western style whoop echoed round the ward as the curtain was wrenched back and Dick leapt out punching the air. Tears of joy poured down my face. A couple of nurses had heard. 'Bravo! Bravo Terry,' they chorused.

Terry, oblivious of us all, had grabbed the grapes and was shovelling them into his mouth. The sticky juice poured down his chin. I couldn't help hugging Dick. Terry had a voice again. The only way forward now had to be up.

After several chats with the young lady doctor in charge of the ward, I realised they wanted to get rid of him as soon as possible and I wanted to get him into a hospital nearer to home anyway. Then he needed rehabilitation. I spoke to our GP who investigated Kingston and Surbiton Hospital. They had no beds. Maybe he could go straight into rehab, I thought. But where? Typically there was a shortage of suitable National Health facilities in the area, in fact in the whole country. Waiting lists were long. I made endless phone calls. Nobody could take him. What on earth could I do? The situation was desperate, I'd have to have him at home. My spirits nosedived.

I had a meeting coming up with writer, Paula Milne, who I hoped would be able to adapt the *Come Home*

Charlie … script. She knew about Terry's accident and encouraged me to talk about it. Writers are like that. I spilled out my worries. Paula was comforting and practical. Her boyfriend was a neurologist. He would get Terry a bed at the Atkinson Morley Hospital in Wimbledon and take him on as a patient. That would give me a bit of breathing space. Next door to the hospital was the Wolfson Rehabilitation Unit. I could meet the matron there and see how soon they could take Terry. My hopes were restored. Nonetheless I asked the specialist at Cuckfield to write a letter to WPA (Western Provident Association), our private medical people, stressing that he needed therapy immediately if he was to make a good recovery. Their rule-book stated categorically that we weren't covered for such treatment. Several strong letters later, they reluctantly agreed that, if necessary, they would pay for interim treatment between hospital and National Health rehabilation for as long as real progress was being made.

The Atkinson Morley Hospital is a Victorian pile of a place with echoing corridors and high ceilings. The ward where Terry was installed was particularly grim and impersonal. The atmosphere was reminiscent of a Dickensian institution. The beds were hard, the sheets were stiffly starched and there was a strong smell of disinfectant. Here all the patients had neurological problems, the variety of which can be endless. Heads were stiff with tubes, shaved, bandaged or encased in strange metal cages. One man had what looked remarkably like a tap coming out of the top of his skull. He fiddled with it and made silly faces whenever the nurses weren't around. Many patients looked utterly gaga, others lost and vacant and a few seemed almost normal. Overall this was somewhere you wouldn't want to linger. Visitors came and went as fast as they could, often in tears.

I was anxious to get Terry out of there as soon as possible. It was so depressing and even he, in his comatose state, seemed to sense the horror film quality of the place. His eyes, bewildered, angry, curious and frightened, would dart around constantly. Trying to focus his attention on me I would hold his right hand, which was at last beginning to have some movement. He managed to close his fingers round mine but then couldn't let go. He got so angry I thought he was going to scream. Finally he succeeded in prising his fingers apart with his left hand. The effort had been exhausting and he became aggressive, grabbing my arm and trying to bite my wrist.

The next day I arrived to find him sitting up in bed looking furious. 'T, what's the matter?' He continued to glare. 'Have you had your scan yet?' He looked confused. 'Have they taken you out of the ward, for a scan?'

'No … yeth … no,' he spat, pulling up his left sleeve with his teeth.

'Oh, God. What a mess!' He'd reacted to the starched sheets by erupting in a livid rash. 'Poor thing! How horrid!' I couldn't help blurting out tactlessly

Terry burst into tears and when he tried to speak, only a gurgle came out, although I thought I detected a 'fuck'. It was progress but so distressing.

The scan was done the following day. Terry was still dopey when I arrived. Apparently the results had been encouraging but very severe head injury could

336

sometimes show nothing wrong on scans. Great! They give with one hand and take away with the other.

My interview with the Wolfson matron was comforting. She said the progress he'd made to date was good and augured well for the future.

'Well, at least that's encouraging, but when will you have a place for him here?' I asked tentatively, fearing I already knew the answer.

'Not for about five months I'm afraid.'

I couldn't help it, I burst into tears. The idea of him staying in that gruesome place for so long was too horrible to contemplate. 'But … where … he can't …'

She reached across the table and took my hand. 'Did you know Dr Jenkins, our rheumatologist, is also the head man at a rehabilation clinic near Godalming?' she said. 'It's called Unstead Park. And if you can find the money, they'll probably be able to take him.'

'Thank God,' I said sniffing and blowing my nose. I put Terry's name down on the Wolfson waiting list, thanked the matron profusely and shot out of the door. I had to get home to contact the insurance people before they closed for the day. For once I got through to the right person and, true to their promise, they agreed to pay. So the arrangements were made. Unstead would have a room for him the following week.

When Jane and I visited Terry that night we tried to tell him, wanting him to know he would be getting out of that dreadful ward and soon be having lots of therapy. He managed a little smile. Had he really understood? We decided he had and drove home in good spirits. It was time to celebrate. Jane and I got thoroughly drunk that night.

41

UNSTEAD BEDSTEAD

I wasn't sleeping well even though I was permanently exhausted. I dropped off quickly enough, but in the early hours I'd wake feeling like I'd just got out of a very hot bath and the sheet beneath me would be saturated. Being alone I could roll over to the other side of the bed where it was mercifully cool, and as long as I could switch off my mind, I'd go back to sleep without too much trouble. But then I'd wake again dripping with perspiration an hour or so later, and would have to fetch a towel to lie on as both sides of the bed were wet. At first I thought it was stress but when I started getting pains in my legs as well, I went to the doctor. 'Are your periods regular?' she asked.

'Sometimes they're later than usual.'

'Sounds like you're starting the menopause. I can put you on HRT, that'll help the night sweats and probably stop the leg pains.' Hormone Replacement Treatment? I was only forty-three, for heavens sake. 'It's up to you. But I can recommend it, especially as you need all the sleep you can get at the moment,' she continued.

I agreed and within a few days of taking the treatment the symptoms stopped. As long as I remembered the pills, I could forget I had reached what Mother referred to as 'the change of life.'

As for Terry, he was facing another change of bed. I had no idea whether he was aware of what was happening but he cried in the ambulance all the way to

Unstead Park clinic. It was the beginning of a tearful phase. I was told not to worry, he would laugh or cry for no real reason and it didn't mean he was either happy or sad. I wondered how the hell they knew.

The clinic was set in beautiful parkland, with mature trees and rhododendron bushes. Patches of crocuses heralded the approach of spring. The ambulance pulled up outside the impressive Georgian country house shaded by two ancient cedars. On the front lawn a tethered goat helped keep the grass under control.

The ambulance driver jumped out, lowered the ramp and wheeled Terry into the main entrance hall. I carried his bag and followed on behind as we were directed to the large modern annexe where most of the rooms were. The quiet, floral-scented corridors were cool and refreshing, such a contrast to the depressing drabness of the Atkinson Morley. We passed a swimming pool and a couple of workshops before going up a carpeted slope to the private rooms. The one next to the nurses' station already had 'T. Balfour' on the door.

Throughout Terry sat hunched in his chair, staring at his feet, unimpressed. To him, I could imagine, it represented another prison, albeit disguised.

His room was light and airy with buttercup yellow walls. Their brightness was echoed by the vase of early daffodils on the table. There was a large en-suite bathroom with double doors and the window, framed by flowery curtains, overlooked a stretch of immaculate lawn fringed with shrubs. The sister and a young nurse came to welcome us. They introduced themselves as Judy and Siobhan. They were jolly and kindly and had Terry into bed in a trice.

Unstead Park, originally a stately home, had been commandeered for wounded servicemen during the last war. It was now a private rehabilitation clinic for post heart-surgery, stroke and a variety of physical injury patients. In fact, head injuries were less common. I was pleased about that, it meant that Terry would be coming into contact with people who were mentally intact. It would help his recovery. I drove home convinced he was in the right place.

Soon there were daily breakthroughs. With some movement coming back to his right side, his capabilities increased and with them his confidence, and his frustration. He was constantly trying to get up and walk, usually falling back into his chair but occasionally ending up on the floor, bruised and disheartened. I insisted he needed to crawl before he could walk. He became pretty efficient with help. I 'patterned' him whenever I could—a process of manipulating his limbs for him so that signals would go back to his brain. Normally it's the other way round. It was a technique Frank Cvitanovich had used so effectively with his brain-damaged son, Bunny.

Terry learned mastery over his body in bizarre but sensible ways. When sitting, calm and in his version of repose, his arms would be folded tightly to his chest to prevent his right hand from flying uncontrollably upwards. And if he was concentrating on something else, the errant arm had to be grabbed by the wrist and pulled back down. It looked quite comical but it drove him mad.

Coherent speech was born of anger or annoyance. His first proper sentence was spat out with enormous effort. The words flew forth like bullets from a machine gun, strung together, barely discernible one from the other. 'I 'o I'll b'awright!'

I bent down and flung my arms round him. He looked most bemused but hugged me back. That was great but he couldn't let go. He struggled to release his grip and I had to slide down and out of his embrace. I wondered if an up would always be tied to a down.

Awareness gradually began to surface and, to help the process, I devised little games and tests. For instance I put together an album of special photos covering the ten years prior to the accident which visitors could look at with him. They were to ask him who people were and where and when the photos were taken. Terry seemed unable to answer, but as soon as names and places were mentioned, he would grin and say, 'Es, 'es. I 'member.' Did he? Did he really? I prayed he did.

A board and chinagraph pen chronicled each day. Visitors left their names and single words denoting what the conversations had been about. Unlikely objects were left in unlikely places to stimulate him into wondering what they were doing there—a key ring with a set of false teeth under the bed, a jar of all sorts—from paper clips to beads to safety pins and badges—on top of the wardrobe. A pair of my knickers hanging off the curtain rail! The nurses and cleaning staff were told not to touch them. They were most amused.

When Terry wasn't watching television, he was sitting opposite the nurses' station silently observing them going about their business. The nurses hadn't put him there, he'd crawled, or rather dragged himself, out of his room, along the corridor and up into the chair. He sat so still he could have melted into the fabric for all the notice they took of him. Occasionally however, one would appear with a small tray of coffee or tea and biscuits. His response was to smile his big smile and kiss their hand. Despite his occasional stroppiness, he could charm them all.

Physiotherapy was beginning to yield results. I arrived early one day and was directed to the gym. There, to my amazement and delight was Terry, propped up between the parallel walking bars. Sandra, his physiotherapist, was holding his right foot straight as he tried to walk. The effort was clearly enormous and, had he had proper feeling, he would probably have been in extreme pain. He was doing well until he spotted me and tried to let go of the bar but couldn't release his right hand. He pulled and pulled until, quite out of breath, he managed to loosen his grasp but then his legs buckled under him and he crumpled onto the mat crying, pathetic and defeated. Cursing myself for not being more discreet and needing to mop up my own tears, I slipped quietly away.

I decided a word with sister Judy might help. At least she could tell me how he was progressing and how he behaved when I wasn't around. I found her in the office. She could see I was flustered and reached down into her desk. Out came a small bottle of brandy and a glass. 'We're pleased with him, he's making good progress, and although he has his moments, everybody likes him,' she said, pouring me a tot. 'He has such a sense of humour and lots of charm, which is more than can be said for most of the patients we have to deal with. And Dr Jenkins says he definitely has potential. But, I'm sorry to have to tell you, your presence can sometimes be disruptive—it seems to affect his bladder for instance.' I couldn't deny he often wet himself whilst I was there, blotting his otherwise dry copybook. 'He's likely to be generally less controlled with you. Husbands and wives often bring out the worst in recovering spouses.' She was gentle but matter of fact.

Oh God, I couldn't bear to think of being a hindrance when I was trying so hard to help bring him back.

'Mrs Balfour, don't look so downhearted. You're doing a grand job. There aren't many wives who are so resourceful.' I smiled weakly, thanked her and downed the brandy in one.

After each visit I felt guilty. Having to leave him just didn't seem right, but he was still so damaged. Would he ever realise that? Would he get much better? Of course, he was getting better every day. The voices in my head argued constantly and it was hard to shut them up. The optimist, strong and cheerful versus the pessimist, feeble, despondent and exhausted by the horror of the situation. When I got really low I would seek out sister Judy for a chat and a tot of brandy. I knew I would leave her office with renewed strength and determination.

The weeks passed and I was well looked after; seldom allowed to be on my own. I adopted as responsive a shell as I could manage and, on that level, was even able to enjoy a social life. It meant falling back on the old technique of thinking superficially, suppressing my emotions whenever I felt them pushing through to the surface.

Work was vital to my sanity and our finances. Luckily Terry was receiving daily insurance payments whilst in hospital which went towards making up for his lack of salary. The salon was staggering along and

343

still just about breaking even. For me casting projects were plentiful and, mercifully, my professional persona functioned as well as ever. Sue Whatmough, Casting Director, was a different person to Sue Balfour, wife of brain-damaged man. I knew I couldn't let the latter creep into the composed demeanour of the former. Diverse and challenging projects came my way—a drama documentary about a controversial court case, *Cats' Eyes,* a tongue-in-cheek version of *Charlie's Angels* and *Across the Lake,* a fascinating film about Donald Campbell's final, ill-fated attempt in Bluebird. Anthony Hopkins, one of my favourite actors, was to play the lead so the rest of the cast said 'yes, please' to a man, or woman. It promised to be a splendid piece of television. Yes, I could be inspired. There was light out in the rest of the world.

42

CANDY AND CAKE

Actors write letters, endless letters: 'I am appearing in *Chips with Everything* at the Oxford Playhouse. Can you cover my performance?' Or 'Please come and see me in Skegness', or even 'I have taken over from Ferdy Falcon in *The Mousetrap*, let me know if you want me to arrange tickets.' Then there is 'Can I come and see you for a general interview.' Some, mercifully, simply send a photo and CV, asking to be remembered for the future. A casting director will receive at least twenty letters every day, more if whatever they are casting is being whispered about. Responding to each one would take a large chunk out of office hours. Letters with CVs and photos would go on file, the rest hit the bin. But I would look at them all.

One morning bright orange writing paper caught my attention. I picked the letter out of the pile. There was a small photo stapled to the top left hand corner. The name at the top was Candida Fawsett; Candy from Mermaid days. The actress who'd been engaged to John, the father of my little Sebastian. She'd been expecting a child when I last saw her, John's child.

'Dear Sue, I don't know whether you remember me. I was in the Greek tragedies you cast at the Mermaid Theatre. Can you spare the time to see me? Not just to say hello but to fill you in on my career since then. Please call. Love from Candy.'

It was irresistible, my curiosity begged to be satisfied. If she'd had a child, he or she would be half-brother or sister to Sebastian. I rang and arranged to meet her for lunch in town.

Candy's story was a mirror of my own, almost. John had left her during the pregnancy and she'd been unable to bring her baby up herself. She'd had her baby boy, Jeremy, adopted. And here the similarity ended. Candy knew the adoptive parents, although Jeremy grew up unaware that she was his real mother.

'How the hell did you cope with that? It must've been impossible for you, not being able to tell him who you were.'

'It was but I got used to it. Anyway, now he's eighteen he knows.'

'How did he take it?'

'He was devastated at first, but he's a bright boy and he's come to understand why. He's devoted to his parents. Yes, he calls them that and I'm glad. I'd like you to meet him one day.'

I was happy for her but envious too; at least she'd seen her boy grow up, known he was well looked after and loved.

'You must have wondered where your Sebastian is now.'

'Of course, not a week goes by that I don't think of him, the strangest things remind me of him. The memory is triggered very easily.'

'Well, if you ever see him again, please tell him he has a brother,' she said.

My eyes filled with tears. How fantastic that would be, but how unlikely.

We parted promising to keep in touch.

Terry was soon having occupational therapy, the stuff of everyday living. He was doing really well until they introduced him to the craft workshop. Then he folded his arms and refused to do a thing. 'Wubbish, all wubbish!'

He was a little less stroppy with the speech therapist, but insisted he'd always had a speech impediment. She nodded and persisted. She would point to random objects in the room, asking him to name them as fast as he could. Mostly he couldn't. He was dysphasic—unable to select words correctly—a pen could be a book, a book a cup, a cup a bag. Often he would muddle up 'yes' and 'no', which could be hilariously confusing.

Regularly I would delve into the pile of Headway literature for any little explanation of his condition. Usually it dealt straight into the hands of my negative self.

Although there can be considerable variability with brain damage, there are likely to be remarkable similarities of effect and the ways in which they manifest themselves will probably depend on the previous personality. Fundamentally there are general trends.

In the post-traumatic amnesic period, where Terry undoubtedly was, the patient is incapable of remembering recent events. Day-to-day information isn't absorbed, this has to come gradually and might never totally return. Following the storyline of a book or film will be impossible. Inevitably concentration is impaired and impeded by such memory problems.

A particularly tiresome aspect of many brain injuries is lack of insight. Whilst the person might recognise physical problems, and it would be hard to refute them, they might deny any change in thinking, speaking or behaviour. Their responses may be slowed and they may lose their ability to make choices. They are likely to be irritable and have outbursts of temper—swearing is common. Huh, I thought to that one! Socially unacceptable behaviour—this worried me horribly. Would Terry become a flasher, be sexually inappropriate or make indecent suggestions? Would he be dreadfully rude to people? In the clinic it didn't matter, he was still a patient and could be excused, but once back in the outside world, this could present a huge difficulty. I put the literature back in its box.

Although Terry insisted on sleeping on the floor, he'd sit on his bed or chair to watch television or eat his meals. No problem with that, you'd have thought. Well, he thought there was. Once when I arrived he was lying on his bed and pulled himself up to greet me, but then he flopped back and had to struggle up again. I tried to help but he pushed me off. Up and down, up and down he went shouting angrily; the bed was in the wrong place, it had a lump in the middle of it. The furniture was all in the wrong place. He wouldn't be calmed. It was all 'naff and wubbish'. He became quite exhausted but not enough to stop him reaching out, grabbing the cupboard door and trying to pull it over. I rescued it and him just in time. 'All wong. Bad news. Crappy bed!' he spluttered, red in the face and shaking with fury and frustration.

I screamed for help. Sister Judy and two of the nurses came immediately. They did their best to sort out the bed but to no avail. Terry got more and more agitated, thrashing the air with his arms. He just wouldn't be pacified. Why couldn't he come home NOW? He needed a happier environment. I told him he'd be home soon but that wasn't good enough. He wanted to come home TONIGHT. It took three of us to hold him down while Judy gave him a sedative. Then came the tears—violent, heart-wrenching sobs. My control clung onto the precipice, I bit my lip so hard it almost bled. It was no good. I left the room to sit in his chair opposite the nurses' station. I simply couldn't handle this one. Dazed and defeated, I stared into the abyss of the future.

Nurses are truly wonderful. Sister Judy appeared on cue with her calming tot of brandy and lots of reassurance. The sedative had taken effect and they would organise his room to his liking in the morning. 'Now, Mrs Balfour, you're really not to worry. It's quite natural he wants to come home and, even supposedly rational patients can have funny turns, convince themselves they're prisoners and that nobody wants them any more.'

I had to accept what she said; it was the only way.

A few days later, Jane took over one of the visits and reported that Terry had gabbled throughout; 'Why am I like this?' he'd said. 'I hate it here. The doctor says I'm not helping. Sue's not coming this weekend. Have we found anywhere to live yet? I feel restricted. How long have I been like this?' Peppered with lots of 'When can I go home's.'

I decided it was time to go to work on Dr Jenkins. 'Terry would make more progress as a day patient,' I said. 'He's so unhappy being away from home that I feel it may be impeding his recovery.'

But Dr Jenkins was adamant. 'I'm sorry, Mrs Balfour, Terry is far from ready and you can't possibly cope with him on your own.'

Thank heavens for friends, the dearest of people. Throughout the months at Unstead, they stood by us, paying regular visits with or without me. Watching Terry's progress and reporting, advising—helping in so many ways. They reacted variously—some were deeply disturbed, others took it well, others were decidedly nervous or embarrassed. But in one thing they were unanimous; he wasn't ready to come home, his brain wasn't yet stable enough and it would be impossible for me. He still needed professional care until his memory and rationality were back. They thought he was unconsciously manipulating me. He wanted to get home at any price, regardless of the consequences. Well, he wouldn't consider those anyway, I thought. He was a prisoner and I was the gaoler. Of course, he had to be better off out of captivity. But, for the moment, as he had no idea of time, whenever he asked, I could simply say 'soon, provided you play the game'. I'd be manipulating him, but there seemed no better solution.

And so I did, for a month, during which he lurched forward and fell back, but each time a little further forward and a little less back. Things were improving, often painfully but sometimes wonderfully.

He made me a cake in occupational therapy, started to stand upright unaided and eventually take a step or two—as long as there was a rail nearby the cling to. He learned to play dominoes, change his clothes without help and to fill in his lunch and dinner menu sheet—ticking the items he wanted and putting his name at the top. In an almost unrecognisable scrawl but that didn't matter. He stopped telling Dr Jenkins his suit was awful and it was time he had a decent haircut. But he refused to make a shelf unit—beneath his dignity, he'd done house conversions after all. He started fantasising, convincing himself of the strangest scenarios – he'd been having an affair and was running away with his new love to Germany and the plane had crashed. He'd been stuck in his car in the school car-park and couldn't get out. Then he accused me of sleeping with every male we knew. He had evidence, he could prove it!

His moods swung between temper tantrums and sweet smiles, miserable moods and jolly unawareness, desperation and acquiescence. He'd complain about everything and everyone then behave like the model patient. He'd talk complete sense followed by a load of gobbledygook. You never knew what he'd serve up next. But usually he could be yanked out of bad moods with jokes. Having refused to be shaved and incapable of doing it himself, he grew a beard. It looked awful. I told him so and thrust the mirror at him. 'You look ancient with that thing!'

'Go' my 'ead on u'side down!' He collapsed in giggles and so did I.

The time came for his first outing. We drove down to my cousin Tim's for Sunday lunch.

The visit went very well, and, apart from refusing a Barbican beer: because it's got 'no alcohol' in it, he behaved beautifully. Sadly though, his return was marred. A very odd-looking old man had commandeered Terry's chair opposite the nursing station. He raised his hand to us as we passed. 'Hello my darlings!'

Terry was not impressed. 'We're not your fuckin' darlin's and tha's my chair!' he snapped.

We were impressed by the clarity of his outburst but he was furious. How dare this man take his seat—his seat! He complained about it daily from then on. I learned later that the man was a bit loopy—a retired judge who thought he was Charlie Drake.

I decided to have another go at persuading Dr Jenkins Terry would be far better off at home. He could become a day patient. The response was not encouraging. 'Mrs Balfour. I've told you before, he's not ready. How would you deal with one of his catastrophic reactions?'

Apparently Terry had thrown a fit when they'd tried to get him to play a video game. He'd shaken with fear, felt faint and sick then screamed for them to get him out of there.

'He hates anything like that anyway.' I sprang to his defence. 'I'm sure there's nothing I would do to provoke him that much.'

Dr Jenkins was becoming weary. I was ready to throw a complete wobbler myself but managed to keep calm admitting patiently that I realised it would be hard, but insisted I was determined to try. After all nobody knew Terry like I did. It would probably be hell, but worth the effort. 'I could get help from friends, organise the house. Do whatever's necessary.'

Finally he agreed I could have him home for a weekend visit soon, to see how things went. I was triumphant. 'Dr Jenkins says you can come home for a weekend soon,' I told Terry.

Immediately forgetting I'd said 'soon' not 'now', he started packing.

'Not tonight, T. But soon.'

From then on he packed his things every day. And I'd have to explain again, and he'd have to unpack again, and again, and again.

Daddy on tank trials

Mother and Tom

Mother & Daddy
1939

Terry post accident

43

TERRY COMES HOME

With Terry at Unstead Park I had more time to concentrate on *Come Home Charlie* … the book I'd been discussing with writer Paula Milne. It was a love-story thriller written by R.F. Delderfield and set in 1930's Wales. Putting together a package involved getting a director prepared to commit to the project. As this was to be my first solo producing experience, I wanted a director I'd worked with before.

Following the success of *Auf Wiedersehen Pet* and *Blott on the Landscape,* Roger Bamford was in a position to pick and choose his projects. Not wishing to be type-cast as a comedy director, he'd moved on to a drama about a failed marriage between an English girl and an Indian.

'What are you doing after *Stolen*?' I asked him over dinner one night.

'There are a couple of things in the pipeline but nothing definite yet.'

I fished in my bag and brought a copy of *Come Home Charlie* … He smiled as I handed it to him. This time he knew why. 'Here we go again, eh?' he chuckled.

I heard back from him pretty quickly. He liked it and agreed to direct if I could get the finance together. So with Paula as adapter, Roger as director and my *Blott* credit, I was pretty confident I had a strong package. As before, I sent out my synopsis to various television companies and wow—result! London Weekend were interested—it could fit neatly into their schedule for the following year. I was delighted at how easily things were falling into place. Prematurely delighted. A few days later Paula rang to say her commitments were too heavy and she wouldn't have time to write the scripts.

Some quick thinking was required to keep London Weekend interested. This meant going through a process of elimination before deciding on Alun Owen, an excellent writer and a Welshman to boot. I approached him. He read the book and was intrigued with the story. However I was a little concerned when we met; having been a highly respected writer in his time, he was somewhat bitter at having slid out of the limelight and he was a heavy drinker. It was likely we'd be in for a rough ride. However we commissioned scripts, crossed our fingers and waited to read the results.

Down at Unstead, Dr Jenkins finally agreed that Terry could come home for a long weekend. Not surprisingly he was overcome with emotion at the prospect and kept bursting into tears.

I knew I was being presented with a real challenge. Dr Jenkins had thrown down the gauntlet when he'd said, 'Terry is far from ready and you can't possibly cope with him on your own.'

The caring was unrelenting. Helping him get in and out of bed, washed and dressed and undressed, up and down stairs on his bottom, across the hall and into the dining-room to eat and the sitting room where I could at least install him in front of the television for a while.

Convinced he would cling onto home, I dreaded the moment when it would be time to return to Unstead. I was sure he would struggle, scream or lash out when we tried to get him in the car. So I prepared for the worst. Neil came, so did Kip. There had to be muscle in case of problems. Terry kept saying he didn't want to go. We kept saying he had to, for the moment. But he could come home every weekend for the next few weeks and then permanently. We promised. Mercifully he accepted and agreed to go back.

After a couple of weekends in Surbiton and a noticeable improvement in Terry's demeanour, Dr Jenkins had to admit he'd make more progress as an out-patient, so I arranged a roster of willing friends to help me ferry him up and down to Godalming.

After four months at Unstead, Terry left. Sister Judy and her team were sad to see him go; they said he'd been a breath of fresh, sometimes very fresh, air.

His first day at the Wolfson Rehabilitation Unit involved various assessments at which I had to be present. As well as physiotherapy, he would need occupational and speech therapy.

'Some hopes,' I said, 'he's a stubborn devil.'

'Don't you worry, Mrs Balfour,' said the sister, 'he'll be fine. We have ways of persuading them, you know.'

Not Terry, you don't, I thought. Oh well, I had warned them. As I'd feared, after one session of occupational and speech therapy, he refused to go any more. He was in total denial. The only handicap he would acknowledge was his inability to walk properly. There was no denying that one. He'd made rapid progress at Unstead, but not great progress. Having insisted on putting weight onto his dead leg too quickly, he now used it much like a stick. He'd been so impatient, where gently-gently would have been a better approach. Now his leg was stiff with hardly any bend at the knee. His foot was rigid and curled upwards and outwards and his hip was in spasm, so the physios had plenty to concentrate on.

After endless manipulation and frequent dunkings in buckets of ice, Dr Jenkins decided a nerve block behind his knee might release the rigidity in the leg and foot. They would then try to twist him into shape. It was as horrific as it sounded. I held his good hand whilst they strapped him face down on a bed-table. There could be no movement as they pumped the gel into his leg. It wasn't over in seconds like an injection, the process took minutes. He cried in agony throughout. It was so painful even a virtually paralysed limb could feel it. Afterwards his foot was twisted into position and set in plaster.

The plaster, whilst showing some improvement, wasn't sufficient. It had to be repeated twice more. I felt so much for the poor man and all he was suffering. As well as the obdurate leg, his right shoulder was frozen and his right hand movement very limited. He still couldn't let go, couldn't control his grip. Often he would have to use his left hand to prise his right apart.

Mentally, his memory was improving, a little, and he developed some day-to-day recall, but it was very patchy. He continued to repeat himself constantly and, to get anything to register for even a moment, I had to do the same. It was exhausting. Notes had to be written and placed strategically around the place to remind him of anything and everything important or relevant. The twelve years prior to the accident were still a blank; only with prompting could he recall anything.

Then I had an inspired idea—why couldn't we go see Victor, the psychotherapist? After all I'd been so impressed with his approach and was confident that he, if anybody, could help us. I was able to introduce the idea as new. The breakdown of our marriage didn't exist in Terry's past reality, he had no memory of it. All that was real for him was the here and now. He was willing to accept that we had difficulties although I was careful to link them to his inability to walk properly.

Victor was brilliant and Terry most impressed. We aired our differences and frustrations and Victor carefully refereed. It was such a leveller and although Terry couldn't remember our visits at first, some of what was said began to stick. Victor and I colluded. The first half hour would be a re-cap of all that had gone on in previous sessions and then we would build on the conclusions. We discussed the pressures on me, Terry's denial of his condition, his partiality to alcohol, the past and the future. Victor's approach worked. In bed one night Terry admitted he wasn't quite himself.

As soon as the pressures began to ease off a little, my body decided it was time for revenge. I was so drained I could feel myself near collapse. I knew if I didn't take a break I'd cave in.

I set off to the Scilly Isles where a film I had cast was now being made. *Why the Whales Came* had a starry cast including Helen Mirren, Paul Scofield and David Suchet, who I knew from *Blott* days. My old boyfriend, Nick Jones, was in it too and although it would be good to see some of the filming, I planned to spend most of my time alone. I was able to stay for the week having left Terry in the care of Em and Kathleen during the day and a rota of friends in the evenings.

A tiny room in a Bed and Breakfast was all I needed and each morning I took lunch in a rucksack and boarded a boat to one or other of the islands. It was May and I was immersed in the warmth of approaching summer as I walked round and round the islands photographing flowers, rocks, sea and sand. All week the sun shone on my recovery. I would pop by the locations occasionally and eat dinner with the actors, but mostly I wanted no other company than my own. It gave me the opportunity to reflect on our lives, what had happened and how we might face the future.

I tried to remember the Terry I'd married, how he'd walked, what his voice sounded like, his laugh. They were fading with every day that passed. Now he was a hobbler with a mouthful of marbles and a throaty cackle. I'd been moved to discover that even though he was still highly sexed, the affection he'd never been able to express had found its way to the surface. He wanted to touch and cuddle and frequently blew lines of kisses at me. Making love was impossible though, we'd tried and he'd been unable to control his right hand and arm. It lashed out in all directions. He'd almost smashed me in the nose and for several days afterwards my back and arms were bruised and sore. After a few attempts I refused and he retreated into a fantasy world and the comfort of his left hand.

Despite the extraordinary beauty all around, my well of tears overflowed daily, on beaches, in meadows, on rocks, by trees. I dreamed up a multitude of tragic scenarios until finally, fed up with all the crying, I decided I should take Daddy's favourite advice and 'just get on with it'. I went home refreshed and received long-awaited news.

Over the past three years I'd received a fileful of updates on the Dalkon Shield case. The trust that had been formed began a regular newsletter informing claimants as the proceedings progressed. The makers, drug company, A.H. Robbins, a family enterprise, had been forced into bankruptcy and obliged to sell. The new owners, American Home, had put into a trust little short of two and a half billion dollars as compensation for successful claims. Mine had at last been evaluated on the basis of the information I'd supplied and evidence from my substantial medical records. I would be classed as Category 10/1, the most severe, with the judgement, *Infertility secondary to pelvic inflammatory disease … probably the result of use of the Dalkon Shield.'*

Apparently the case notes of the doctor who'd performed the laparoscopy had brought the P.I.D. to light as well as the evidence of considerable internal scarring. I was livid. Had I not had the right to know? How dare he tell me my failure to conceive was due to a psychological block. What possible reason could he have had to conceal the facts from his patient, the person into whose body he'd intruded? Contrary to popular belief, it seemed the conduct of the medical profession could be deeply unhealthy. But at least I had a case and, of course, a further wait. Heaven knows long though; it could take years for my hearing to come up.

By now the salon was in terminal decline. I knew we couldn't carry on. Then, totally unexpectedly, I received a letter from the landlords of the building, the Public Trustee. They wanted to redevelop the place into flats.

The time had come to take Terry down to Brighton. I chose a weekday. I didn't know how he would react and didn't want too many people exposed to him—either to his condition or his behaviour. He wasn't keen to go, he didn't seem in the least interested. But I was adamant. I felt he should decide if he wanted to be bought out or carry on. Even though there was really only one course, it had to be his choice.

He was completely traumatised by the journey; in some dark corner of his damaged brain the accident lurked like a ghost. On arrival at the salon, he refused to go in. Finally I persuaded him. The two remaining stylists, a new junior and a couple of clients were there. They were visibly shocked to see the change in him and when he opened his mouth to try and speak, one of the girls had to turn away she was so horrified. Terry didn't notice, he was watching the new junior who was shaking with nerves. She was so inept he hobbled over to the basins waving his arms. 'No, No, No! No' like 'at,' he shouted.

The client didn't know where to put herself and the junior ran off in tears. I apologised profusely and steered Terry through to the staff room where he informed me loudly he didn't want to know about the place. I could do what I wanted with it. He didn't want to be a hairdresser ever again. The whole experience was distressing and embarrassing for everyone concerned. Except Terry, who was oblivious. Nonetheless I was glad I'd insisted on taking him there. The next day I wrote to the Public Trustee saying we would be interested in the offer of a buy-out.

A few letters went back and forth before a figure of eight thousand pounds was agreed upon. It was very low but as there was virtually no business left, no good will to sell on, I accepted. Poynters was to close down at the end of the summer. A huge weight had been lifted from my sagging shoulders. Terry couldn't have cared less. It was as though, for him, the place had never existed. If he talked about hairdressing at all, he talked about his days in Belgravia. The twelve years between were like a gaping hole in his consciousness.

—44—

CHARLIE COMES HOME

Come Home Charlie … was at last coming to fruition. An overall schedule was prepared and pre-production began.

Locations were found in the Isle of Man, where a whole street was commissioned, yellow lines were painted over, houses redecorated and buildings restored to 1930's style. Among other things this included taking television aerials down. I never thought the occupants would agree but they did. I imagine the idea of having their street featured on the screen and all the ensuing excitement must have seemed worth the sacrifice of a week's viewing.

Roger and I cast three unknowns as the young leads—Tom Radcliffe, Mossie Smith and Jennifer Calvert. They were backed up by such names as Peter Sallis, Gary Olsen and, because of his Welshness and my conviction that he'd make a brilliant deputy bank manager, Nick Jones.

Pre-production was soon over and we were ready to begin shooting, which meant I would be going out to locations whenever possible. It was thrilling and rather frightening. Would I be able to hold the reins effectively, make the buck-stopping decisions when they arose, keep everyone heads-down and happy? I was determined.

Below me the Irish Sea sparkled through gaps in the clouds. The flight had been bumpy and my tummy, already churning with nerves, complained all the more. We were coming in to land at Douglas, Isle of Man. It was unreal—filming for *Come Home Charlie* … had begun and was scheduled from day one to the final wrap. We hadn't been pulled at the last minute, none of the unions had called a strike, everyone had arrived on time and the weather was behaving itself. I'd come to location to witness the first stage of filming. A unit car would be waiting to ferry me via the hotel to the location in Port St. Mary, where I planned to slip surreptitiously into a suitable vantage point until the afternoon tea break. Then I would go and say hello to everybody.

As we dropped down through the misty layer over the airfield, I tried to calm my nerves. Throughout the flight I'd been envisaging how it would be and how I should behave. I'd come to realise that the producer is often considered a perfect nuisance, constantly wittering on about the budget, contingency plans, or weather cover. It was essential to strike the right balance and I was determined my inexperience wouldn't show me up too much. I wouldn't get under feet or in the way of cables, I'd keep out of shot and quiet, not interfering unless absolutely necessary. Above all, no matter what, I wouldn't panic.

The driver introduced himself and took my bags. The unit car was no big deal and he wasn't wearing the right hat but he was my chauffeur and I was important, apparently. After the appropriate pleasantries, I concentrated on the passing countryside. Well, it was very pretty and appreciating it occupied my mind. On arrival we parked in a side road close to where they were filming. I crept round the back of some houses and emerged behind the sound man. They were setting up for the next shot, I hadn't arrived mid-take.

Forget hiding—someone called out 'Hi, Sue,' and I'd entered the party, only unlike so many parties, people stopped their conversations or whatever they were doing to say 'hello'. I felt instantly welcome and my stage fright dissolved. The atmosphere was good and the first few days had gone extremely smoothly. This had all the makings of a happy shoot.

The week sped by and I managed to keep calm when things went adrift and had to be ironed out. Twice the weather threw us badly off course. And there were minor but cumulative hold-ups—the local flying club deciding to practice stalling overhead, someone's hairstyle collapsing mid-take, an untimely cough, actors forgetting their lines or a hair in the lens … the list was endless. It was a marvel the perfect take was ever captured.

My other role was supportive—being mum, checking out grievances and problems and resolving them where I could as well as dishing out love to the thesps. Any new arrival found a basket of fruit and a note of personal welcome in their room and I made a point of complimenting performances. But most of the time I just watched and marvelled at the efficiency, the teamwork and expertise of everyone involved. The results looked fantastic, Roger and crew were putting together a gem of a serial, even better than I'd envisaged, and I was thrilled.

Of course there could be personal downsides, such as teasing whispers: 'Shh, here comes the prod', 'Better be careful, prod's on the warpath,' or, 'What have we done to deserve such distinguished company?' when I sat down to lunch in the chuck-wagon. It was pathetic letting their comments get to me but I wasn't sure whether they were sending me up rotten because of my inexperience or it was a genuine light-hearted tease.

At times I suffered from that lonely outsider feeling. The crew were mostly London Weekend television staff, so everyone knew each other well, the actors were instant, if not old friends and the freelancers stuck together. I didn't quite fit in anywhere. I supposed it was inevitable and just had to be endured. Luckily, when he wasn't being monopolised by the lighting man, the designer or some actor or other, there was Roger, always full of warmth and encouragement. 'I think we've got something really special here. And you put it all together. Well done,' he said as we chinked our glasses at dinner on my last night.

At the end of a successful shoot at our second location in Wales, the unit came to London to complete the interior scenes. Silly really, but as schedules are rarely if ever sequential, we'd done the exterior street in Port St. Mary, some of the rooms in Wales and, for logistical reasons, the rest had to be shot in London. It's amazing that actors maintain continuity of performance.

By the summer Roger and I were into editing and dubbing and I had the ideal connections for the music. Studio-owners, Tony and Gaynor Sadler, the couple Kip worked with, came from Wales. He was a talented composer, she had an exquisite soprano voice, and they were both high on energy. As they mostly worked in the commercials world, they welcomed my proposal with enthusiasm. I explained we wanted exclusively vocal choral and incidental music.

'No problem,' they chirruped in unison. 'Just up our alley.'

And it certainly was. They found us a choir of superb Welsh voices. Tony composed some haunting sequences and Gaynor led the singing as well as voicing for our female co-star in the chapel scene.

In complete contrast and because a good part of the story was set in a cafe whose main attraction (apart from the waitress, played by Jennifer Calvert) was a Wurlitzer jukebox, we needed a package of 1930's jazz and popular hits. I asked my mate, Jane, whose knowledge of music was encyclopaedic, if she could help. She ran her own company locating and licensing recordings for film and television soundtracks. 'I'd love to be involved,' she said.

Roger was happy so she joined the post-production team putting together a mixed package of famous as well as little-known titles to suit the mood of the individual cafe scenes.

Finally *Charlie* was ready to be presented to an audience At the press showing I was as nervous as hell. I had to make a speech to a large audience of cast, crew, press and guests, then suffer through the full three hours, trying not to keep glancing round for reactions to interpret and agonise over. As the final titles rolled, the applause rose above the music. Our little three-parter had been well received. It was due to go out on air at the end of the summer, now we could be hopeful of good previews and respectable audience ratings.

The day came and I was in a lather of excitement again. But when I looked as the Radio Times my spirits plunged. It felt as though a clash of airtime had been deliberately planned by the BBC. I knew instinctively we were to be eclipsed by their new and innovative political satire, *House of Cards*. Sure enough it captured the bulk of the audience. I was very disappointed.

'Oh well, just one of those things,' said Roger philosophically. 'It was fun to make and I had a great producer to work with.'

'Thank you, Roger, that's a wonderful compliment. You've cheered me up no end.'

'Good. And now I think you could do with a break. Have a holiday or treat yourself to something you've always wanted. Or both, whatever … and let's work together again soon.'

LOST AND FOUND

That night I couldn't get to sleep. I'd been thinking about Roger's suggestion and had decided he was right. Surviving so many months of emotional upheaval and physical exhaustion, managing to keep my career not just intact but moving forward, surely that deserved a reward.

On every visit to France, Terry and I had gazed longingly at the photos of houses for sale in the windows of *les immobiliers* and dreamed of buying a place in the country we'd come to love, not just for it's beauty but for the quality of life the rural French enjoyed and into which we slipped so easily. It was time to do something about it. I put the idea to Terry the following morning. 'Terry, shall we buy a house in France?' I said lightly, knowing what his response would be.

'Es!'

'We can get a second mortgage on this place, we can afford it.'

'Es.'

'Okay, I'll call Beth. I'm sure we can stay there while we're house-hunting.'

'Es,' he said again.

I knew it was a good idea, not just because it had always been our dream, but because we needed a new project, something to take our minds off the tragic accident that had played such havoc with our lives. Somewhere we could escape to and be who we were now, not who we had been but weren't any longer. Where nobody knew us and would accept us at face value, and where folk spoke another language, had different values, a better, more leisurely, quality of life.

I'd become disillusioned with life in London. Like a gathering squall, speed was overtaking our lives; people were always busy, rushing here or there. 'Sorry, can't stop now, I've got to …' became the excuse for not doing anything they considered unnecessary. Inevitably, I'd become a far more patient person and, by comparison, others appeared to have little time for anything that didn't come easily.

Socially, mentally handicapped people are hard work, and Terry could be particularly tiresome. Visiting us had become a chore. I realised it was inevitable that even the closest of friends were likely to become weary of him. After all, his company was extremely taxing. You had to strain to hear what he was saying and try to respond appropriately. He'd developed a repertoire, which would be trotted out whenever we had company. It was nearly always word for word the same little stories and the accompanying facial expressions and gestures never varied. Everyone got to hear about men from outer space only needing to learn three languages to get by on earth and the fourth cousin to the queen who'd been a client in his Belgravia days and not averse to making tea for everyone when she came in to have her hair done. This splendid lady's relationship to HRH ranged from second to fifth, so I suppose there was a little variation. There were more such stories and it was hard not to laugh but it was extremely tedious. And so was I, constantly telling him he was repeating himself.

In particular I noticed that Neil, who'd been my mainstay through hospital and Unstead days, was frequently 'too busy' to come round. Then his visits tailed off completely and he began to avoid contact. Terry said nothing but I'm sure he noticed and was hurt.

Shocked and saddened, I tried to rationalise why and came to conclusion Neil just couldn't cope any more. He too was worn down. And I felt there was another, more significant, reason. Whilst Terry was in hospital and then at Unstead Park, it was possible to imagine he'd return to some sort of normality. Now, back at home, it was obvious he wasn't Neil's old mate any more; Terry was somebody else, somebody irreparably damaged. Perhaps too, Neil realised that there, but for God's grace, he could have gone himself more times than he cared to remember. Finally I had to accept it was the end of their friendship. We never saw him again.

Mother usually rang me on Friday evenings; she liked a detailed account of my week. For me it was a way of putting a full stop to work before the weekend. I was in the office when the phone rang that night. I knew it would be her. 'Hi, Mother, how are you?'

'I'm alright, but I have some news.' She sounded extremely ominous. Death flashed through my mind. 'I've had a very strange call. A man trying to get in touch with you.'

Instinctively, I knew who it was. 'Mother, it's all right. I know what you're going to say.' My whole body was shaking but my voice was surprisingly firm. I was going to stand my ground this time. 'Did he give you his number?'

'Yes, dear, but …'

'What is it?'

Reluctantly she gave it to me. I didn't recognise the code. 'Now, before you do anything hasty, think of what this could mean, think of Terry.' Mother's doom-laden tones were indelibly associated with the painful memories I'd tried to bury forever.

'For God's sake, Mother! This is what I've always wanted. You must understand that.' Nothing was going to stop me from obeying what my emotions dictated, however foolhardy.

'But, he might be after your money. He might have seen your name on the television and think …'

I cut her short. I didn't want to hear. 'Look, I don't feel like talking any more now. I need a stiff drink. Lots of love and please don't get yourself into a state. I can handle this. Bye.' I put the phone down before she could say any more. She was bound to get herself into a state but I was in too much of a turmoil to worry about how anyone else might be feeling.

I ran up to the kitchen and poured myself a large whisky. Terry was watching television and oblivious, as usual.

Back in the office and several cigarettes later, I was staring at the phone trying to find the courage to pick it up. Finally, I just grabbed it and dialled. My hands trembled with nervous anticipation. I prayed my voice would be steady.

A man answered. 'Hello.'

'This is Sue. Sue Whatmough. You've been trying to get in touch with me.'

'Yes, yes. Thank you for ringing back.' There was a long pause. 'I'm sorry, this might come as a bit of a shock to you, but I have every reason to believe you could be my mother. I was born in Windsor on the second of February 1964. My mother's name was

Whatmough.' He had an Essex accent and spoke rather formally, like a salesman. Could he really be my son, my little lost Sebastian? 'I'd like to meet you, if that's convenient,' he added.

I snapped back down to earth. This was no longer a fairy tale this was true. Flesh and blood true. 'I think I'd like that too but there are complications. My life isn't exactly … straightforward.' I stumbled over the words.

'I'm sorry. I don't want to alarm you. I haven't got any unsavoury motives or anything. I just want to know who I am.'

'Yes, of course. It's okay. I have a friend who can explain. I'll ask him to ring you.'

I couldn't wait to get off the phone, to breathe.

'Great. Thanks. I'll wait to hear. By the way, my name is Nigel.'

A friend. What friend? The words had just slipped out; without forethought I'd come up with a delaying tactic. I sat back and lit another cigarette. I needed to calm down and think clearly before arranging to meet him. I wondered if he'd thought about the emotions we'd have to confront and if he'd addressed the idea of the guilt that might have plagued me. And would he have suppressed anger to deal with? How would his adoptive parents react? There were a lot of issues to be considered—those I could immediately imagine and those I couldn't. Talking to a go-between would give him the chance to back out.

Who would be prepared take on this role? I reached for my address book and there, on the first page, I saw the name—Arnold, Phil. He was an old mate of both Terry and I. A self-employed cabinet-maker and free spirit who'd had never joined the material world and preferred to spend his days with *The Archers*, the Guardian Crossword and his beloved wood. A gentle, alternative character who couldn't intimidate anybody. Phil was the ideal person to act as our go-between. I rang him and explained what had happened.

'That's amazing. What fantastic news. I won't just call him, I'll go and see him if you like. Then I can report back.'

'Phil, you're an angel, thank you.'

As soon as I was able to rein in my excitement, I realised there were other practicalities to consider. Mother was right, I had to think about Terry. He knew I'd had a baby, a son, but after I'd told him in the very early days of our relationship, we hadn't discussed it again. Now he was damaged, how would he take it? What would he think? I had to admit he probably wouldn't take it at all well. I decided it would be wisest not to say a word until I'd met Nigel and ascertained what kind of person he was. After all, we could have little to say to each other. If I told Terry, there'd very likely be a huge row, I'd end up in tears and probably come out with hurtful stuff I didn't really mean. It was best to find out first if there was any future in our meeting.

Phil was wonderful. 'I've got a couple of day's work then I can drive down to Essex to see Nigel.'

Those two days dragged slowly by. I found it impossible to concentrate on anything, needing desperately to confide in somebody but reluctant to tell the girls in the office until after Phil's trip to Chelmsford. I'd arranged to go down to a location in Kent where Roger was filming a new series. At dinner that evening, I could contain my excitement no longer.

I spilt out my story to Roger and the two actors we were dining with. By the time I'd finished, we were all sniffing into our hankies; they were as thrilled as I was. All being well, I was to meet my twenty-five year-old son for the first time—how utterly bizarre, how wonderful, how terrifying.

Phil rang me immediately he arrived home. They'd got on very well, and I wasn't to worry. Nigel, a thoroughly straight guy, was anxious not to upset anybody and very understanding of my situation and Phil had a cassette for me, a song Nigel had written to commemorate discovering me! I couldn't wait to hear it. 'Phil, can you come over tonight? Come for dinner.'

'I'll be there in an hour,' he said.

I sped off to the kitchen to organise the food—something easy, not needing thought, concentration or complication. A *bolognaise* or something, who cared?

Phil slipped me the tape when he arrived.

'Terry doesn't know anything about this,' I whispered.

'No problem. I promise I won't put my foot in it.'

'He's in the sitting room. There's some wine in the kitchen, pour yourself a drink. I won't be long.'

I ran down to the office. My hands were trembling so much I could hardly press the start button on the cassette player.

It was a simple song, beautifully sung and piano-backed. The sound quality was lousy but that was totally unimportant. To me no song could have been more precious.

> *I just want to see your face so I know*
> *the look that's in my eyes is in your own*
> *I just want to see your face so I can see*

the very special reason why I'm me.
And if in twenty-five years in the line of our duty
We've covered the fact with our tact sounding truly fulfilled
then we've lied to ourselves—'til now.

'Til now there's never been a choice
to understand my make up and the sound of my voice.
'Til now there's never been a reason or a how
'cos I've never known you and I've never seen you—'til
now.

I just want to see your eyes and fill the space
that spans this life so empty until I've come to trace
the one who gave me life in '64
and ever since that moment she has been a closed door.
I don't mind how it happened, we all do what's best
in our lives when it's hard or we're put to the test.
As for us we can catch up on the rest—right now.

The tears poured down my face as I played the song over and over again, each time reading more into the underlying meaning. Finally, I returned to the present, blew my nose and went back upstairs. I knew that what lay ahead would throw me once more into emotional turmoil and I was ready.

And so it happened, on the twenty-first of February 1989, a quarter of a century after I'd given birth to him, my son walked into my life.

TO BE CONTINUED

ACKNOWLEDGEMENTS

A big thank-you to friends and family who read my story in various draft stages and who contributed a critique: Roger Bamford, Michelle Beresford, Hassanah Burton, Susi Fielding, Dorothy Gruszczynski, Allen Harbinson, Sally Hughes, Rosemary Humphries, Ali Jackson, Claire Jefferson, Jerry, Jane Jones, Nicholas Jones, Catherine Lovering, Carol Meaden, Nigel Morris, Angie Page, Beth Shorter, Keith Tate, Patricia Taylor, Clara Villanueva, Christina Verbeeck, Karyn Willie, Fronza Woods and to Richard Kelly and CPI Anthony Rowe for their help with the 'review' copies.
Special thanks to Frankie Bailey of The Literary Consultancy for her extraordinary critique, for her endorsement and for her constant support, to Bernard Krichefski for his help and for wanting to direct 'No Copy …' for radio and not least to Lynda Bellingham for her encouragement and wonderful endorsement.

The biggest thanks to Leaf for being my sternest critic and my inspiration.

Sue Whatmough now lives in an old farmhouse near the Pyrenees in South West France where she runs creative writing courses and helps her partner, Leaf, with his organic food business. She is also a correspondent for The French Week newspaper.

She is currently working on 'ANOTHER LIFE', the sequel to 'NO COPY OF THE SCRIPT' in which she gets to know her long-lost son, moves to France and spends time in an African township on a project to house Malawian street children.